Tillie Olsen

Twayne's United States Authors Series

Warren French, Editor
University College of Swansea, Wales

TUSAS 581

Tillie Olsen

Mickey Pearlman

and

Abby H. P. Werlock
St. Olaf College

Twayne Publishers • Boston
A Division of G. K. Hall & Co.

Tillie Olsen
Mickey Pearlman and Abby H. P. Werlock

Copyright 1991 by G. K. Hall & Co.
All rights reserved.
Published by Twayne Publishers
A division of G. K. Hall & Co.
70 Lincoln Street
Boston, Massachusetts 02111

Copyediting supervised by Barbara Sutton.
Book production by Janet Z. Reynolds.
Book design by Barbara Anderson.
Typeset by Compset, Inc., Beverly, Massachusetts.

10 9 8 7 6 5 4 3 2 1

The paper used in this publication meets the minimum requirements
of American National Standard for Information Sciences—Permanence
of Paper for Printed Library Materials, ANSI Z39.48-1984.∞™

Printed and bound in the United States of America.

Library of Congress Cataloging-in-Publication Data

Pearlman, Mickey, 1938–
    Tillie Olsen / Mickey Pearlman and Abby H.P. Werlock.
        p.   cm. — (Twayne's United States authors series ; TUSAS 581)
    Includes bibliographical references (p.   ) and index.
    ISBN 0-8057-7632-X
    1. Olsen, Tillie—Criticism and interpretation.   I. Werlock, Abby
H. P.   II. Title.   III. Series.
PS3565.L82Z84   1991
813'.54—dc20
                                                        91-8623

For my nephews, Gary Heiman and Bill Glaser.

—M. P.

For my husband, Jim Werlock, and my parents, Tom and Abby Potter.

—A. W.

Contents

Authors' Note

This volume has been written jointly. The major responsibility for the interview with Olsen, the chapters on *Yonnondio* and "Requa," and the Bibliography lies with Mickey Pearlman. Abby Werlock wrote the chapters on the four *Tell Me a Riddle* stories and *Silences,* as well as the biographical sketch.

We would like to thank the New York Public Library, Astor, Lenox and Tilden Foundations, for providing us access to Tillie Olsen's manuscripts in the Henry W. and Albert A. Berg Collection.

We would like to thank Liz Fowler for her good nature, sharp ear, and patience. We gratefully acknowledge the support of Connie Gunderson, Rojean Fall-Vetsch, and Jean Parker of the Rolvaag Memorial Library of St. Olaf College; Thomas Raich of the Microcomputer Center at St. Olaf College; Dorothy Deming of the Rice County (Minnesota) Historical Museum; and the patience and encouragement of Mia Bess Pearlman. Finally, we thank Katy and Alexander Gottschalk, John Paul, and Ted Pearlman for solving last-minute emergencies with "summer camp" housing, computers, external disk drives, and Macintosh programs.

Introduction

Any writer who is a woman and a feminist approaches Tillie Olsen with a jumbled sense of awe, excitement, and trepidation. Tillie Olsen, after all, is widely regarded as an icon: as Margaret Atwood said in her *New York Times* review of *Silences,* "'respect' is too pale a word: 'reverence' is more like it."[1] Olsen would be the first, however, to object vehemently to both the almost religious fervor of her followers and the exalted status that has been accorded her relatively small body of work. Instead Olsen claims (with her usual emphasis on commonality, not individuality) that she is "not as good a writer as some of you think I am. It is you and what you bring to it . . . the common work that we do together"[2] that she celebrates. In spite of these disclaimers, however, Olsen remains an icon to large numbers of women in and out of academia, feminist critics in particular. Certainly she deserves this approbation for the myriad ways in which she has encouraged women and minorities to write their own stories and to break through the encoded silences that surround the lives of the powerless. To this day her appearances across the country, where she talks about such silences, empower, support, and encourage writers and women in ways that she herself was not empowered, supported, or encouraged until very late in life.

Every woman now writing in America has felt the subtle effects of Olsen's groundbreaking insights into her own life and work—insights that may finally surpass her own writing in fame and influence—because she has forced us to pay attention to the influence of economic circumstance and social class; the meaning of limited time, money, energy, and space on the productivity of women; the nature and pain of imposed silence; and the often debilitating effects of "otherness" in a society that equates difference with disability, sameness with safety.

Having said that, we should add that it is difficult to write a critical study of Olsen's work for several reasons. Great as two of her short stories may be, Olsen is known and admired much more because of what she represents than because of what she has written. The fragmented quality of her sparse output and the unexplained fallow periods in her writing life challenge interpretation. And much of the extant

ix

criticism is so adulatory that it impedes rather than enhances a straightforward understanding and appreciation of her work.

To begin with, Olsen's oeuvre—five short stories, one unfinished novel, one nonfiction book (*Silences*), two edited collections of work or photographs by others (*Mother to Daughter, Daughter to Mother* and *Mothers and Daughters: That Special Quality*), and several essays—is small, and the best of it was written between 1953 and 1960. Olsen's one novel, *Yonnondio: From the Thirties,* is unfinished: it was found some 40 years after she began it and was finally published, largely as she found it, as a fragment. After the highly acclaimed *Tell Me a Riddle* she published only one piece of fiction: the unfinished novella "Requa." Although "Requa" was first published in 1970, the story remains in its original form. Since then she has published few pieces of non-fiction beyond "Dream Vision," a brief but poignant tribute to her mother (in *Mother to Daughter,* 1984). Consequently, it is important to remember that we are working with writing that ranges from the production of a very young person a very long time ago to the stories of a middle-aged woman—being published for the first time in middle age—as well as with the nonproductive and undocumented periods in between.

For someone who has built a reputation addressing the issue of silence, Olsen herself has remained oddly silent about the specifics of much of her own life. What has prevented her from publishing fiction since the publication of "Requa" in 1970, and what caused the long silence between the publication of *Tell Me a Riddle* (1960, 1961) and *Yonnondio* (1974)? We know that Olsen abandoned *Yonnondio* the year that the witch-hunting Dies committee swung into action and the Communist party in the United States began to disband as a result of the heightened awareness of the Stalinist purges in the Soviet Union. We know that she returned to writing in earnest, enrolling in a Stanford University creative writing class in 1955, a few months after the Senate disciplined Joe McCarthy. Whether these events are related, however, is conjecture. What we do know from Olsen's essays and talks is that four children and very little money—circumstances that permeate the plots of the four *Tell Me a Riddle* stories—are heavy burdens. But we do not know, for instance, about events of the years between the publication of "Requa" and the present. In fact, one writer has uncharitably called Olsen's *Silences* (1978) a "well-known apologia, a lamentation for her own sparse literary output."[3] Speaking of the silences of many writers, Olsen said in 1978, "I'm embittered about the whole situation, inconsolably. I'm more and more in a rage about it. . . . I'm bitter about all those books that are unpublished or unfinished."[4] In *Silences,* she writes of "myself so nearly remaining mute and having let writing die over and over again in me."[5]

Other critics, however, do not find these issues of fragmentation and silence as disturbing as we do. Elaine Orr, for instance, says that "one of the great paradoxes of Olsen's texts is the sympathy their incompleteness evokes in the readers."[6] Likewise, Elizabeth Meese, following the lead of the French feminist critic Hélène Cixous, believes that because "feminine" texts are "without ending," the "pages' blank spaces" constitute "open invitations to the reader to participate in the text's creation."[7] We cannot concur with this attitude toward the "unfinished" quality of Olsen's writing because we think it leads to a damaging syndrome not previously noted—critics frequently adding to or subtracting from the stories. Olsen's admirers, many of whom are writers and critics, seem to be interpreting her fiction as saying more than it does, and consciously or unconsciously they fill in the gaps, essentially rewriting the stories.

Much of this criticism, unfortunately, is poorly written. More than a little of it contains minor errors, such as characters' names spelled incorrectly, and major ones of fact and interpretation. For example, in "Literary Foremothers" Rose Kamel writes of *Yonnondio,* "It is small wonder that Anna loses her baby, takes sick, and dies" (Kamel, 59). In fact, at the end of the book Anna is alive, on the mend, and making jelly.[8] Another critic states that "the children [in *Yonnondio*] find the women at the mine and Mazie's father trapped beneath" (Orr, 55). Needless to say, Mazie's father is not trapped beneath anything in the mine; Mazie finds him in a bar, where he is drinking with his cronies. As implied by the title of *The Modernist Madonna: Semiotics of the Maternal Metaphor,* which contains a lengthy discussion of Eva, critic Jane Silverman Van Buren has literally changed Eva into a victimized saint. In her description of Lisa, Eva's childhood friend, Van Buren says that Lisa "defied authority and tradition to teach Eva to read. The woman was executed for her treason while Eva herself spent a year in prison,"[9] an explanation mistakenly implying that Lisa was put to death for teaching Eva to read. In fact, Lisa was almost certainly executed for her murder of another person, an informer in the prison with Lisa and Eva. The "gentle" Lisa's attack on the betrayer is rendered in a highly dramatic scene, fragments of which surface several times in Eva's consciousness.[10] This critic also believes that at the end of "Tell Me a Riddle" Eva "lies dying at Jeannie's Santa Monica apartment" where together the two women "reveal themselves" to each other. She makes the astonishing statement that each woman has had an abortion (Van Buren, 166). Not only does Eva not go to Jeannie's apartment (Jeannie finds rented rooms for her grandparents, which are not in Santa Monica), but, far more important, nowhere is an abortion either mentioned or implied for Eva or for Jeannie. The character of Eva, in fact, emerges repeatedly as a focus for misinformation. This kind of literary criticism does not serve Olsen well. Such analyses, especially of women characters, often seem generated by a critic's desire to fit Olsen's work into a given political or feminist rubric. Such misreadings derive not from Olsen's description of the characters but from the critic's own worshipful perception of Olsen.

It is astounding that so much of the criticism of the work of such a pivotal figure consists of reviews, many of them unsigned. Of the remainder, most are both outdated and rehashed from several substantial essays written by Selma Burkom and Margaret Williams, Deborah Rosenfelt, Catharine Stimpson, and Joanne Frye.[11] There also seems to be a mistaken or misguided tendency to publish only laudatory or eulogizing criticism.

While working on this book we also became aware that Olsen's name is often absent from contemporary studies of mothers and daughters, feminist criticism, and American literary histories. She rarely merits her own chapter or section in such works, and her name is frequently missing from their indices. Although most critics agree on the genuine artistic strengths of her two most widely reprinted stories, "I Stand Here Ironing" and "Tell Me a Riddle," and although writers from Margaret Atwood to Tim O'Brien have admired her considerable talent, she is often not a reference point in discussions of American writers of either gender. It is unusual, to say the least, that a writer so admired by a large number of other writers and general readers is missing so completely from scholarly studies by Americans.[12]

With this book we suggest new directions for further study and redress the imbalance in Olsen's critical and popular reputations. Without doubt, a significant number of novels, short stories, essays, and anthologies—as well as the criticism and canon reforms spurred on by sweeping changes in academia and the culture at large—exist partly because of the vision, talent, and determination Olsen has released and encouraged in her contemporaries. Her singular prescient vision and constant attention to those on the margins of society ennoble her to her "fellow" writers in and out of academia. Through a 1969 course she taught at Amherst College on "The Literature of Poverty, Work, and the Human Struggle for Freedom," the reading lists she published in 1971 and 1972, and her subsequent writings about lost manuscripts and forgotten writers, Olsen, more than any other American writer, has disabused the reading public of the notion that literature is written exclusively by and about white, upper-middle-class Protestant men and convinced them that it can (and should) "be made out of the lives of despised people" as well. Her insistence that we consider how women's lives are "instantly interruptible" (and the price of that interruptibility) and that we pay attention to the working class and the working writer encourages us to read and reread the writings of a diverse and usually marginalized majority. This is her most powerful and empowering legacy.

Chronology

<table>
<tr><td>1912 or 1913</td><td>Tillie Lerner born in Wahoo, Omaha, or Mead, Nebraska, on 14 January, the second of six children of Samuel and Ida (Beber) Lerner, immigrants from czarist Russia after the 1905 rebellion.</td></tr>
<tr><td>1928</td><td>Finds three dilapidated copies of Atlantic Monthly in junk shop for 10¢ each. April 1861 issue contains Rebecca Harding Davis's unsigned "Life in the Iron Mills."</td></tr>
<tr><td>1929</td><td>Leaves Omaha Central High School without completing her studies.</td></tr>
<tr><td>1930</td><td>Jailed in Kansas City, Kansas, for trying to organize packinghouse workers. Contracts severe case of pleurisy, then incipient tuberculosis.</td></tr>
<tr><td>1932</td><td>Begins Yonnondio in Faribault, Minnesota, during recovery. Daughter Karla born.</td></tr>
<tr><td>1933</td><td>Moves to Southern California, then to Stockton and finally to San Francisco. Lives for 40 years in Mission and Fillmore districts of San Francisco.</td></tr>
<tr><td>1934</td><td>Involved in San Francisco Maritime Strike. The 5 July strike-breaking attempt results in a battle, known as "Bloody Thursday," which leaves several strikers dead and others injured. The Hearst Press labels the unions "Commie" front organizations. Olsen arrested; bail set at $1,000. Writes two essays chronicling her involvement. "The Iron Throat," a portion of first chapter of Yonnondio, appears in second issue of the Partisan Review while Olsen is in jail. "Thousand-Dollar Vagrant," an account of her encounter with the judge, appears in the 29 August New Republic. "Literary Life in California," a description of her arrest written at the request of Lincoln Steffens, appears in the 22 August New Republic.</td></tr>
<tr><td>1935</td><td>Attends the American Writers Congress in New</td></tr>
</table>

York. The October–November issue of *The Anvil: The Proletariat Fiction Magazine* announces that "Skeleton Children," a novelette by Tillie Lerner, will appear in the next edition. *The Anvil* merged with *Partisan Review* and "Skeleton Children" never appeared.

1936   Begins living with Jack Olsen.

1937   Abandons work on "Yonnondio"; devotes two decades to rearing daughters and to working numerous low-paying jobs to support the family.

1938   Daughter Julie born.

1943   Daughter Katherine Jo born. Marries Jack Olsen.

1948   Daughter Laurie born.

1953–1954   Writes "I Stand Here Ironing."

1953 and 1955   Writes "Hey Sailor, What Ship?"

1955   At 42, enrolls in creative writing course taught by Arthur Foff at San Francisco State College.

1956–1957   Receives Stegner fellowship in creative writing at Stanford University; writes "O Yes."

1957   "I Stand Here Ironing" appears in *The Best American Short Stories of 1957.*

1958   Discovers that Rebecca Harding Davis is the author of "Life in the Iron Mills" ("The Korl Woman").

1959   Receives Ford Foundation grant in literature.

1960   "Tell Me a Riddle" published in volume 16 of *New World Writing.*

1961   "Tell Me a Riddle" wins O. Henry Award first prize for best American short story.

1962   *Tell Me a Riddle* published.

1962–1964   Receives fellowship from Radcliffe Institute for Independent Study.

1967   Consultant on literature; reader and lecturer. Receives National Endowment for the Arts award.

1968   Begins "Requa."

1969–1970   Visiting professor and writer in residence, Amherst College.

1970   "Requa I" appears in the *Iowa Review* and in *The Best American Short Stories of 1971*, which is dedicated to Olsen.

1972   Visiting instructor at Stanford. Participates in the Modern Language Association forum, "Women Writers in the Twentieth Century." Jack Olsen finds manuscript of *Yonnondio* while searching for other papers. Works on the old manuscript and her afterword to *Life in the Iron Mills* at the MacDowell Writers' Colony in Peterborough, New Hampshire.

1973   *Life in the Iron Mills* published.

1973–1974   Writer in residence, Massachusetts Institute of Technology.

1974   *Yonnondio.* Distinguished visiting professor, University of Massachusetts, Boston.

1975   Receives American Academy & National Institute of Arts & Letters award for distinguished contribution to American letters.

1975–1976   Guggenheim fellowship.

1977   Copeland fellow, Amherst College.

1978   *Silences.* Board of Regents visiting lecturer, University of California, San Diego.

1979   Awarded honorary Litt.D. by the University of Nebraska.

1980   Receives Ministry to Women Award, Unitarian Universalist Federation. Named international visiting scholar to four Norwegian universities and Radcliffe centennial visitor and lecturer. Selected by British Post Office (and Business and Professional Women) for a special award to honor her work. "Tell Me a Riddle" filmed (screenplay by Joyce Eliason; produced by Susan O'Connell, Rachel Lyon, and Mindy Affrime; directed by Lee Grant).

1981   Mayor and Board of Supervisors proclaim 18 May "Tillie Olsen Day" in San Francisco.

1982   Awarded honorary Litt.D. by Knox College, Galesburg, Illinois.

1983   Tillie Olsen Week and Symposium, 5 Quad Cities
            Colleges, Iowa and Illinois.

1983–1984   Awarded Senior Fellowship, National Endowment
            for the Humanities.

1984   Visits Soviet Union as guest of Writers' Union. Vis-
            its China with group of women writers which in-
            cluded Paule Marshall and Alice Walker. Awarded
            honorary degree, Hobart and William Smith Col-
            leges, Geneva, New York.

1985   Awarded honorary degree, Clark University, Wor-
            cester, Massachusetts.

1985–1986   Bunting Fellow, Radcliffe College.

1986   Awarded honorary degree, Albright College, Read-
            ing, Pennsylvania. Hill Visiting Professor, Univer-
            sity of Minnesota.

1987   Gund Professor, Kenyon College, Gambier, Ohio.
            Regents Lecturer, University of California at Los
            Angeles.

1988   Special session at Modern Language Association in
            New Orleans called *Silences*: Ten Years Later." Ol-
            sen, along with May Sarton and Gwendolyn Brooks,
            is honored at Clark University in Worcester,
            Massachusetts.

1989   Jack Olsen dies.

1990   Spends September and October at Leighton Arts
            Colony, Banff, Canada.

Chapter One

Interview with Tillie Olsen*

There is no doorman or glitzy California-style entranceway at Tillie Olsen's San Francisco apartment building, just a simple white card downstairs that says "Olsen." I rang the doorbell and as I stepped inside, I heard a voice from the third floor call out, "Is that Mickey Pearlman? Come on up." I had very much looked forward to sitting with her in her own space, an apartment built by the longshoremen's union in the 1930s as an experiment in cooperative housing. It is in a neighborhood known as the Fillmore district, near Japantown, where she has lived with her husband, Jack Olsen, since 1965. [Jack Olsen died in 1989.] This is a cozy, comfortable space, full of books, patchwork pillows, snapshots of children and friends, Grandma memorabilia, and colored glass mobiles twinkling in the sunlight that streams in from her terrace.

Tillie Olsen takes the stairs two at a time, as I found out when we went to lunch at a nearby Japanese restaurant, where she was greeted by waiters and owners as only a familiar is. She doesn't stroll—she strides—and you are amazed (as you are each time you meet her) by her small size and slender frame, from which emanate the ideas of determination, morality, and fortitude that are linked to her name. Olsen is a natural teacher, as much as she is a writer, and while she is gracious and forthcoming, and has been widely and rightly praised for her intellectual generosity, you are always aware of the fact that she does not allow her time or her energies to be dissipated by moral or mental triviality or by unsolicited and unwanted praise. Moreover, she is precise and even fierce in her choice of words, and in her replies to an interviewer's questions; it is clear that every word and every idea matters. You are reminded of the way she values time when you are asked both to submit questions in writing before the interview and to call her in California for an initial, albeit long-distance, interview. But when you sit with her at her small, round dining table, Olsen con-

*Conducted in 1987 by Mickey Pearlman.

centrates on that conversation entirely. If the telephone rings during the interview, she simply picks it up, says "call back later," and hangs up.

Tillie Olsen does not talk "off the tape." You get no sense, as with some writers, that there is a prepared, formulaic public response, as well as a possibly less-assured one for private consumption. Now 75, she has lived through three wars, the birth and the rearing of four daughters, pleurisy, poverty, several social revolutions, the unfinished civil rights struggle, the ongoing labor–management struggle, the continuing women's rights struggle, and a stint in jail for organizing packinghouse workers in Kansas City. She has experienced the birth and death of many dreams; she knows what she thinks and she tells you just that. She expects an interviewer to have the wide-ranging knowledge of social, economic, and literary phenomena that she, indeed, has, and there is an energizing influence in her unspoken expectation that the listener will be sensible and sensitive, especially to the political realities that have sometimes defeated and always defined the ongoing struggle for world peace, workers' equity and women's rights.

Tillie Olsen is interested in the silences shared by all people, and not in what she sees as the current overemphasis on ethnicity and race and the other subdefinitions of human experience, which, in her opinion, serve only to divide us further. "We recognize the terrible divisiveness of old human bigotries and religious hatreds in the Middle East or India," she says, "but we don't recognize the subtler forms [like] the ethnic mystique." At the 1988 Modern Language Association Convention and elsewhere she has told audiences to "leap beyond race, class, and sex," to "recognize what is common between us," and to remember "that your only power is in working with others."[1]

Olsen has spent over 50 years investigating the wellsprings of strength and "human resilience," ideas often reflected in her stories, and she believes that it is "one of the great characteristics of the human race" that "we do not remain forever in degrading circumstances, circumstances that are harmful, circumstances that are unpleasant, if we can find a way out." What, she asks, is "the source of that in human beings? What does it feed on when there seems to be little for it to feed on, and what does it have to do with what a human being is, the nature of being human? What's the relationship of human caring in all that?"

We talk initially about her last, unfinished story, "Requa," published in 1970 in the *Iowa Review* and republished as "Requa I" in

Martha Foley's *Best American Short Stories of 1971,* a volume dedicated to Olsen. The story takes place in the town of Requa (which, according to Olsen, means "river mouth" [Werlock interview, 1990]). Requa is in the Klamath Valley of northern California, an area Olsen knows well. "Requa," also a Native American word for "broken in body and spirit,"[2] is a story about the survival in the 1930s of a young boy, Stevie, who is informally adopted by his bachelor uncle, Wes, a junk-yard worker, after the boy's mother dies. "Requa," Olsen says, is not only about Stevie; the real story is embedded and, as with the stories of *Tell Me a Riddle,* is exemplified by the mother: " 'stained words that on her working lips came stainless.' I'm writing about this kid who gets picked up after his mother has died, [the mother who] has been his parent, and his companion and his primary source of the bond to life and to wholeness."

These ideas about resiliency and survival were partially shaped by one of Olsen's "great influences," Dorothy Canfield Fisher, and by Fisher's "wonderful fable for parents, 'The Forgotten Mother,' " which is about "the hardest of all jobs in our society—having to raise kids on your own," often without the benefit of educational or financial resources. Olsen frequently reminds audiences that "of the 50 percent [of us] who are women, only a tiny percentage is not working class. I often think we should feed into a computer all the [existing] literature and see how little of it is about human work and, for that matter, the work of women, including raising children."

For me, "Requa" is a story profoundly about loss, exhaustion, and disorder, but Olsen believes that "within it is 'order twining with dis-order' ["Requa," xx]. The idea of order is not implicit in the [nuclear or extended family]" represented by Wes, as I had suggested. Rather, "Order is implicit in human history and human progress and human growth, and it's essential. Human beings cannot function without that underpinning."

Stevie, whose uncle calls him a "ghost boy," Olsen continues, does have "a physical look, like people in deep mourning who have not been eating well—the kind of transparent look that people get." But, she says, "I'm taking one aspect, and a very obscure one at that," and showing "that people are able to pick themselves up, to try either to get away from something that's intolerable, or to make changes to something that is better. . . . The younger you are when you are re-moved from all that's familiar, including your sources of strength," the more poignant the struggle is.

Olsen says she still "plans to finish" "Requa," but that "when I first sent it out, nobody wanted to publish it." In 1969 "there was all that scorn about material things [and] technology," she explains. "It was very much against the current. If I'd used language in the service of more 'acceptable' subjects"—if, that is, she had written about subjects akin to "the slaughterhouse or Anna in the kitchen"—". . . there would be a kind of place for it [and] a recognition" that "Requa" has yet to receive.

Olsen says she doesn't "think in terms of style" because "style comes out of the material I'm trying to convey. 'I Stand Here Ironing' was really beginning writing, and 'Hey Sailor' was already somewhat different. 'Requa I' was on its way if you look at [these] differences. . . . There is a section [in 'Long Ago Yonnondio'] about what's going on in the slaughterhouse on that intolerably hot day, . . . about human work and human tasks," about "Anna and her assembly line in the kitchen doing the canning." These ideas about work and what work means are reflected in "Requa." She talks about the disparaging and continuing "upper-class attitude[s] about maintenance of life, menial or lower-class work."

In this context she recalls Robert Coles's groundbreaking *Children of Poverty.* "Freud and Eric Erickson had not prepared him for those little children in New Orleans, some of whom came from what seemed to be terrible families who never provided what kids had to have for all those stages when [Erickson said] you get your identity. . . . Here were these amazing strong children and these amazing strong parents, and [Coles] asked himself, 'What are the sources of human strength?'" And asking himself this question changed him, she says. Certainly the human seedbed of strength and resistance is one of the messages encoded in "Requa," particularly in the discussions there of the junkyard workers and the attempts to eke out a barebones livelihood by the occupants of the roominghouse where Stevie and Wes live.

Whenever you examine the meaning of human work, Olsen says, "the implications are revolutionary implications, because it bespeaks the common background of humanity instead of the split into colors" and social divisions. It is work "and the bearing and rearing of kids which has consumed most of human life." And Wes, she says, "is a working man" who has "to be organized," has "to have a strong sense of order." It "has to do with the *kind* of work you do; . . . you have to be competent, you have to be skilled. Don't forget, this is set in the 1930s, half a century ago, and much has changed in the nature of work and in the nature of the Weses," to whom people stop to sell their belongings just to stay alive, or to be able to travel a few more miles with that money to a better future in the West.

Olsen reminds me that "Wes had been in the army during World War II. You remember how he keeps his tools and his boots?" There is an inherent beauty in the names and the rhythms of tools and tasks reflected through the characters in "Requa." And, she says, "Wes knows a lot." Her point is an important one: "So much is covered over about the human past and human genius, about the achievements throughout the centuries, and the development that has taken place. That development did not take place out of inventors who graduated Cal Tech or MIT but from people who were doing the work and found, thought of, [and] invented, an easier way, a more efficient way, [or] a new thing. And that's not in people's heads at all: how we got chairs and pencils and pens and lamps and lighting and containers for flowers or anything else. Look at your clothes. Human genius went into that. . . . When we talk about women, I say it often (and I think I was one of the first who said it [since] there was a lot of scorn about these 'nothing' women, these so-called ordinary women) . . . in kind of a shorthand, 'Who needs goddesses in the past to sanctify us?' The fact is that women were most responsible for food, for the development of shelter, probably language and music, and everything they did in clothing and in food was decorated" with an artistic sense. "These were creatures who died when they were young" and who "were cold and didn't read and write."

Olsen says she "was very struck, after all those years, when the pieces of *Yonnondio* [begun in 1932] showed up along with those first four chapters" of "Requa." (The manuscripts were found by accident in 1972.) She cites a scene from "Requa" that she had rewritten in a different form. She asks if I remember "when Stevie wakes up Wes [and] startles him (Wes has fallen asleep after work and is snoring), and the boy remembers his own hard-working mother and the way her feet hurt her so much, and how he rubbed her feet, and Wes's reaction. That, by the way, has to do with a need so deep in human beings—the need to have hands on," what psychologists now call "skin hunger," the need to be physically touched. "I wrote that [same passage] in *Yonnondio* with Mazie and Anna, many years before. Evidently, it went very deep with me. . . . In those days people worked so hard, there wasn't much of you left." In a scene from *Yonnondio* Jim falls asleep on the front porch when his young daughter Mazie wants his attention, but, as Olsen says, "we think of exhaustion [now] more in emotional terms. Now again how tired women are—women working full-time jobs with kids under three years old, and with crummy care for their kids."

"Anyhow," she says with the tired sigh of a longtime fighter, "I don't think of 'Tell Me a Riddle,' 'I Stand Here Ironing,' 'Oh Yes,' 'Hey Sailor, What Ship?' or 'Requa' as primarily about 'loss,' 'exhaustion,' 'displacement,' and 'emotional fatigue' [all words that I had used in my list of questions]. It's interesting that you do. That's legitimate and that's your right." It is clear that with Tillie Olsen the emphasis is always on humankind's predilection to persevere and to overcome rather than on the innumerable opportunities that an inhumane society presents for failure and defeat.

I ask her how the mother in "I Stand Here Ironing" could create order in a world seemingly suffused with chaos, disorder, tumult and sadness. Olsen says she "would not have thought of 'Ironing' [which has been anthologized more than 90 times] in that way. Do you remember the point when the mother breaks down and can't go on? Here is this lovely 19-year-old and she says, quite lightly, 'In a couple of years when we'll all be atom-dead they [my exams] won't matter a bit.' It's interesting that [you see that as] loss, but I didn't write it to hit people over the head" with what has been lost in the lives of this mother and daughter. "Rather, as the mother in 'Ironing' says, 'Only help her to know—that she is more than this dress on the ironing board, helpless before the iron,'" which, Olsen says, "is partly what 'Requa' is about too." She points out again that the characters I saw as defeated she had created as survivors, because "it is not the nature of human beings to just lay down and be victims."

"It's interesting how the literature about the Holocaust has begun to change too as we come to know more. What is resistance? How, in one way or another, do we uphold human dignity?" How active must resistance be in order to be called resistance, I ask. Sometimes it appears to be passive but is still resistance, depending on how you define that word. "Well," she says, "often you define it from where you sit. And it has very deep political implications. It is the difference between the terrorists who take things in their own hands and the people who try to give organized voice and action to masses of people, so that [action] is effective. It has to do with what used to be called 'Uncle Tomism' and gauging [action] by the enormous forces arrayed against it, and [planning] the only way to survive for a period. I'm thinking of Sylvia Plath's phrase, 'the courage of a shut mouth against artillery.'" In political struggles, Olsen asserts, "you have to be close enough to understand what's going on. As seen from the outside, we women were nothing. Whose names do we know from history? Who got worshiped? This is the first century in which some of us have become equipped with the capacity to write the reality. We'll never recapture what went on in times past. We don't know and we have no idea of knowing even about the resistance that existed against the Nazis. Most of that is lost forever. We only have indications here and there.

In 1987 Olsen and her husband traveled for three weeks in Russia, where "Riddle" has been published. She "was invited by the Writer's Union" and went to her mother's birthplace, Minsk. She visited a museum with pictures of hundreds of people who "make the point that history is made by numerous human beings, not by a few great leaders." In another museum Stalin's picture was still in place among "pictures of the 'brass.'" Olsen says she was looking at those faces of the revolution of 1905 "for a face like my mother's to see if my mother [was there]. The only other time that I remember [seeing such faces] was when [I] saw what the organized faces of resistance looked like on 'Eyes on the Prize' [about the civil rights struggle in America] on PBS. It was overwhelming and wonderful. Those were times of actual movement." Moreover, Olsen says, "we only understand and know [resistance] in our own lives and in the lives of those around us." For her this is exemplified in "the Sanctuary movement, the [anti]nuclear movement—what's taking place on campuses, even elite campuses where kids can graduate owing $100,000, and on [those] like Cabrillo, City, State [all colleges in California]. It's academe that started hiring people [on a part-time basis without health benefits or pensions], and industry has" copied it. On these campuses are "good people who exhaust themselves because they care about their students, they take time out of their tired bodies and their personal commitments. They have their own aspirations and dreams and intentions that die—silenced! Silences are worse now than ever before, because there are more people who have [these hopes and aspirations], . . . the will, the desire, but the circumstances are not there. This country is full of marvelous resisters who try to keep the human compact"—that is, theirs is "much more the story of humanity [even] in benighted and bigoted times, even if it only exists within [their] own tribe, [their] own family, or [their] own religion. Every single time I hear that some woman has thrown this birthday party or graduation party or other celebration and I know what her life was like, I think, 'My God, human resistance against being dehumanized.'" Resistance, she reminds me, "doesn't create isles of peace—maybe just aisles—what you walk down to get through."

I ask Olsen if that breakdown in the relationship between mothers and daughters alluded to in "I Stand Here Ironing" and in "Tell Me a Riddle" was inevitable. "It is the societal problems that make [human] relationships so hard," she says. "In this our world, the only ones we can hope to depend on (and that doesn't always happen) are the people—whether blood kin or 'arterial' kin (Emily Dickinson's word)—on whom we have some claim or who have some claim on us. Those are the facts. When it comes to dying, to breaking down . . . or just having somebody to take your place in the carpool, the chain of human relationships and human connections is very strong and more necessary than ever in our [nonrural] society. And those acts are not given recognition either." These human relationships, which sustain life and energize the human capacity for resilience and strength, emerge in all of Olsen's stories, whether they are about Stevie and Wes, about the mother and daughter in "Ironing," the two adolescent girls in "O Yes," the disaffected friends in "Hey Sailor," or the pain and recriminations of the family in "Tell Me a Riddle." Like "Requa," they all express "one small aspect of what human reality is."

What "human reality is" for those people whose lives and visions have been inexorably altered by access to Tillie Olsen is problematic because, after four hours of conversation, I am motivated to see hopefulness and continuity where I initially saw despair and depression, and to concentrate on the viability of the human spirit instead of on its fragility. "You can't talk about loss without talking about gain," Olsen says. She has not let her readers ignore the sadness and the desperation of much of human experience, but at the same time she is a woman whose belief in humanity, in energy and compassion, remains undiminished. She has come to represent to her readers that inextinguishable force for progress and peace we continually admire but on which we are often ourselves too exhausted, spiritually and physically, to draw. In breaking through those silences she has consistently decried, she has compelled the rest of us to listen and to speak.

Chapter Two
Biographical Sketch

"I shall write stories when I grow up, and not work in a factory." So says the youthful protagonist in an unpublished story—now part of the Berg Collection in the New York Public Library[1]—by the 18-year-old Tillie Lerner.[2] That the real Tillie Lerner Olsen succeeded in her dream, despite nearly overwhelming obstacles, is implicit in Robert Coles's perception that "everything she has written has become almost immediately a classic" (quoted in Turan 1978, 56). In David Dillon's words, "Among women Tillie Olsen is something of a saint, although she has done her best to avoid canonization."[3] Margaret Atwood declares that for American women writers, the word *respect* is simply inadequate to describe the feelings Olsen evokes: "'reverence' is more like it. This is presumably because women writers, even more than their male counterparts, recognize what a heroic feat it is to have held down a job, raised four children and still somehow managed to become and to remain a writer" (Atwood, 1).

Olsen's life, the inspiration for her fictional subjects, began in almost mythic American fashion on the Nebraska plains. Some details about her early years are uncertain or ambiguous, lending a touch of mystery to her origins. A first-generation American daughter of Russian immigrants, she was born in either 1912 or 1913 in Wahoo, Omaha, or Mead, Nebraska, to a Jewish father, Samuel Lerner, and a mother, Ida Beber Lerner, who probably was nominally Jewish. In any case, although Olsen comments that "no birth certificate seems to exist,"[4] she affirms that she was the second of six children (Werlock interview, 1990).[5] Not until 1979, when Olsen needed a passport, was the matter resolved—after a fashion. In lieu of a birth certificate, government officials told her they would accept two records or statements by older members of the family. Olsen's brother Harry, a lawyer, found two conflicting documents: according to the 1920 census, she was born in 1912; according to the Omaha school records, she was born in 1913. Her father wrote her a note saying, "You was born in Wahoo in 1913" (Werlock interview, 1990). Together, these statements affirming her Nebraska birth secured a U.S. passport for Tillie Olsen.

Both her parents had been involved in the 1905 Russian revolution against the czar and had fled to the United States when the uprising failed (Rosenfelt 1981, 375; Orr, 24). Atheists and committed socialists, Samuel and Ida began living together after their arrival in the United States (Werlock interview, 1990). According to Olsen, Samuel Lerner escaped from Russia after he had been imprisoned and was scheduled to march to Siberia (Orr, 24). To support his family once he arrived in the United States, he had held a series of jobs as farmworker, packinghouse worker (Yalom, 57), painter, paperhanger (Martin, 7) and candy maker; for years he was state secretary of the Nebraska Socialist Party (Werlock interview, 1990; Rosenfelt 1981, 375). In the early 1920s he was blacklisted after the failure of a packinghouse strike (Orr, 23). His experiences greatly influenced his daughter, one of whose youthful memories involves her father organizing men to go to Tulsa, Oklahoma, to help blacks rebuild their homes, which had been razed by fire in a violent 1920s race riot (Orr, 25).

Of Ida Lerner we know less, but we can intuit much from her presence in Olsen's fiction: Olsen dedicated the short story "Tell Me a Riddle" to Ida, Samuel, and the Russian revolutionaries "Seevya and Genya," and Olsen acknowledges that Eva, the main character in the story, is a composite of Ida, Seevya, and Genya (Werlock interview, 1990). In all likelihood Ida was born Jewish but, like Eva, preferred to think of herself in Eva's words: "Race, human; religion, none." Olsen's 1984 story, "Dream Vision," in *Mother to Daughter, Daughter to Mother*,[6] is her most recent tribute to her hard-working immigrant mother who, even on her deathbed, saw hope for the future in a community unhampered by divisions of sex, class, or race.

Whether Bonnie Lyons is correct in her assertion that Ida Beber was not Jewish and thus "for Orthodox Jews Olsen is not, in fact, Jewish," Olsen considers herself a Jewish atheist. In an unpublished interview in 1983, Olsen commented, "I still remain with the kind of *Yiddishkeit* I grew up with."[7] Olsen believes her Jewish socialist background provided her with two important insights: "knowledge and experience of injustice" and "an absolute belief in the potentiality of human beings" (quoted in Lyons, 91). Moreover, Olsen acknowledged that "what is Yiddish in me . . . is inextricable from what is woman in me, from woman who is mother" (quoted in Lyons, 91). Thus as in Olsen's fiction, everything interconnects and intertwines: her roots are not only in her gender, her connection with her mother, and her own role as mother, but also in Jewish humanism and Communist politics. Olsen remembers herself as a young girl sitting in Eugene Debs's lap when he visited Omaha to speak at a socialist meeting; she has never forgotten his statement that "under socialism society would be like a great symphony with each person playing his own instrument" (quoted in Duncan 1984, 36).

This image of a mass of individuals each contributing to the communal harmony of humanity becomes central to the adult Tillie Olsen's fiction. Indeed, Olsen seems to have threaded into her fiction each incident that she found remarkable. Nearly all the memories she has shared, whether with individual interviewers or large audiences, have woven their way into even her very earliest and unpublished writing. In the second and longer version of "Not You I Weep For," the young protagonist is called Nena Asarch, the first name clearly an anagram of Anne, precursor to Anna of *Yonnondio,* the surname suggesting a search or quest. Nena's nickname is Fuzzie because, as she writes in her diary, she can never explain the exact nature of her desires (Berg, 2, 1), just as the youthful Tillie worries because, she says in her journal, "there are so few things we can be sure and definite about—so often I am pulled both ways" (quoted in Rosenfelt 1981, 377–78). Fuzzie is the first of many youthful characters whose names echo "Tillie": Mazie in *Yonnondio,* Jeannie in "Hey Sailor, What Ship?" and "Tell Me a Riddle," Carrie and Parry in "O Yes," Stevie in "Requa I," and even the sensitive androgynous male characters Whitey in "Hey Sailor, What Ship?," and Lennie in "Hey Sailor," "O Yes," and "Tell Me a Riddle." At the very least, these echoes of the author's first name demonstrate the American addiction to nicknames. They may also indicate a longing to create a feeling of community or camaraderie that did not really exist—a longing that surely must have characterized the lonely and sometimes bitter Tillie Olsen.

The first-person narrator, a high school girlfriend of Fuzzie, notes that Fuzzie poetically views nature through "Katherine Mansfield eyes" (Berg, 2, 5), her "sensitive face" registering an "enormous fecundity of reaction" (Berg 2, 6). Numerous references to Katherine Mansfield establish her influence on the young Fuzzie, who even hangs a picture of "Katie Mansfield" in her otherwise pathetically bare room (Berg 2, 7). Again, the substitution of "Katie" for Katherine seems a touching rendition of a desperate young girl's attempt to bring an admired figure into the realm of her pitifully circumscribed experience. When the young woman narrator unexpectedly drops by her home one day, Fuzzie, the eldest of seven children of a poverty-stricken family, is humil-

iated to think of the "dog meat begged from the butcher" that her
mother then "trim[s] and dice[s] for soup to feed a hungry family,"
painfully aware of the "shame of having to haggle for every penny"
(Berg 2, 9–10). Olsen either recalled from memory or actually used
these passages for Eva's recollections of the humiliations of poverty
when, as recounted in "Tell Me a Riddle," she had tried to feed her
seven children.

Like the young Tillie Lerner who read almost all the way "through
the M's" in the Omaha Public Library (Rosenfelt 1981, 376), Fuzzie
loves libraries, repositories of "the volumes with all that wisdom waiting to be read" (Berg 2, 12–13). And, like Tillie who even from a
young age felt there was "never enough time" (Duncan 1984, 36),
Fuzzie observes despairingly, "There isn't time" for all she would like
to read (Berg 2, 13). Fuzzie's reading interests echo Olsen's, which
included Katherine Mansfield and Olive Schreiner; Fuzzie "had devoured every accent, every inflection of their personalities" (Berg 2,
12). Just as Tillie Lerner was frequently ill with childhood diseases
(Duncan 1984, 39), then contracted pleurisy after she began factory
work, Fuzzie is stricken with pleurisy. Moreover, Fuzzie keeps diaries
that she calls the "manifestation of this disease"—but what she means
by "disease" is the desire to write. Similarly, when Olsen kept her
"Faribault journal" while recuperating from pleurisy and incipient tuberculosis in Faribault, Minnesota, she was aware of her fragile physical
condition, but a very different sort of disease preoccupied her: "I don't
know what it is in me, but I must write too. It is like creating white
hot irons in me & then pulling them out . . . so slowly, oh so slowly"
(quoted in Rosenfelt 1981, 384). As in Olsen's life and as often depicted in her published fiction, illness or disease presages or facilitates
an awakening or a release in the character.

When Fuzzie reads aloud from portions of her work, the narrator
privately finds Fuzzie's writing maudlin and trite. In an interesting
parallel, Rosenfelt, to whom Olsen has shown some of her early poems,
finds them the "effusions of an intense, imaginative young woman as
influenced by the romantic traditions of nineteenth-century poetry" as
by social concerns (Rosenfelt 1981, 376). In the story Fuzzie blurts
out, "It was so hard writing that, hammering it out. I wanted so desperately to express the pity of us in this world" (Berg 2, 19). Likewise,
in her Faribault journal Olsen records the intensity of her feelings as
she labored over *Yonnondio*: "At last I write out all that has festered in
me so long—the horror of being a working-class child—& the heroism, all the respect they deserve" (quoted in Rosenfelt 1981, 389). At

the end of the story, Fuzzie dies of pneumonia and is mourned by the narrator who recalls the "lightness of her body" and the "radiance of her face" (Berg 2, 21), a description that prefigures the description of Jeannie in "Tell Me a Riddle." The narrator weeps not for Fuzzie, but "for all our vanished youths" "before we were ever young" (Berg 2, 21).

The companion Berg Collection manuscript is marked "earlier draft (?)" (Berg 1); although only eight pages long (two pages are torn fragments), in some ways it is far more interesting than the later one just discussed. Written in the third person, this manuscript continues the story of Fuzzie and, in addition to drawing obvious parallels between her adolescence and Olsen's, it ventures on romantic and sexual matters that Olsen herself never includes in her published fiction. Here, too, Fuzzie's voracious reading interests echo Olsen's, particularly Katherine Mansfield, along with "the lyricists" and Edna St. Vincent Millay, but the 18-year-old author parenthetically comments that this is "the literature which has such appeal for adolescence" (Berg 1, 1). The high school classmate who was the first-person narrator in the other version is here named Ruth, and the class difference between the two friends is more pronounced. Olsen has frequently spoken of the painful experience of "crossing the tracks" to the academic high school of Omaha, and of the social distinctions she found there. Likely drawn from Olsen's own high school acquaintances and experiences, Ruth is "quick, vivid, witty" and self-confident, unlike poor Fuzzie (Berg, 1, 1). Together the two girls read copiously, but Fuzzie in her anxious love of her friend and her burning desire for knowledge reveals too much of herself, and Ruth abruptly leaves Fuzzie's house. Their friendship cools, and Ruth departs for New York, writing only twice. Fuzzie hears nothing more from Ruth for the rest of the story.

Meanwhile, Fuzzie, like Olsen, leaves high school and finds employment in a tie factory. She has vague desires to improve herself and for a while takes art lessons from a "mediocre artist"; she also continues to read a great deal and for a time "becomes" the characters from her reading. Olsen's publicly stated admiration for Hardy's Jude and Schreiner's Lynadall in *Story of an African Farm* are evident in her inclusion of them in Fuzzie's reading. Fuzzie then attends business college and becomes a stenographer in the factory (Berg 1, 3, 4). At this point the factory girls, led by Communist women, go on strike. The manager agrees to their demands but tells Fuzzie that he plans to fine the strike committee. Because she has great admiration for "Ann, the red," Fuzzie reveals the manager's plan to the Communists and he subsequently fires her for her betrayal (Berg 1, 4). Olsen, too, worked in a tie factory and she, too, formed friendships with Communist women such as Fern Pierce and "Red" Allen after she joined, at age 17, the Young Communist League (YCL) and attended the Communist party school in Kansas City, Kansas (Rosenfelt 1981, 378, 375). Olsen's involvement in a strike landed her temporarily in jail.[8]

Fuzzie, called Nena most of the time now, becomes a model for an artist named Britton whose studio occupies the top floor of the factory. Olsen, too, had been a model for a time, although whether she modeled for an artist with a studio in the tie factory is unknown. She describes Nena's reaction to modeling: "soon she grew to love it, sitting quietly, for hours, in an attitude of beauty, the quietness, downstairs the hum of the the [*sic*] machines" (Berg 1, 4). She had read so much that the "attitudes toward sex she found in books—which romanticized it, made it more intense, more emotional—than it is in most people's lives—had become her attitudes" (Berg 1, 4). Here is an area the mature Olsen explores in neither her published fiction nor her public statements, although apparently she did so in her early unpublished poetry. In the story Britton seduces Nena: "She never forgot his face when he discovered she was a virgin. The amazement, joy, and pride written upon it. She did not know a value was set upon it" (Berg 1, 4). Apparently Tillie Olsen, too, had a romantic interlude with someone at the tie factory where she worked—an unhappy, disillusioning relationship (Rosenfelt 1981, 378).

The next two pages are torn fragments; some crucial lines are missing or indecipherable. Certainly Nena had been pregnant, but whether she has had a miscarriage or an abortion is not clear when she says, "Today I became the most miserable of females. One who cannot talk about her operation" (Berg 1, 5). Rosenfelt, in reading Olsen's early unpublished verses, found poems centering on "the anguish of an abortion or miscarriage and the bitterness of misplaced or betrayed love" (Rosenfelt 1981, 378). Shortly thereafter a fragment describes Nena running into a cemetery and lifting up her hands in a gesture of joy and freedom as she screams, "I'm alive" (Berg 1, 5). Because of the time she spends in the cemetery she contracts pneumonia. As she tries to write during her illness and recuperation, the words do not come easily; they are "damned [*sic*] in." In an early use of Olsen's music metaphor, Nena explains, "Always I long for music, beautiful, beautiful music. In my mind I hear the melodies, great symphonies, enormous choirs of human voices, the run of a piano" (Berg 1, 6). Then the words begin to flow. For Nena, as for many future fictional characters of Olsen, through illness comes a breakthrough or a revelation. The "fence of her pain" breaks her inarticulateness, and now she knows she will write about factory girls *"and* life as it could be" (Berg 1, 7). That is, like Olsen, she will write about both the horror and reality of poverty-stricken, working-class life and the wondrous potential within each human being. Tillie Olsen found at age 18 the major themes and metaphors of her lifetime.

Having decided to write of her paradoxical vision of life, Nena runs outside and looks for Orion, prefiguring Mazie's running toward a star on the farm in *Yonnondio*. When she returns to the house, she sees a baby (whose baby is not clear; several of her sisters are present) "bubbling, blowing soft shining bubbles of sound" (Berg 1, 7). The baby in "I Stand Here Ironing," which Olsen wrote over 30 years later, blows those same "shining bubbles." In a refrain, Nena murmurs to the little four-month-old boy, "little future, love for you" (Berg 1, 7). But the effort of leaving her bed is too much and she faints. As she lies down again, in her thoughts "she lived over the factory, long dim hours of labor, with the iron growing out of the center machine; she became a part of the machine, a hand, every girl around it, also a part of the huge body" (Berg 1, 7). In the image—a familiar one recurring in "The Iron Throat" and "I Stand Here Ironing"—the oppressive and in this case phallic suggestions of the iron twine with the communal image of the united body of women. Suddenly "the child that she could not have was forgotten" (Berg 1, 7), and Nena attempts to write a "poem of thanks." But as she writes "a bubbling sound" begins, and "when it ended, life itself was ended" (Berg 1, 8). Readers of "Tell Me a Riddle" will have no difficulty equating the freeing nature of her illness with the loosening of her tongue and her bursting out of silence, or identifying the image that describes Eva as she grows closer to death.

Tillie Olsen, who as a child had jobs taking care of her numerous brothers and sisters (Duncan 1984, 36) and shelling peanuts after school even at age 10, managed to stay in school through the eleventh grade (Yalom, 57; Rosenfelt 1981, 375). Today, Olsen suggests that critics have neglected the importance of her junior high school and high school education, and believes that her academic training harmonized with her American midwestern roots and her socialist background. After all, she points out, "I was born in William Jennings Bryan's state," and she grew to maturity hearing and reading the oratory of politicians such as Bryan and Clarence Darrow, who visited Omaha (Werlock interview, 1990). Olsen speaks admiringly of the McGuffy Readers she studied in the 7th and 8th grades, textbooks which, with their selections by American writers ranging from Long-fellow and Whittier—whom she knew by heart (Orr, 28)—to Abra-ham Lincoln, one of Olsen's heroes, and Edwin Markham—"who could ever forget 'The Man With the Hoe'?"—not only gave her a rock solid educational base, but also portrayed the United States as "a beacon of liberty and justice" (Werlock interview, 1990).

Olsen still recalls her move to the Omaha Central High School with a pride tinged with awe: it was, she emphasizes, a truly academic high school where Omaha's leading families sent their children to be edu-cated. Its halls were lined with classical statues, and it offered one the opportunity to study Greek as well as Latin. Tillie Lerner was a student in English IX, a special academic class; she vividly remembers her studies in Milton and Wordsworth. During these years Olsen also formed her habit of reading at the Omaha Carnegie Library.

However, her years at the high school also provided their share of difficulties for Tillie Lerner, who alternately pleased and irritated her teacher, Sara Vore Taylor. She remembers, for example, Miss Taylor's displeasure with her habit—"in the days before Kleenex"—of wiping her nose on her sleeve (Werlock interview, 1990). Olsen's published fiction, particularly "I Stand Here Ironing" and "O Yes," laments for the children of the poor the lack of space, time, and motivation to study. That she had firsthand knowledge of this educational dilemma is evidenced in Olsen's failure notice dated 30 April 1929. Signed with a stamp reading "Sara V. Taylor," it is addressed to Mr. Samuel Lerner, 2512 Caldwell St., Omaha, and reads: "The work of Tillie Lerner has not been of passing grade in English IX during the past month."[9] No comment is given in the space under "reason." We know that she wrote a prize-winning humor column called "Squeaks" for the high school paper, and she wrote skits and musicals for the Young People's Socialist League (Rosenfelt 1981, 382, 375). But these accomplishments might not have satisfied the requirements of the English teachers of the pe-riod; in fact, her extracurricular writing successes may have exacerbated whatever image Olsen had already projected. She also stuttered a good deal, so she spent a large share of her time observing and listening (Duncan 1984, 37).

Ultimately, however, Olsen's gratitude to this teacher is evident in her inclusion of Sara Vore Taylor in the acknowledgements section of

Silences, and in her genuine love of the traditional "great" British and European writers. Olsen also read widely in American literature, of course, and she acknowledges a particular debt to Harriet Munro's *Modern American Poetry.* She certainly read Edgar Lee Masters, Vachel Lindsay, Elinor Wylie, Jean Toomer, Hart Crane, Conrad Aiken, Stephen Vincent Benét, Robinson Jeffers, Robert Frost—these were the "big poets at the time," she says, "and I read them avidly." Moreover, during this time Olsen read Katherine Ann Porter and Louise Bogan, as well as such socialist and Marxist journals as the *Liberator* and *Modern Quarterly* (Orr, 27) and *The Comrade* and *The Masses.*[10] According to John L'Heureux, she also "studied the Little Blue Books that the publisher Haldenman-Julius designed for self-tutoring workers" (quoted in *First Drafts,* 62).

Olsen emphasizes that her reading of past as well as contemporary writers influences her own writing to some degree (Werlock interview, 1990). Almost apocryphal now is the story that, while browsing through an Omaha bookstore, Olsen picked up the *Atlantic Monthly* issues containing Rebecca Harding Davis's "Life in the Iron Mills" (Werlock interview, 1990), a novella that affected Olsen for the rest of her life—although she did not discover the name of the author until 1958. The message she received was that even a poor girl like herself could write—and publish—a tale of the lives of the "despised" and ignored people for whom she would continue to speak for more than half a century.

After leaving high school, and for much of the next several decades, Olsen would have to work at all sorts of everyday jobs merely to survive. Over many years these jobs included packinghouse worker, waitress, punch press operator (Rosenfelt 1981, 376); trimmer in a slaughterhouse, hash slinger, mayonnaise jar capper in a food-processing plant, checker in a warehouse (Rosenfelt 1980, 17); shaker in a laundry, secretary, transcriber in a dairy equipment company, and "Kelly 'Girl'" (Burkom and Williams, 74). She joined the YCL in 1931 and remained a member well into the decade (Rosenfelt 1981, 378, 375). In an undated draft of a letter to Philip Rahv, editor of *Partisan Review,* she writes,

Father state secretary Socialist party for years
Education, old revolutionary pamphlets, laying around house, (including liberators), and YCL.
Jailbird—"violating handbill ordinance" [a reference to her arrest and impris-

onment in the Argentine Jail in Kansas City for her work in organizing a
strike in the packing houses].
Occupations: Tie presser, hack writer . . . model, housemaid, ice cream
packer, book clerk. (quoted in Rosenfelt 1981, 376)

Thus as she began submitting serious writing for publication, Olsen
in a somewhat cavalier fashion summarized her youthful background.
Although some question exists as to whether she contracted pleurisy as
a result of factory working conditions or while she was in jail,[11] Olsen
recently confirmed Rosenfelt's statement that the pleurisy resulted
"from working in front of an open window at the tie factory with a
steam radiator in front of it" (Rosenfelt 1981, 378); in jail she became
ill with incipient tuberculosis (Werlock interview, 1990), and in 1932
she was sent back to Omaha before moving to Faribault, Minnesota,
to recuperate (Rosenfelt 1981, 378, 380; Orr, 31). Some confusion
also arises about where she was living when she began writing *Yonnondio*: Olsen says that the pleurisy and incipient tuberculosis "meant that
I had to be taken care of and was given thinking-writing time. I began
Yonnondio the same month that I became pregnant" (quoted in Yalom,
58).[12] Olsen recently stated that she became pregnant and started *Yonnondio* in March 1932 in Faribault where she lived with and was well
cared for by Karla's aunt, Ray Schochet (Werlock interview, 1990). In
any case, Olsen's temporary residence in Faribault also produced the
journal in which she writes: "I shall only care about my sick body—to
be a good Bolshevik I need health first. Let my mind stagnate further,
let my heart swell with neurotic emotions that lie clawing inside like
a splinter—afterwards, the movement will clean that out. First, a
strong body. . . . I don't know what it is in me, but I must write too"
(quoted in Rosenfelt 1981, 384).
   This passage may help to explain what seems a rigid self-control, if
not actually an emotional coldness, that sometimes emanates from Olsen's characters. The primary importance of this journal entry, however, is in its demonstration of Olsen's priorities. Before she was 20
those priorities had formed the woman writer familiar to us today: her
political commitment was ineluctably bound up in her urgent need to
write—and things would become even more complicated when her
daughter Karla, named for Karl Marx, was born the end of 1932 in
Minneapolis, where Olsen lived at 616 University Avenue, N.E. (Werlock interview, 1990). Thus when Olsen left Minnesota for California
in the spring of 1933 (Duncan 1984, 40), she took with her the com-

mitments of a political activist, a writer, and a mother—and probably in that order.

Olsen's travels when she reached California were as frequent as they were sporadic. As she told one interviewer, "When you didn't pay your rent you just moved" (quoted in Duncan 1984, 40); and move she did—from Stockton to Venice and back, and finally to San Francisco in late 1933. After the peaceful life of Faribault, Olsen seems to have thrown herself into political work that provided a voice for her writing, published prolifically in 1934. Sometimes she would bring her baby daughter to work with her at the office of the *Waterfront Worker,* a mimeographed union publication (Werlock interview, 1990; Orr, n. 14, 70, Duncan 1984, 40). Only once did she send Karla to relatives (Werlock interview, 1990). Olsen has said she missed Karla when she was away, but she was simultaneously aware of global struggles in the Philippines, Spain, Guatemala, Africa, Chile, China (Orr, 32). For Olsen as for many others, the thirties was a time of the heady excitement of revolt and desire for change; she felt she belonged to an international, intellectual and political community (Rosenfelt 1981, 386).

Olsen today believes that politics has been "over-emphasized in the whole handling of my life" (Werlock interview, 1990), but, as Rosenfelt argues, "few of Olsen's contemporary admirers realize the extent to which her consciousness, vision, and choice of subject are rooted in an earlier heritage of social struggle—the communist Old Left of the thirties" as well as the largely socialist and anarchist tradition of radical thought she experienced in the teens and twenties (Rosenfelt 1981, 373–74). The year 1934 saw the publication of "The Iron Throat" (part of what is now chapter 1 of *Yonnondio*); two poems, "I Want You Women up North to Know" and "There Is a Lesson"; and two articles, "Thousand-Dollar Vagrant" and "The Strike."

"The Iron Throat," published in the *Partisan Review,* is described by Burkom and Williams as "leftist polemic" in which the "protagonists are proletariat and the 'message' is Marxist" (Burkom and Williams, 71). Stylistically, it looks back to Olsen's earlier concern with the lives of impoverished, trapped workers fighting hopelessly against "fat-bellied capitalists," but it also looks forward to Olsen's "hallmark"—the linking of tragedy with hope (Burkom and Williams, 71). It foretells the rebellion of the working classes: "Someday strong fists [will] batter the fat bellies, and skeletons of starved children batter . . . the fat bellies" (quoted in Burkom and Williams, 71; now *Yonnondio,* 6). Olsen never completed the novel, but when she published the "incomplete" *Yonnondio* in 1974, she declared that her outline for the rest of it included "killing off" Anna (Rosenfelt 1981, 390), just as she had "killed off" Fuzzie/Nena in "Not You I Weep For." Significantly, though, the hope of the novel was to lie in Mazie and her brother Ben. The novel *Yonnondio* opens with the image of Mazie intuitively understanding both the darkness and the wondrous potential of life, and ends with the image of her baby sister Bess ecstatically banging jam jar lids and asserting herself: "*I can do, I use my powers; I! I!*" (*Yonnondio* 132). Mazie, a strong, talented young woman, was supposed to become an artist and to help improve the lives of those around her (Rosenfelt 1981, 290).

The image of woman is central to most of Olsen's other publications in 1934. In "I Want You Women up North to Know" the protagonist begins her polemic by referring to herself in the lowercase "i." But as the poem grows in intensity, she pleads the case of the oppressed seamstresses Maria, Catalina, and Ambrosia, switches to the uppercase "I," and implies serious consequences if the wealthy northern women do not heed their sisters' plight:

> i want you women up north to know
> how those dainty children's dresses you buy
>   at macy's, wanamakers, gimbels, marshall fields,
> are dyed in blood, are stitched in wasting flesh,
> down in San Antonio, "where sunshine spends the winter."

After eloquently cataloguing the litany of their woes, the narrator warns, "Women up north, I want you to know / I tell you this can't last forever. / I swear it won't" (quoted in Burkom and Williams, 67–69).

According to Charlotte Nekola, Olsen's poem is "unusual in that it not only details the conditions of work itself, but also outlines the relationship of third-world workers to a capitalist economy."[14] Moreover, a poem of this sort was highly unusual from a woman writer. Nekola explains:

The ideals of proletarian poetry embraced work and the workplace as central subjects, yet relatively few poems by women on work appeared in the 1930's. Poetry by men in this decade is full of worker-heroes, complaints of displaced workers, political-organizer heroes, and of accounts of strikes and the physical facts of coal mines and steel mills. The "brotherhood" of "workmen" found a noisy outlet in such lines as Joseph Kalar's "Once I rubbed shoulders with sweaty men/pulled when they pulled, strained, cursed."[15] Though women fiction writers and journalists wrote about the mechanics and politics of the workplace, the female equivalent of the male work poem is hard to find. (Nekola, 132).

The middle of 1934 was a momentous time for Olsen and other Communist activists, including Jack Olsen, whom she had met in 1933 (Orr, 31). A violent clash on July 5 1934—known as Bloody Thursday, the worst day of the San Francisco Maritime Strike—"left several strikers dead and many injured on both sides" (Burkom and Williams, 72). Along with Jack Olsen and others, Tillie Olsen was arrested on a vagrancy charge. To protect her family, she says she used the same false name (Teresa Landale) she had used for her previous arrest (Werlock interview, 1990) and a false address, which in fact was the address of the *Waterfront Worker* (Burkom and Williams, 73; Rosenfelt 1981, 384). Her arrest captured the attention not only of the press, but also of Lincoln Steffens, who invited Olsen to visit him and Ella Winter at their home in Carmel. There Steffens convinced Olsen of the need to describe the brutality of her arrest. Olsen wrote two pieces as a result: "Thousand-Dollar Vagrant," which describes the violent behavior of the police toward Olsen and her comrades, and "The Strike," an eloquent account of the strike itself and her position as activist and writer—and woman.

At the beginning of "The Strike" she describes her dilemma: she is not actually on the "battlefield" but behind the lines. Sounding notably like the ironing mother of the later "I Stand Here Ironing" who tries to make sense of, to "total," the fragmented meaning of her life, Olsen writes that if she had had time, peace and quiet, and solitude she might have been able to understand and explain the significance of the strike: "All that has happened might resolve into order and sequence, fall into neat patterns of words. I could stumble back into the past and slowly, painfully rear the structure in all its towering magnificence, so that the beauty and heroism, the terror and significance of those days, would enter your heart and sear it forever with the vision" (quoted in Rosenfelt 1981, 385). The essay ends with the image of a pregnant woman, full of life as she looks at the devastation in the wake of the strike: "She might have been a marble, rigid, eternal, expressing some vast and nameless sorrow. But her face was a flame, and I heard her say after a while dispassionately, as if it had been said so many times no accent was needed, 'we'll not forget that. We'll pay

it back . . . someday'" (quoted in Duncan 1984, 42). As would become typical of Olsen's fiction, the answer to oppression, the hope of
the future, is embodied in young women who will fight to improve
life for their children.

Of all her 1934 publications, "The Iron Throat" was especially well
received; it was called a work of "early genius" by Robert Cantwell,
who tried to locate Olsen through a note in the *New Republic,* saying
four editors and a literary agent wished to contact her. Of the many
publishers trying to ascertain her whereabouts, Bennett Cerf and Donald Klopfer of Random House actually succeeded in reaching her. After
learning of her arrest, they offered her a monthly stipend if she could
send them a chapter a month. Olsen at first agreed and sent Karla to
stay with relatives, but she then became involved with her job as a
typist, and eventually she decided not to pursue the project. Years later
she told an interviewer that she felt like a "failure" for not finishing
the novel (Duncan 1984, 41). The guilt she must have felt at leaving
Karla is movingly depicted in the ironing mother's similar thoughts
about her daughter Emily in "I Stand Here Ironing."

The year 1935 proved to be a similarly active one for Olsen, for she
was invited to attend the American Writers Congress in New York City
with such luminaries of the left as Mike Gold, James T. Farrell, Nelson
Algren, Richard Wright, Theodore Dreiser, and Nathanael West, some
of the many who either signed the call to the congress or actually
marched with their compatriots in the parade (Rosenfelt 1981, 387,
n. 405). At the congress she was one of a small number of women
invited to address this body, which included "most of the major writers
of the day" (Rosenfelt 1981, 387). Olsen still owns a copy of a car-
tooned sketch that appeared in the *New Masses* issue covering the congress: it depicts the "profile of a lean, intense young woman" (Rosenfelt
1981, 387) whose name was beginning to be known not only because
of her articles but because of her stint in jail for her participation in
the events of Bloody Thursday.

But Olsen published nothing in 1935. Of her many friends, she has
mentioned three in particular who seem to mark that period of her life:
Georgie Kaye, Jack (Julius) Eggan, and Jack Olsen. Kaye, who had
been Olsen's "beloved friend since 1936," was the youngest member
of the Abraham Lincoln Brigade that went to Spain to fight Franco
and fascism during the Spanish Civil War. Kaye's death in the spring
of 1990, Olsen notes sadly, is another in "my series of great losses"
(Werlock interview, 1990).

Eggan was the young seafarer to whom she would later dedicate "Hey Sailor, What Ship?" She recalls him as one of the most remarkable men she has ever known. Apparently emblematic for Olsen of almost limitless human potential, Eggan took root in indifferent soil and bloomed in myriad directions. He spent his early years with his younger brother in a Montana orphanage. A tall and impressive-looking young man, he lied about his age and joined the Navy, becoming at age 16 the Navy welterweight champion. He evinced a strong sense of responsibility and concern for his younger brother, whom he helped to leave the orphanage and acquire an education. After his naval discharge, Eggan became a seafarer, attended the YCL school, and met people who interested him in fiction, poetry, and music. According to Olsen he had an engaging manner with others, inspiring them to go beyond their limited beliefs in their capacities and earning the respect of all who knew him. Olsen recalls that, in addition to his leadership abilities, he "flowered" in every way—intellectually, culturally, socially. During the Spanish Civil War Eggan, like Kaye and numerous other seafarers, volunteered for the Abraham Lincoln Brigade. He was killed at the age of 24 during the 1938 retreat across the Ebro. In 1988 Olsen's daughter Julie, who is named for Eggan, visited the Ebro and brought back some soil from its banks, eliciting Olsen's affirmation that despite his early death, Eggan "has kept on living for me and for everyone who knew him" (Werlock interview, 1990).

Olsen's other close friend during this period was Jack Olsen. By 1936 Tillie Lerner had begun living with him; by 1937 she was pregnant with her second child, Julie (Duncan 1984, 42); and in 1943—after the birth of her third child, Kathie, and before Jack left with the U.S. Army—Tillie and Jack Olsen were married in a San Francisco church (Werlock interview, 1990). Altogether she would bear four daughters: Karla, born in 1932; Julie, in 1938; Katherine Jo, in 1943; and Laurie, in 1948. Olsen notes that her husband was "in some respects" similar to the admirable Lennie of "Hey Sailor" and "O Yes" (Werlock interview, 1990). Glimpses of their life together seem to appear to the relationship of Helen and Lennie in their recollection of the events of Bloody Thursday, in which Tillie and Jack Olsen participated, as well as in their affectionate concern for their daughters. Certainly Olsen's commitment to politics and her need to work to support her growing family gradually "eclipsed" her writing (Rosenfelt 1981, 382; Orr, 31). Recently Olsen commented that during the 1930s, as well as the 1940s and 1950s, her concerns centered on "my family, my workplace, my community, and my world" (Werlock interview, 1990).[16]

As president of her PTA, Olsen worked relentlessly with others to improve conditions in the public schools. She fought for and succeeded in adding a playground and a library to the school her daughters attended. During this period she also researched and unearthed information about the early-nineteenth-century educator Kate Kennedy, after whom her children's school was named. Olsen discovered that Kennedy, "one of the most beloved of all principals in San Francisco," was the first woman to run for state superintendent of education—long before women were eligible to vote—and was the author of numerous influential articles, including "The Teaching of Ignorance in Our Public Schools." She taught herself Italian in order to communicate with the many Italian students—and their parents—in her school, and she was instrumental in the fight to allow Chinese children into the public schools. Kennedy also brought to court the case that established teachers' tenure in California. Emphasizing Kennedy's significant contribution to U.S. history, Olsen points out that Elizabeth Cady Stanton traveled all the way to San Francisco to meet the Irish-American woman responsible for the first decision ordering equal pay for equal work.

In addition to her work with the public schools, Olsen helped form a separate women's division of the International Longshoremen's and Warehousemen's Union (ILWU) to which Jack Olsen belonged, enrolled in a class on "The Woman Question" at the YCL headquarters on San Francisco's Haight Street, and for a few months in 1946 wrote two columns in *People's World*. In addition to a piece on Benjamin Franklin, her articles for that publication included "Wartime Gains of Women in Industry" and "Politically Active Mothers—One View," which argued that motherhood should be considered political work (Rosenfelt 1981, 399, 400, 406). She also wrote occasional pieces for the CIO auxiliary paper (Werlock interview, 1990).

The activism and communal sense of those years seems embodied for Olsen in her admiration for Agnes Smedley, whose *Daughter of Earth* influenced Olsen even more profoundly than did Rebecca Harding Davis's "Life in the Iron Mills" (Werlock interview, 1990). Smedley demonstrated an enviably clear purpose as, arriving in China in 1929, she lived and worked with her Chinese comrades for a decade (Rosenfelt 1980, 16). During the Long March with the Red Army, Smedley, her "typewriter strapped on her back," lived alongside such high-ranking Communist officials as Chou En-lai and Mao Tse-tung in the çaves of

Yenan (Werlock interview, 1990). She eventually saw Mao's victory over the Kuomintang army in 1949 (Rosenfelt 1980, 16). In a perhaps less exciting but nonetheless significant protest at home, Olsen, with thousands of other women, boycotted silk stockings to protest the Japanese invasion of Manchuria and other parts of China. After her stint with the YCL, Olsen became a member of the Communist party "for several years in the late 30s and again in the 40s after World War II." From the beginning she disagreed with the party's "treatment of people within its ranks." Olsen recalls her dislike for the "party line" and its "verbiage." Particularly abhorrent was the chasm dividing the party leaders from the workers—the people who "knew what was going on." Equally disturbing were the party's charges of heresy for those who disagreed with its policies, and its expulsion of such people. Ultimately, however, Olsen has few, if any, regrets: she is glad to have been a YCL and party member during those years, and says that, even today, "I still feel that socialism is, must be, the future" (Werlock interview, 1990).

As the United States passed through the years of the Dies Committee[17] and entered the McCarthy era, Olsen remembers that, during the hearings held by the House Un-American Activities Committee (HUAC), she "was standing there ironing" when a neighbor called to ask if her radio was on. When Olsen replied no, the neighbor advised her to listen to it "because," she said, "it's about you." When Olsen switched on the radio she heard a voice saying "Tillie Olsen, alias Tillie Lerner, alias Teresa Landale" is an "agent of Stalin working in San Francisco public schools to take over the public schools." Her accuser was the host of a weekly 15-minute radio gossip show that, Olsen says, was used as a vehicle for blackmailing the wealthy (Werlock interview, 1990).

Olsen was never subpoenaed, but Jack Olsen was not so fortunate. His accuser, Leo Rosser, testified in December 1953 before the HUAC, at that time chaired by Rep. Jack H. Velde of Illinois. Rosser, a former Communist party member disillusioned with the party's hypocritical treatment of "Negroes," identified Jack Olsen among the Communists he had known while working for the party in California between 1932 and 1944. Rosser testified, "I was on the county committee of the Los Angeles Young Communist League with Jack Olsen. He was the head of Los Angeles County. I was on the state committee of the YCL. He was on the State committee, and he later became head of the YCL in California, and then he was an open Communist, and then he later became an official in the Local 6 of the Warehousemen's Union."[18]

According to Tillie Olsen, Jack Olsen, after spending a year or so as the union's business agent, had become director of education because he had been teaching literacy skills through the union newspaper (Werlock interview, 1990). During his testimony, Rosser offered up as exhibits pamphlets and posters describing the San Francisco Workers' School at 121 Haight Street as "the only school in San Francisco which authoritatively bases its education on the theory of Marxism-Leninism under the official guidance and leadership of the Communist Party of the United States of America and the Communist International" (Hearing, 1953, 3074). The first three names on the Advisory Council list are "Langston Hughes, writer; Ella Winter, writer; Lincoln Steffens, writer" (Hearing, 1953, 3078). The cost for 12 sessions, over a period of three months, was $1 for employed and 50¢ for unemployed workers; courses included such subjects as Principles of Communism, Marxian Economics, Leninism, History of the American Labor Movement, and History of the Russian Revolution (Hearing, 1953, 3075–76). Jack Olsen's course, meeting during the spring term (5 March–31 May) of 1934, was entitled "History of the Youth Movement and Program of the Young Communist International" (Hearing, 1953, 3076). In its annual report, the HUAC had indexed Jack Olsen, "also known as Jack Olshansky," as "Official of Local 6 ILWU; Communist Party Functionary."[19]

In Jack Olsen's appearance before the HUAC—which he characterized as a "wholly un-American committee"—he explained his reasons for standing on "the Bill of Rights and particularly its First and Fifth Amendments"[20]:

All of my adult life I have tried to be a good citizen, a good neighbor, a good shopmate, a good union man and a good father to my children. I have tried to exercise my duties and my rights as a loyal American citizen—by interesting myself in and speaking out on public issues, by voting for candidates who seemed to me to be right, by serving on public committees and in organizations working for the common welfare, and by serving in the Armed Forces of my country. . . . I believe that I would be less than a good citizen if I did not resist with all of my power efforts of this committee to curtail our freedoms, to smear, intimidate and punish citizens without due course of law; to attack and villify legitimate trade unions and their leaders, and to make meaningless our Constitution and our Bill of Rights. . . .

I cannot with good conscience testify before this committee in such a manner as to open me, my friends or my acquaintances to further attacks which inevitably follow from this committee. I cannot with good conscience place in jeopardy organizations to which I may or may [not] have been affiliated. I cannot with good conscience allow my testimony to endanger the jobs and livelihoods of others. (Jack Olsen's HUAC statement)

Tillie Olsen points out that during the McCarthy hearings, being named or subpoenaed did not destroy one's chances for employment; but if one were on the so-called blacklists issued by the Office of the Attorney General, he or she could not hold a job (Werlock interview, 1990). No one with a "record" could work around ships or hold jobs in places that delivered or warehoused supplies for the armed forces. Jack Olsen was therefore ineligible to return to his union job or to work in the warehouses, and at the age of 40 he found himself apprenticed to a printer (apprentices were called "boys") for the requisite period of six years (Werlock interview, 1990). Tillie Olsen could not hold a job for more than a month before the FBI would appear and speak to her employer, who would then fire her. One job she especially remembers was in an antiquarian bookstore specializing in first editions. When her employer reluctantly told her he would have to let her go, he said, sotto voce, "You have to learn to live low like a blade of grass. . . . You have to be invisible—bend with the wind—be trodden underfoot" (Werlock interview, 1990).

At home, the Olsen family experienced both good times and bad. The children were sometimes discriminated against by those whose fear of communism was fueled by the McCarthy hearings, but they were also helped by others who went out of their way to "defend or protect them" (Werlock interview, 1990). Kathie and Julie share amusing as well as painful memories because during these times they were bolstered by family "solidarity" and the inevitable "family jokes" (Werlock interview, 1990). This sense of humor, evident in Olsen's fictional families, no doubt helped the Olsens weather this difficult time. When Jack Olsen died more than three decades later (26 February 1989), other members of the St. Francis Square Apartments recalled his "familiar chuckle" and his "rock-solid wryly philosophical response to the human condition," noting that the "years of struggle and inevitable disappointment seemed to enrich, rather than embitter him."[21] A more formal tribute was made less than a month later when San Francisco Mayor Art Agnos officially proclaimed 25 March 1989 "Jack Olsen Remembrance Day in San Francisco." Praising Olsen for his contributions to the "betterment" of the city, Agnos called him "an esteemed, trusted, and outstanding labor leader, having served as a longtime member, organizer, and educator in the I.L.W.U., [International] Typographical Union, and the Labor Studies Program."[22]

Tillie Olsen recalls "endless stories" of that era and is adamant about the need for those who still remember the events of the period to record them (Werlock interview, 1990). The impact of the McCarthy era on the lives of workers is unrecognized by most people who tend to think only in terms of the "Hollywood Ten" and Lillian Hellman. Much of the McCarthy experience has not been filmed, studied, or discussed because, as Olsen points out, very few of those whose lives were "damaged" during that time possessed the tools with which to write their version of events: most of them were not from professional or educated families and therefore did not write their accounts (Werlock interview, 1990).

In her own story, the year 1954 was a memorable one for Tillie Olsen. The family traveled to Washington, D.C., and in a vivid image Olsen recalls "all of us on the train sitting up" during the 3,000-mile trip as she and Jack pointed out to their daughters such sights as the steel mills of Gary, Indiana and Pittsburgh, Pennsylvania. In Washington they spent what would be the last time with Olsen's mother, Ida, who had moved there with Samuel shortly after World War II (Werlock interview, 1990). Olsen had also begun to write again. Although she had, since the 1930s, continued to try to write by day while riding the bus to work and by night when the children were asleep (Burkom and Williams, 74), her efforts had resulted mainly in "notes made on file cards, kept in pockets" (Werlock interview, 1990). Arthur Foff of San Francisco State University was, says Olsen, "Karla's dearest instructor. She urged my enrollment in his evening writing class" (Werlock interview, 1990). Although she recalls that by taking the course she had even "*less* time—I had to fit in the class along with my job and other responsibilities"—she wrote and submitted an early version of "I Stand Here Ironing." Foff "read it to the entire class," and his praise rekindled her belief in her abilities. In fact, so great was his respect for her talent that he later told her not to come to class, for he felt he had nothing more to teach her. "He believed in me as a writer," Olsen states, and "I loved him, am indebted to him—and know my luck that it was with him I enrolled and not someone else" (Werlock interview, 1990).

The following years were impressively productive for the woman who had subsumed her writing talents for two decades. Always a voracious reader, she continued to add to the list of authors she admired. A "very partial," by no means inclusive, list of writers not previously mentioned cites Elizabeth Madox Roberts, Ethel Voynich, Sarah Teasdale, H.D.; the midwestern writers Selma Lagerlof, Susan Glaspell,

Mari Sandoz, and Ruth Suckow; also Mary Wilkins Freeman, Sara Orne Jewett, Mary Austin, Zora Neale Hurston, Josephine Johnson, Adelaide Crespey, Dorothy Richards, Anna Seghers, Kate Chopin, and Toni Morrison, whose novel *Beloved,* suggests Olsen, may be the best book of the last two decades (Werlock interview, 1990). Of the many writers she admires for character as well as for talent, Olsen singles out two: Grace Boynton, "the last white woman to leave China," only one of whose books has been published (*The River Garden of Pure Repose* in 1952), although her unpublished manuscript, "The Secret Springs," is, according to Olsen, required reading for John Fairbanks's classes at Harvard University's Center for Asian Studies; and Nobel Prize–winner Pearl Buck. When Buck, this "important" and "prolific" writer, spoke at the Palace Hotel in San Francisco in the 1930s, Olsen recalls having been "torn apart" because she was working as a waitress at the hotel and was thus unable to hear Buck's entire speech (Werlock interview, 1990).

In addition to Edna St. Vincent Millay, Olsen also read Carl Sandburg, Walt Whitman, Victor Hugo, the early D. H. Lawrence, W. E. B. DuBois, Langston Hughes, Willa Cather, Ellen Glasgow, Upton Sinclair, Katherine Mansfield, Olive Schreiner, John Dos Passos, Agnes Smedley and Rebecca Harding Davis (Rosenfelt 1981, 376); Theodore Dreiser and Jack London (Orr, 28). Moreover, she continued to read the modernist male writers now firmly established in the canon. Of Steinbeck, with whose *Grapes of Wrath* her *Yonnondio* has such obvious parallels, she says she is "happy he was writing in the 1930s": he is, she believes, a "valuable influence in his time." Although Hemingway has little appeal for her, she has read all his major works; and she began reading Faulkner in the late 1930s. She notes further that she did not care much for Wallace Stevens or Ezra Pound, but she admires the Eliot of *Four Quartets* and the Joyce of *Dubliners.* As is obvious in her numerous literary commentaries in *Silences,* she has read widely among European writers, reserving a special place for her "beloved" Chekhov (Werlock interview, 1990).

From 1955–56 she held the Stegner Fellowship in creative writing at Stanford University, where she was the only "unknown" among the group that year, which included James Baldwin, Bernard Malamud, Flannery O'Connor and Katherine Ann Porter. 1956 saw the publication of her first work in over 20 years: "Help Her to Believe" in the *Pacific Spectator.* It was reprinted that same year in *Stanford Short Stories* and appeared the following year as "I Stand Here Ironing" in *Best American Short Stories.* 1957 also saw the publication of "Hey Sailor, What

Ship?" in *New Campus Writing* and "Baptism" in *Prairie Schooner*. The short story "Tell Me a Riddle" appeared in *New World Writing* in 1960 and was reprinted that same year in *Stanford Short Stories*. All four stories, including "Baptism" under the new title "O Yes," were collected and published in 1961 as *Tell Me a Riddle*.

Olsens burst of creativity in the mid 1950s, crowned by a Ford Foundation grant in literature in 1959 and the O. Henry Award for *Tell Me a Riddle* in 1961, unquestionably owes a great deal to the spirit of her participation in the events of the 1930s and 1940s. Although she has said that later she "had a different understanding of the ways in which the party was so wrong in how it handled people" (quoted in Duncan 1984, 52), there can be no doubt, according to Rosenfelt, that Olsen's "Marxian perspective and experiences ultimately enriched her literature." In her study of Olsen in the thirties, Rosenfelt cites three contradictions in Olsen's involvement with communism. First, it "required great commitments of time and energy" but "it also validated the study and production of literature and art." Second, although much Marxist literature and criticism was "narrowly prescriptive," it nevertheless encouraged "a social consciousness." And third, although "profoundly masculinist," communism simultaneously paid "serious attention to women's issues" (Rosenfelt 1981, 381).

Clearly, all four of Olsen's stories in *Tell Me a Riddle* are rooted in her experiences of the thirties and later. "I Stand Here Ironing," the most overtly autobiographical fiction she has ever published (Werlock interview, 1990), mentions neither Olsen's passion for politics nor her gift for writing but instead focuses on the third of her twined interests in that period: motherhood and the price that women and their children pay for the circumstances of both personality and history. Olsen's feelings of anguish and longing when leaving Karla with relatives is surely significant in her depiction of the ironing mother who, like Olsen, lacked the means to encourage and enhance the talent of her eldest daughter. Olsen naturally considered higher education important for her children: "But we did not know much about how to go about it till Laurie. Kathie used to say, 'Why should I go to college. I did better than you did, Ma. I got through high school.' But in her mid-30s she did enroll, graduated" (Werlock interview, 1990).

"Hey Sailor, What Ship?"—although, as will be shown, apparently influenced by Eliot's *Waste Land*—obviously owes much to Olsen's involvement with the ILWU and the 1934 San Francisco Maritime Strike, not to mention the *Waterfront Worker* in whose service she spent a good deal of time, performing a variety of jobs (Rosenfelt, 1981,

384). However, the story also acknowledges the phenomenon of the postwar suburban movement when, spurred by the G.I. Housing Bill, "the calyx of the cities opened" and moved outwards (Werlock interview, 1990). Although Whitey's youthful potential is reminiscent of that of Jack Eggan, to whom the story is dedicated, the similarity seems to end with their bright youth and their seafaring lives. The Whiteys of the world, muses Olsen, were a "remarkable breed," even "tragic" in a way. Olsen's sympathetic portrayal of Whitey's alcoholic decline was honored in 1989 when "Hey Sailor" was included in an anthology on alcoholism and the short story.[23]

"O Yes," like "Hey Sailor," also provides insight into a woman's changing sense of responsibility when concern for children and family gradually eclipses that for politics. Additionally, however, "O Yes" derives from Olsen's childhood and adolescence in Omaha, where she attended black church services and was exposed to the affective tones of "black language" (Duncan 1984, 37–38), as well as from her similar experiences in black churches in San Francisco. Olsen considers it part of her "good fortune" that after the Lerners left their farm they lived in two partly black neighborhoods in Omaha where Olsen sang for a time in a black church choir (Werlock interview, 1990). Alva and Parry of "O Yes" were created out of women and children with whom Tillie Olsen was friendly, while Alva's "vision" or "song" is, Olsen says, a "composite of three versions" she heard over the years in the form of "musical teas." These "musical teas" consisted of music and rhymed narrative recitations by black women, "some of whom could barely read and write." Alva's vision is a sort of "folklore" that Olsen brings up to date in the story. The story is also partly rooted in the experiences of Olsen's daughter Kathie, who was in junior high school just after *Sputnik* and just before the civil rights movement when administrations imposed "tracking" systems on the students. "O Yes" very movingly describes the painful divisions imposed by "class/sex/race," separating us from "those with whom we are most deeply bonded" as white people move to different, sometimes more privileged, worlds, frequently leaving close friends behind (Werlock interview, 1990).

And certainly "Tell Me a Riddle" has a basis in Olsen's mother and father's political involvement in the 1905 revolution, as well as in their move to the United States and the effects of American life on their children. Like the fictional Clara, Olsen recalls that she herself had "a singing mother" (Werlock interview, 1990). Many of Ida Lerner's grandchildren, like Eva's, were separated from her by half a continent or more. Although Karla spent time with her grandparents when she was 3 and visited them again when she was 19—Jeannie's age when she takes care of her grandmother Eva—Laurie, the youngest, saw her grandmother Ida only twice: when she was three months old and, for the last time, when she was 6.

Indeed, despite her subsequent lack of affiliation with the Communist party, Olsen speaks publicly of her admiration for its goals, many of which she believes were, like those of her parents, honorable and humanist: recently she stated, "I profoundly believe that the vision that came out of people like my parents is the most realistic one for our time," adding that she hopes to see what Nelson Mandela calls a "'nonracist' society" (Werlock interview, 1990). In 1984 she visited the Soviet Union and was extremely moved to see pictures of workers in that 1905 revolution—the "hundreds and hundreds of faces" (Pearlman interview) that she had described in terms of chorus, voice, and song in so much of her fiction.

Ultimately Tillie Olsen eschews labels and is suspicious of any description that is "inherently exclusionary" (Yalom, 59). Perhaps Burkom and Williams come closest to an accurate portrayal of the woman and the writer when they describe her as "neither sexist nor leftist" but instead a "passionately committed humanist" (Burkom and Williams, 66). Unlike many of her modern and contemporary peers who espouse individualism and the cult of self, Olsen believes in Matthew Arnold's communal "human struggle bursting the thick wall of self." In answer to Duncan's question about the central position of a "core of self" in literature, Olsen erupted angrily: "It is irrelevant to even talk of the core of self when circumstances do not sustain its expression or development, when life has tampered with it and harmed it" (quoted in Duncan 1984, 39). A much less polemical writer in *Tell Me a Riddle* than she was in her writings of the thirties, Olsen's artistic achievements, in Catharine Stimpson's opinion, are reminiscent of Edith Wharton's in *The House of Mirth*: "Olsen wants to teach us about the vileness of a system by dramatizing the indifference with which it victimizes human beings" (Stimpson 1977, 1).

It may be that Olsen has drawn as much as she could from the remarkable events of the twenties and thirties that influenced and shaped her. Even the Ford Foundation grant in 1959, according to Olsen, "came almost too late (*Silences*, 20)." She has published little fiction since *Tell Me a Riddle*—"Requa" appeared in 1970 in the *Iowa Review* and was reprinted as "Requa I" the following year in *The Best American Stories* and "Dream Vision," a brief tribute to her mother, was published in 1984 in *Mother to Daughter, Daughter to Mother,* edited by Olsen. Yet Olsen's humanistic vision has never wavered, as evidenced in her tremendous academic and public commitment in the 1960s and 1970s. She was a Radcliffe Institute fellow from 1962 to 1964 and during that time used the Schlesinger Library there to make a tape about Kate Kennedy (Werlock interview, 1990). Between 1969 and 1974 she was visiting professor or writer in residence at Amherst College, the University of Massachusetts (Boston), Stanford, and the Massachusetts Institute of Technology. In 1967 she received a National Endowment for the Arts grant and in 1972–73 she lived and worked at the MacDowell Writers' Colony in Peterborough, New Hampshire, where she worked on her afterword to Rebecca Harding Davis's *Life in the Iron Mills* and on *Yonnondio.*

Olsen's admirable humanism reserves a place for feminism, a conviction that is traceable to her earliest work. She is one of the first writers "in the past quarter century to bring a consciously gendered voice to literature" (Yalom, 60), and that voice emerged particularly after 1972 when, while searching through her old papers, Olsen's husband Jack rediscovered the fragments of the manuscript of her "lost" novel *Yonnondio* (Werlock interview, 1990). Although Olsen published *Yonnondio* in 1974 without completing her plan to depict Mazie as a successful artist who could tell the story of workers like herself and her family, particularly her tragic mother Anna, Olsen's demonstration of the human creative quality especially through women added "a significant dimension to the largely masculine and public world of the proletarian novel" (Rosenfelt 1981, 399). In Stimpson's words, Olsen "seems to reserve a special respect for the mother who . . . keeps the home going. Such a mother is a major symbol of the battered, ennobled will, and when she fails, Olsen assigns to her fall the dignity that tragedy once reserved for kings" (Stimpson 1977, 3). In the early 1980s, referring to the disdain that women feminists in the seventies displayed toward their mothers' lives, Olsen observed that nothing or little had been written to express the "true content" of those lives, of the "real achievement in motherhood" (quoted in Orr, 34). Olsen had addressed that problem from the view of women writers in her essay "Women Who are Writers in Our Century: One Out of Twelve," delivered as a talk at the Modern Language Association in 1971 and published in *College English* in 1972. Her 1972 "Biographical Interpretation" of Rebecca Harding Davis, published as an afterword to the reissued *Life in the Iron Mills,* decried the lack of attention to women writers in the United States, as did the 1978 publication *Silences,* a collection of Olsen's previous talks as well as quotations from writers on the creative process, with particular attention to women writers.

A number of critics pay tribute to Olsen's writings about mothering, crediting her, in Rosenfelt's words, with helping "a new generation of women writers to test the subject" of the painful complexities of motherhood "with a fullness and honesty never before possible in American literature" (Rosenfelt 1981, 397). Olsen's most recent story, "Dream Vision," consists of barely three pages of narrative, but is an immensely affecting description of her mother Ida's last hours before giving in to cancer. On Christmas Eve her mother sees a vision she takes to be the three wise men coming to visit her. Once they remove their veils, however, they reveal themselves to be three wise women. They wear not jewelled robes but "the coarse everyday shifts and shawls of the old country women of her childhood," and they ride not camels but "farm beasts" (in *Mother to Daughter,* 262). Finally Olsen's mother realizes that the three women are holding a little baby and she weeps so that her words can barely be understood, speaking of "the human baby, before we are misshapen; crucified into a sex, a color, a walk of life, a nationality . . . and the world yet warrings and winter" (*Mother to Daughter,* 263). Once again Olsen demonstrates her humanity through a woman and a baby.

Even when she is writing primarily about women, Olsen's humanism and generosity shine through her words. Throughout her career, readers, critics and admirers have noted her fairness: she writes about women, but "never loses compassion for the victimized male"; men who are poor are just as likely to be "victims, too" (Yalom, 60; Stimpson 1977, 3). About relationships between men and women, Olsen declares: "Sex and love *are* in my fiction as they appear in my created peoples' lives: childbirth, rape, miscarriage; deep caring (as best they know how) in long-term relationships between wife and husband, physical attraction; sexuality as it is expressed, understood, by young children; sexuality as expressed in the old; and sex as gender—the difference in the shaping into 'female' and 'male' as children; the differing circumstances, tastes, lives as women or men" (Werlock interview, 1990). In 1978 she had surprised students at Stanford University by telling them that we are all formed and shaped by our class, gender, and race (Yalom, 59). That in the end she cannot be neatly pigeonholed as "working class" or "feminist" is a sign of her wide appeal and genius. After all, as one critic, at first approaching her from a feminist perspective, points out, Olsen is "no politician but an artist."[24]

Although the feminist movement of the 1960s and 1970s helped Olsen—as did the socialist and Communist movements of the 1930s—ultimately it is her style that, in Yalom's words, "accounts for her prestige in literary circles" (Yalom, 61). Richard Scowcroft, editor of *Stanford Short Stories,* in which Olsen was published, recalls her "pouring not months but years into an anguished and constant reshaping, reappraising of any story."[25] The density and richness of her poetic prose is the result. A 1989 Stanford University Writers exhibit of a page draft of "Requa I" included the comment that Olsen's use of different-color pen and pencil marks "suggest that she has revised it no less than four times" (L'Heureux, *First Drafts,* 65). Olsen herself admits to reading aloud so that "it sounds right"; moreover, she warns, "Don't have contempt for people, don't have contempt for your readers, trust them, they are intelligent, they have lived as profoundly as you have. Maybe they haven't articulated what you the writer have, but they'll fill it in with their own lives, they'll write it along with you. . . . I assure you I am not as good a writer as some of you may think I am. It is you and what you bring to it . . . the common work that we do together" (quoted in Yalom, 64).

Always Olsen stresses community, solidarity, and common humanity. She continues to travel around the United States, filling huge rooms with audiences eager to hear her read and speak. And she continues to write: as recently as September and October of 1990, she took up residency at the Leighton Arts Colony in Banff, Canada. She says she's "still working, writing" and that there is "an infinite amount" she still intends to do. Moreover, she has endured a great deal over the past few years, including the illnesses and deaths of family members and close friends. She probably needs someone such as George Eliot had, a being who "'protects and stimulates in me the health of highest productivity'" (Werlock interview, 1990), but as she notes in *Silences,* "No one's development should any longer be at the cost of another's" (222). So she continues her active life, trying to balance her responsibilities in her home, her community, her profession, and her world.

Yet even if Tillie Olsen does not write another book, we are the richer for having read the major works—*Yonnondio* and *Tell Me a Riddle*—and for the way Olsen's voice has touched the lives of writers, workers, and women. We are the richer for her thoughtful public addresses and nonfiction writing in which she has urged more diversity in the curricula, more attention to nonprivileged, ethnic and women writers, and more time and credence to the stories of those who, until recently, have been silenced. It is Olsen, among others, we must thank for our increased awareness of these issues and for the profound changes her writing has encouraged not only on our campuses and in our class-rooms but in the very tenor of our thinking. An indomitable figure on the vast California landscape that she has made her home, Olsen has a voice that, like that of Eva in "Tell Me a Riddle," still pulsates and resonates as, aware of the imperfect society in which she lives, she teaches us that we have the potential to become that "loftier race": with Eva and with Tillie Olsen, we believe that "these things shall be."

Chapter Three

Yonnondio

Tillie Olsen began to write her only novel, *Yonnondio: From the Thirties,* in Faribault, Minnesota, in 1932 when she was 19. She finished and polished the first four chapters, and a portion of chapter 1 was published as "The Iron Throat" in a 1934 issue of *Partisan Review*[1] to the approbation of reviewer Robert Cantwell. Among other publishers, Bennett Cerf and Donald Klopfer, who founded both Modern Library and Random House, tried to locate her in order to publish more of her work, but they were initially unsuccessful because "she was in jail, charged with vagrancy (translate: 'being a Communist')."[2] According to Erika Duncan, the two publishers "offered her a monthly stipend" so she would be able to "complete one chapter every month" (Duncan 1982, 212), and she "sent her [newborn] daughter home to relatives and went to Los Angeles to work." But Olsen felt very separated from her compatriots in the socialist/labor and prodemocracy movements, and "from her own child," and in retrospect Olsen says "that most of her best writing was done after she moved back to San Francisco, when she was living alone with her daughter" (Duncan 1982, 213).

By 1937 Olsen was pregnant with her second daughter and immersed and enmeshed in a decade of strikes, "terror, arrests and jail," and she realized, as she has written in "The Strike" (1934), that "the songs in the night must be written some other time, must be written later . . . there is so much happening now."[3]

So, like many of the unrealized dreams and short-circuited expectations of Olsen's characters, *Yonnondio* was set aside, relinquished, almost "gone and still, and utterly lost," prophetic words from the Walt Whitman poem from which the novel takes its title. As Olsen has written, "The simplest circumstances for creation did not exist" (19), although she was "always roused by the writing, always denied. What demanded to be written, did not; [although] it seethed, bubbled, clamored, peopled me" (*Silences,* 19, 20). And *Yonnondio* fell victim to what Olsen has called the "unnatural thwarting of what struggles to come into being, but cannot" (*Silences,* preface).

Around 1972, 40 years after Olsen began *Yonnondio* and 12 years after the publication of *Tell Me a Riddle* (1961), the four finished chapters, plus pieces of the novel typed on sales slips and scribbled on the backs of envelopes,[4] surfaced among other misplaced papers from the past—and the rediscovered vision of a 19-year-old woman was delivered into tired but more experienced hands. *Yonnondio* (published in 1974), became, in Catharine Stimpson's words, a "recovered" text.[5] This event allowed Tillie Olsen to retrieve a part of her past, not only through the transfiguration of memory, as all readers and writers recover the past, but through the double visions of then and now. Despite the inexorable passage of time, she had received a tangible, unscathed product of her youth. Then, as she explains in "A Note About This Book," a preface to the 1974 edition, she was faced with "two to fourteen versions to work from: 38 to 41 year old penciled-over scrawls and fragments to decipher and piece together. Judgment had to be exercised as to which version, revision or draft to choose or combine; decision made whether to include or omit certain first drafts and notes; and guessing as to where several scenes belonged. In this sense—the choices and omissions, the combinings and reconstruction—the book ceased to be solely the work of that long ago young writer and, in arduous partnership, became this older one's as well" much as any nonyouthful reader's life is reenvisioned as the distance widens between actuality and memory. She worked on these "scrawls and fragments" for five months during 1972 and 1973 at the MacDowell Colony, but *Yonnondio,* as we know it, remains "all the old manuscripts—no rewriting, no new writing" (viii).

This unusual recovery is remarkable in itself, but it seems particularly ironic as part of the biography of a writer who so often writes about loss—of opportunity in "Ironing," of idealism in "O Yes," of time in "Riddle," of hope in "Hey Sailor," and of family in "Requa"—but who believes unequivocally in the human potential for recovery. As Deborah Rosenfelt has remarked, "In *Yonnondio,* as in Olsen's later work, the most powerful theme is the tension between human capacity and creativity—the drive to know, to assert, to create, which Olsen sees as innate in human life—and the social forces and institutions that repress and distort that capacity" (Rosenfelt 1981, 389).

As always, the sense of loss and disillusionment in *Yonnondio* is encased within the story of a family. The story revolves around Anna Holbrook, the mother, who bears the name (as do many women in

literature) of St. Anne, the ultimate mother of Mary. Anna, her husband, Jim, and four children are exploited in turn by the mining,
farming, and meat-packing industries that sucked the blood of the
unorganized and nonunion workers in the 1920s and 1930s and by the
systemic disenfranchisement of the underrepresented, the working
class, and nonwhites—in an economic system gerrymandered to en-
franchise the powerful. Concomitant with this trap of poverty are the
linked and related entrapments of gender, since women are always underrepresented, and the intellectual impoverishment that often pre-
cludes any opportunity for people of the "underclass" to pull
themselves out of the downward spiral into which they have fallen. As
Olsen has repeatedly explained, talent, vigor, and potential are destroyed by a combination of enormities, not by the lack of will or
strength inherent in individuals. As Anna tells Mazie, her eldest
daughter, in one of the novel's most polemical but haunting exchanges,
"An edjication is what you kids are going to get. It means your hands
stay white and you read books and work in an office" (3). Additionally,
as Anna is suggesting, "an edjication" gives you some means of determining your own destiny, and it is a message Olsen constantly reiterates in the novel.

Anna and Mazie are trapped, too, by the actual physical spaces that
define the novel—the mines in Wyoming, where boys go to work at
12 or 13 and men die "buried under slaty roof that the company hadn't
bothered to timber" (1) or are asphyxiated because "the new fire boss,
the super's nephew, never made the trips to see if there was gas" (3).
These images resonate from Olsen's immersion in Rebecca Harding
Davis's "Life in the Iron Mills," which she read and reread after finding
it in an April 1861, water-stained copy of the *Atlantic* in 1928, and
for which she wrote the Feminist Press afterword in 1972.[6] In both
stories the disregard of the absentee owners is conflated with the despair of the workers, and one provokes and energizes the other. In both
stories the women and children wait, even when they are not apparently waiting, for "the paralyzing moment when the iron throat of the
whistle shrieked forth its announcement of death" (2), because their
own lives are inexorably bound in helplessness to the male providers.
Mazie, for instance, knows already that the mine is the "bowels of
earth . . . Bowels is the stummy. Earth is a stummy and mebbe she
eats the men that come down" (4).

Anna is also trapped by the brutalizing effect of the mine, particularly on her husband Jim, who is terrified by both imminent disaster and unmeetable responsibilities, and because of whom "the whole household walked in terror. He had nothing but heavy blows for the children, and he struck Anna too often to remember. Every payday he clumped home, washed, went to town, and returned hours later, dead drunk. Once Anna had questioned him timidly concerning his work; he struck her on the mouth with a bellow of 'Shut your damn trap'" (6). Inevitably, his brutality engenders her own: "If one of the children . . . did not obey her instantly, she would hit at them in a blind rage, as if it were some devil she was exorcising" (6–7). Mazie, at six and a half, but "like a woman sometimes" (2), is caught between what she already knows—that "all the world is a-cryen"—and what she cannot understand and should not even be obligated to address—"I don't know for why" (7).

The entrapping configurations of space are underscored in several telling images. Olsen says that Mazie daydreams under "the hot Wyoming sun, between the outhouse and the garbage dump," since "the one patch of green in the yard was between these two spots" (3). Both are images of refuse, decay, and death, images with which the book is suffused. The earth smells of rotting garbage, and the house reeks of unwashed diapers and uncleaned rooms. The large industrial city (perhaps Omaha or Kansas City) where the family ends up will be defined by "human smells, crotch and underarm sweat, the smell of cooking or of burning, all are drowned under, merged into the vast unmoving stench" (47). The images of bowels, outhouse, dump, and stench resonate, emphasizing a pivotal message: that one of the repressions that always accompanies poverty is demarcated by the oppression of a certain place, or, in this case, the sense of no place. Poverty means, simply, that there is no safe place, and therefore no safety—a state from which the impoverished are always noticeably excluded. Olsen, delineating the exigencies of her own life, has said that "'when you didn't pay your rent you just moved. There was a lot of wandering up and down California in those days'" (Duncan 1982, 40), and that sense of spatial tenuousness resonates throughout her work, particularly in "Requa."

Mazie, like many children of poverty, is often unattended if not unloved. By innocently following her father to the neighborhood bar one night, she nearly becomes the victim of Sheen McEvoy, a victim "of the gas explosion that had blown his face off and taken his mind"

(10). McEvoy decides, in a moment of utter (but understandable) craziness, to feed Mazie to the mine, that "thousand-armed creature" who "was hungry, for a child . . . she was reaching her thousand arms for it" (11). McEvoy, who "mistakes her frail white body fluttering against the blackness of the culm for an angel" (Duncan 1982, 45), is ready to "lift [his] arms and throw her down the shaft and the mine'll forget about men" (12). The reader should not miss Olsen's point that no matter how desperate the lives of these men, one way to assuage the hunger of the mine, at least in the demented vision of McEvoy, is through the sacrifice of a girl child, an action for which fiction, never far from "lived experience,"[7] can provide endless examples. Mazie is saved only by happenstance (once again underscoring both the serendipitous and nonserendipitous nature of these lives). This incident contributes to the reader's realization that a painful destiny is often the product in part of bad luck and worse circumstance and that, in this environment, innocence and spirit are crushed early and repeatedly, particularly for children.

The experience with McEvoy is an "initiation into sexuality [and although] the awareness of death" comes to all children and "to all adolescents," it comes "too early and in a mangled form" for Mazie (Duncan 1982, 46). Again by chance, a "nightman" hears her cries, almost splits McEvoy's head open with an ax, and "bloody of face and clothes" he delivers Mazie to her drunken father. The nightman tells Jim that "the mine done the job for you. [McEvoy] fell down the shaft he was aimin to throw her down" (12). Jim's response is to shake the almost unconscious Mazie, blame her ("What you been doin? . . . What did you run away for?" [13]) until the shock of near disaster and the recriminations of the watchman ("Why didn't you watch her, if she's your kid?" [13]) leak into his sodden brain and he cradles her in a borrowed coat and carries her to the already overwhelmed Anna, a woman living under a sky "so thick with clouds, heavy, gray, . . . it had the look of an eyelid shut in death" (17).

This incident energizes Jim and Anna to dream of a "new life in the spring" (16) in the open space of Dakota farmland where the air is "pure and soft like a baby's skin. . . . breathe it in, kids" (23). The open spaces here are important because the structure of this 191-page book, from the closed spaces of the Wyoming mines to the final, totally vicious enclosures of the packinghouses, in part replicates the closed-open-closed spaces of life itself—from womb to existence to tomb. But the middle portion on the farm—brief, foreshortened—is also inevitably doomed, like the creativity of "the lives of despised peoples" (a line coined by Rebecca Harding Davis) about which Olsen always writes. As Stimpson remarks, Olsen becomes "their voice as well as their witness" (Stimpson 1974, 565). Since the Holbrooks do not own the farm, they are subject to the voracity with which the banks and the absent owners, like the mine owners and the mine itself, swallow their meager earnings. "Earth" again becomes a "stummy" and "eats" the Holbrooks. It is a foregone conclusion that as tenant farmers on someone else's land, they will lose the farm, their savings, the proverbial cow, and even Nellie, the horse that brought them.

Once again someone has prospered through the labor of the workers about which Olsen earlier has spoken directly to the reader:

"You will have the cameo? Call it Rascoe, Wyoming, any of a thousand mine towns in America, the night of a mine blowup. And inside carve the statement the company already is issuing. 'Unavoidable Catastrophe . . .'" (20). "(*Dear Company. Your men are imprisoned in a tomb of hunger, of death wages. Your men are strangling for breath—the walls of your company town have clamped out the air of freedom. Please issue a statement; quick, or they start to batter through with the fists of strike, with the pickax of revolution)*" (21).

The middle portion of *Yonnondio*, which begins with chapter 3, opens with a three-day wagon ride (the Christian reverberations inherent in the number three are probably both symbolic and unintentional) through Wyoming and Nebraska when Anna "felt like a bride" and Jim "whistled or sang with her in a depthless bass voice" (23). The family is "intoxicated" with the whirling snow, the wind that stirred the dust "into a dervish dance" (25), and the "blue hazes and dull mists" (26). The family arrives in South Dakota to find their "stoop-shouldered" neighbor, Benson, doom leaning on a fencepost, who says, "I tell you, you cant make a go of it. Tenant farmin is the only thing worse than farmin your own. . . . the bank swallows everything up and keeps you owin 'em. You'll see" (29), the effect of which is to suffuse even this hopeful interlude with the expectation of despair. His pessimism is somewhat offset by another neighbor, "Old Man Caldwell," who functions here as a wisdom figure who introduces Mazie and Ben to the life of the mind. He tells Mazie "why the stars seemed dancing, how old stars were," of the Greeks and of "eternal things that had been before her and would be after her" (33). On his deathbed

("Goodbye my wonder-gazer companion" [38]), he asks his daughter Bess to make sure that Mazie gets his books and tells Mazie to "learn from your mother, who has had everything to grind out life and yet has kept life" (37). Indeed, during the happier time on the farm Anna psychologically tries to protect "the happiness with which she brims [so] it will not jar and spill over" (29). "Mazie," writes Olsen, "never got the books—Jim sold them for half a dollar when he got to town, though Anna cursed him for it" (39).

This section of *Yonnondio* includes an almost perfect description of an enervated family snowed in for four days by an unrelenting blizzard. The mounds of whiteness surround the house, "blinding white at noon, yellow and old at dusk, ghost white at night" (39). Again the ideas of enclosed space as victimizer permeates the text. Even distance was "enormously magnified by the cold" (39), and the ills of the dejected family huddled around the stove are exacerbated by closeness: "Will's staccato cough" mingled with "Baby Jim's ceaseless sniffling" (39). Anna, pregnant again with the fifth child, "drugged by the warmth" (40), slips into a miasma of ineptitude, a "dream paralysis," while around her "dirty clothes [gather] into a waiting pile, bacon drippings coiled greasy in the bottom of the pans, bread went unmade, and the smell of drying diapers layered over the room" (40). Jim grows intermittingly violent and contrite: "snowed in like this leaves a man too much with himself . . . he starts asking why, and what for, like a kid" (40).

Anna's fertility is again contrasted with the barrenness of her family's future, and the reader is reminded that repeated and often unwanted pregnancies degrade women, particularly poor, undernourished women, and that the actuality of pregnancy contrasts markedly with its usual (and usually male-created) Madonna manifestations in literature and art. Almost 20 years later, this message has not penetrated the minds of some critics. A recent essay by a Fulbright lecturer in American literature assures us that in *Yonnondio* "a theme emerges: that women and girls of the working class will never identify their own concerns at home or in the society at large, and will never be able to change their lives for the better, until they can create forums where their individual stories are heard, shared, and debated, . . . [that Mazie] descends into a trancelike madness over the course of *Yonnondio* . . . [and that her] speechlessness results in her identity confusion."[8] If this were not such a supercilious misreading of a novel about poverty and its attendant infringements on the human spirit, one could dismiss

it as merely annoying. But apparently one needs to assert repeatedly
that *Yonnondio* is a novel about struggle, not "selfhood," and that families like the Holbrooks, "In the Thirties" (and now), are worried about
survival, not about style. Their problems will not be solved by a lot of
psychobabble about "identity confusion" but by legitimate work under
humane conditions at fair wages. Olsen herself has said that her "vision
is very different from that of most writers" and that she does not "think
in terms of quests for identity to explain human motivation and behavior"; she feels that "in a world where class, race and sex are so
determining, that has little reality . . . circumstances are the primary
key and not the personal quest for identity" (quoted in Rosenfelt 1981,
404).

The climactic incident on the farm concerns the death of a brood of
chicks (foreshadowing Anna's next childbirth). Jim and Mazie have
tried to save the chicks from freezing by putting them into the oven
"to warm." They are "roasted to death" by the lethargic family because
"nobody noticed when the cheep became hysterical, and finally ceased"
(41). Jim's physical reaction to the loss of these chicks is to grab the
pregnant Anna, "[force] her down by the open oven," and to couple
this with an outpouring of emotional abuse: "no wonder nothing ever
comes right. Lots of help I get from my woman . . . Who asked for
your goddamn brats? . . . No wonder we're starvin. Look at the
woman I got" (41). He deserts the family: "It was ten days before Jim
returned. Where he went or what he did, he never told" (42). Olsen's
point is that Jim blames Anna and her "goddamn brats" for his failure,
and she blames him ("Can't even make a living" [42]). Olsen rightfully
blames the system.

The tension and the winter storms both finally subside, but the
thawing spring and melting snow still leave "the ground like great
dirty sores" and the trees with "oily buds" (43), and bring forth also
the subsequent miscarriage of Anna's next pregnancy. Mazie hides in
the henhouse—nauseous, vomiting, alone—the tableau a kind of up-
ended, reversed manger scene of the joyous birth of Christ. This birth
also ends with a journey, but here the journey follows the loss of the
farm and the despairing move to the slaughterhouses adjoining an industrial slum. Chapter 5 opens with a cacophony of "skeleton children," a "fog of stink," and streets "bulging [with] the soiled and
exhausted houses" (47–48), into one of which this family will. soon
move. For Jim and Anna the streets are "old and familiar . . . their

childhood, rearranged. . . . [T]he human dumpheap where the name-less FrankLloydWrights of the proletariat have wrought their wondrous futuristic structures of flat battered tin cans, fruit boxes and gunny sacks, cardboard and mother earth" (48).

The children are surrounded by futility at home and hostility at school: "MazieandWillHolbrookhavecomefromthecountrywherethey growthecornandwheatandallourmilkcomesfromsayhellotoMazieandWill children" (49). Encoded in this supercilious welcome is the usual de-nigration of the outsider by the insider, which is always expressed more savagely by the children in the schoolyard. Anna's exhortations about education are similarly mixed: "I catch you not doin good and I'll knock the livin daylights out of you, you hear?" (49), as is her reaction to Will's "failure report" from school: "'You bring another one and I'll beat you to a pulp,' she said to the empty room" (67), as she fantasizes about happy children and "learnin."

The point here is that Anna Holbrook, in ways both similar to and dissimilar to her husband, Jim, has her own problems with violent behavior that are clearly exacerbated by her captivity within an op-pressive social system and a violent marriage. Her illnesses and depen-dency on her young daughter Mazie and her son Will energize a kind of arbitrary meanness directed toward these same children: "Dont you know [your brother's] sick? . . . [G]it in there with this drink of water afore I skin you alive" (55). Even when she is writing about the happier times in the country, Olsen includes the emotions of Mazie, "hungry, degraded, after a beating from Anna for some mischief" (32) in jux-taposition to one of Anna's rare memories: "her grandmother bending in such a twilight over lit candles chanting in an unknown tongue, white bread on the table over a shining white tablecloth and red wine" (27), which evoke a Jewish Sabbath tradition probably more pertinent to the encoded memories of Tillie Olsen than to the history of Anna Holbrook. These memories raise interesting questions too about the absence of extended family for the Holbrooks and contribute to Anna's sense of helplessness; she has no one to turn to except her neighbors, who are as bereft and bedraggled as she is.

Similarly, as sunny days on the farm move to a "wild hungry dark-ness" (42), even Mazie begins to "hit Will, hard, ferocious" (43). Anna's realization that "life never lets anything be" (46) sinks in, and what is left of her spirit exhorts the children to breathe in the smell of the hay "so's not ever to forget" (46). So many critics have commented on Anna as uncontaminated saint figure,[9] but a closer reading reveals that Olsen's portrayal of her is less celebratory but is an infinitely more realistic portrait of a woman under siege.

A similar polarity exists in Mazie, who like all poor children, feels the degradation of poverty (symbolized by her "scuffed shoes" [35]) and later suffers terrible discordant daydreams of "a monster thing with blind eyes and shaking body that gave out great guttural sobs, . . . just a truck . . . suddenly she would see before her a woman with her mother's face grown gaunter, holding a skeleton baby whose stomach was pushed out like a ball, and behind was a wall like darkness and misshapen furniture" (59). Mazie, who at eight years of age cannot read (34) (because no one has had the time, energy, or the education to teach her), is, at the same time, knowledgeable about the catalog of life's evils far beyond her chronological and emotional capacity. At an age when even daughters of the depression were thinking about hair ribbons and hopscotch, she has a clear view of sexual abuse, degradation, and near starvation. She is her mother's left and right hand, and, as her mother's closest ally, she also receives the almost constant residue of Anna's anger and frustration. It is clear that the mother wants a life for her daughter better than the one in which the family is trapped, but it seems clear too that Mazie is in many ways her mother's victim— trapped repeatedly, like Anna, in closed physical and emotional spaces from which there is no exit.

Anna pointedly, if inarticulately, understands the implications in the family's move from the country's open space to the Dantean inferno of the city, but she is "shrunken and ill" (53) with a "familiar faintness" (54). Jim is "back in the earth again, sewering"; Bess, "shrank and yellowed" (56), is "tugging at [Anna's] breast and pulling away and tugging again and giving out small frantic cries" (54), and Ben, who "can't breav, Momma" (55), knows "there was a darkening where had been light . . . a weight where had been lightness" (57). Mazie lives in her memory of the farm where "a voluptuous fragrance lay over the earth" (58). There is no beauty here.

The circumscribed nature of the Holbrooks's lives is juxtaposed against the supposed options of Jim's fellow worker, Tracy, a younger, less burdened man who stands up to his bosses and ends up on a chain gang in Florida. Jim and Tracy are fellow workers in the sewers, but they are not unlike the slaughterhouse workers, whose destinies are controlled by the Beedo system, which Olsen defines in a footnote as "a speed-up system of the 1920's" (114), that was inflicted on the slaughterhouse workers by a corrupt foreman enforcing the policy of an inhuman ownership. Tracy quits his job and Olsen addresses this directly in one of her more didactic passages:

And Tracy was young, just twenty, still wet behind the ears, and the old blinders were on him so he couldn't really see what was around and he believed the bull about freedomofopportunity and a chancetorise and ifyoureallywant toworkyoucanalwaysfindajob and ruggedindividualism and something about pursuitofhappiness. . . . So he threw it up, the big sap, not yet knowing a job was a straw and every man (having nothing to sell but his labor power) was the drowning man who had no choice but to hang onto it for notsodear life. . . . He learned all right, the tortures of the damned: feet slapping the pavement, digging humbly into carpets, squatting wide apart in front of chairs and the nojobnojob nothingdointoday buzzing in his ears; eking the coffee . . . shuffling along the frozen streets, buddy (they made a song out of it) can you spare a dime . . . Oh he learned alright. He never even got a chance to have a wife and kids hang round his neck like an anchor and make him grovel to God Job. . . . And there's nothing to say, Jim Tracy, I'm sorry, Jim Tracy, sorry as hell we weren't stronger and could get to you in time and show you that kind of individual revolt was no good, kid, no good at all, you had to bide your time and take it till there were enough of you to fight it all together on the job, and bide your time, and take it till the day millions of fists clamped in yours, and you could wipe out the whole thing, the whole goddamn thing, and a human could be a human for the first time on earth. (62–64)

The "Beedo" system, however, was far more than an isolated incident in the history of the Holbrooks. As Carolyn Rhodes has discovered,

[the] actual Bedaux system . . . was devised by Charles E. Bedaux and sold by him to many American and foreign companies during the 20's and 30's. Bedaux measured work in units which he called (in his own honor) B's and he defined the normal rate of work as one B per minute, or sixty B's per hour. The system was adaptable by Bedaux's-efficiency engineers . . . [and] when employed by a company, [the experts] were supposed to base the acceptable 60-B rate on a good worker, yet one whose speed of work represented what an average person could do. Such a worker's output became the standard. After the standard was set, all workers who produced from 45 to 60 B's per hour would receive standard wages. Any faster worker earned a proportional bonus,

not only for himself or herself, but also for the foreperson and higher officials, in progressively smaller percentages for people higher up the managerial line. . . . Bedaux's method of payment had the obvious advantage of making his system very attractive to management, including the lowest level of bosses. And it had a corresponding and equally obvious disadvantage for workers: it meant that the bosses at every level, even those who directly supervised the workers, had a vested interest in speeding up production."[10]

It is obvious, too, that this nefarious system also served to pit the workers against each other, as well as against the so-called management. Rhodes adds that "Charles E. Bedaux himself was an entrepreneur who made a fortune out of his system for efficiency but died in disgrace as a collaborator with the Nazis during World War II" (Rhodes, 25). According to Rhodes, he planned to give the Duke and Duchess of Windsor a tour of the United States "with the intention of showing the Duke American working conditions. But representatives of labor protested so vehemently that Bedaux was persuaded to give up his plans and even to dissociate [sic] himself from the management of his American branches" (Rhodes, 25). In 1943 he was "captured in Algiers and handed over to the United States Army as a probable traitor, since he had managed a number of projects for the Nazis. . . . He committed suicide early in 1944" (Rhodes, 25).

At the same time that Jim is caught in the maze of exhausting work and inevitable poverty, Anna sickens with still another pregnancy, the children watch as life devours their mother, and Jim feeds, like a ravenous cancer, on hate, anger, and frustration. His rage will be spent on Anna. It is through Mazie's ears that the reader understands: "What is happening? It seemed the darkness bristled with blood, with horror. The shaking of the bed as if someone were sobbing in it. . . . And the words, the words leaping. . . . 'Dont, Jim, dont. It hurts too much. No, Jim, no.' . . . 'Cant screw my own wife. Expect me to go to a whore? Hold still'" (75).

The rape of Anna by Jim ends with "blood on the kitchen floor, the two lifeless braids of hair framing her face like a corpse . . . [Mazie says,] 'Poppa, come in the kitchen, Momma went dead again, Poppa, come on'" (75). The miscarriage leads to an "awful sick" woman, who "needs everything she cant get" and who, says Jim, "tells me everything she needs, but not how to get it (cry from a million swollen throats)" (78). Anna falls into a "merciful numbness that was half sleep, half coma" (80). Even the doctor thinks they "ought to sterilize the whole lot of them after the second kid" (77).

Deborah Rosenfelt says it is Anna's "apparent apathy and incompetence [that] make her a target of her husband's rage; he strikes out at and violates her because he has no other accessible target for his frustrations and fears, until her miscarriage forces him to a pained awareness and reawakened love. Few other American novels . . . reveal so starkly the destructive interactions of class and sex under patriarchal capitalism" (Rosenfelt 1981, 402). Rosenfelt and other critics have noted that *Yonnondio* is "far more reticent" on sexuality than Agnes Smedley's *Daughter of Earth* (among others) but, in spite of the rape scene, Olsen's "silence may well have something to do with the rather puritanical and conservative attitudes of the Communist party on sexuality throughout the 1930s" (Rosenfelt 1981, 401). Cora Kaplan, in her introduction to the 1980 Virago edition of *Yonnondio,* adds that "the absence of familiar discussions of love and passion in the text is deliberate, not the result of puritanism—rather a desire for us to see women's lives and needs outside, beyond, sexual desire" (quoted in Martin, 37).

These comments are not meant to soften or to de-emphasize the ways in which Jim has brutalized Anna but to underscore how Olsen was unconsciously writing class literature from a woman's point of view, incorporating a dimension that she saw ignored and neglected in the works of most contemporary male leftists. "All of Olsen's work, in fact, testifies to her concern for women, her vision of their double oppression if they are poor or women of color, her affirmation of their creative potential, her sense of the deepest, most intractable contradiction of all: the unparalleled satisfaction and fulfillment combined with the overwhelming all-consuming burden of motherhood" (Rosenfelt 1981, 397).

These issues dominate the novel after Anna's physical breakdown, which is accompanied by a spiritual dislocation, following the miscarriage. She exists with the help of her female neighbors in a "merciful numbness that was half sleep, half coma" (80), and even Jim admonishes her to "go back to sleep . . . best sleep again" (81), as if years of deprivation and privation could be assuaged by an extended nap. "[S]he never answered, answered or looked at him or questioned why it was that she was lying there, or what had happened" (81). Mazie, who is supposed to be the "little mother now" (80), runs off with her friends;

she is more afraid to *be* her mother than to *see* her mother. Anna is roused from this state to visit the clinic where she is further traumatized by the public health signs that admonish that "Dirt Breeds Disease," "Flies . . . Spread Germs. Germs Breed Disease," and "You Make Your Children Sick" (84, 88). With only the memory of strength, she decides that "the house . . . It needs cleanin" (82), and in an attempt to impose order on chaos, which is familiar to all women, she tries to sweep the cobwebs from the corners and to scoop the "garbage up into a pot" (84). She is surrounded by unpatchable clothes, shoes that cannot be resoled, by mess, clutter, and responsibility that are "too far gone" (87). Her four children sleep "here in this closet bedroom, three on a mattress on the floor" (88), and her only rational thought is that she must "do something" (89). To Mazie's question, "What, Momma," Anna answers, "I dont know" (89). The agony seems exacerbated by Jim's offer "to help," which is sarcastically (but understandably) rejected by Anna. Meanwhile, the children grow increasingly "defiant" and "contrary."

The configurations of enclosed space are again pronounced. "A need was in [Anna] to be out under a boundless sky, in unconfined air, not between walls, under the roof of a house" (93). That "need" is an early declaration of the effect of enclosed space on female characters in fiction written by women, an idea that resonates everywhere now in novels by Joan Didion, Toni Morrison, Joyce Carol Oates, and others. As Anna's son Benjy reminds her, "We got to go in. Its suppertime. Don't talk goofy, Momma. Mommas always goes in" (97). In fact, the only scene in *Yonnondio* where Mazie feels the "strange happiness in her mother's body" happens on the family's walk through better neighborhoods to collect dandelions and nasturtium leaves because Anna suddenly "hanker[s] for greens" (97), and the public health charts say, *The Wheel of Nutrition: One Serving: Green Leafy Vegetable Daily*" (97).

This interlude, and a trip to Anna's "Temple of Learning" (107), are only brief relief since the children, having been judged "poor learners, dumb dumb dumb" (107) by their teachers, are already emotionally protected from the lure of the library. Mazie, described earlier as "homely," is much more attracted by descriptions of the "Sheik of Araby. Broken Blossoms. Slave of Love. She Stopped at Nothing. The Fast Life. The Easiest Way" (109), tales of "gigolos" and "ecstasy," and whiffs of Blue Waltz cologne provided by her 12-year-old friend Jinella. Olsen's underlying message is that girls are easily trapped by

unattainable fantasies that contrast sharply with ugly reality. That dichotomy was particularly great in the depression years.

At the novel's end, the family is not only imprisoned by poverty and
illness but by the suffocating heat of the city where "the heat is en-
tombed deathly still" (112) and the children sicken from lack of sleep
and fresh air. The packinghouse is, of course, even worse; Olsen calls
it a "Hell [populated with] figures half-seen through hissing vapor,
live steam cloud from great scalding vats" (114) where young girls and
women work in Casings, "where men will not work" (115). Part of the
power here emanates from a list (replicating the "speed-up" of the
Beedo system): "*Geared, meshed*: the kill room: knockers, shacklers,
pritcher-uppers, stickers, headers, rippers, leg breakers, breast and
aitch sawyers, caul pullers, fell cutters, rumpers, splitters, vat dippers,
skinners, gutters, pluckers. . . . Ice hell. Coolers; freezers. Pork trim:
bone chill damp even in sweaters and overshoes; hands always in icy
water, slippery knives, the beedo piece work speed—safety signs a
mockery" (115). It is 110 degrees in Casings and "in the hog room,
108" (125). Marsalek, a worker, falls from a heart attack, "is carried
away, docked, charged for the company ambulance" (125). Olsen describes the main steam pipe that breaks open, "hissing live steam in a
magnificent plume" (125), which scalds ("I forgot *scalded*" [125]) Peg
and Andra and Philomena and Cleola, who "fall and writhe in their
crinkling skins" (*Yonnondio*, 125).

Yonnondio's final scenes are of Anna making jelly and canning peaches
in the "humid kitchen . . . Jimmie and Jeff asleep under the kitchen
table," the baby, Bess, cranky from "oozing sores on the tiny body"
(128). The misery is unrelieved. At the novel's end Jim staggers in
after a day spent working in a 106 degree slaughterhouse. What sep-
arates Anna's misery from his is that she is at least needed, while Jim
only needs.

Bess bangs a fruit jar lid on the kitchen table and "a look of nean-
derthal concentration is on her face. That noise! In triumphant, as-
tounded joy she clashes the lid down. Bang, slam, whack. Release,
grab, slam, bang, bang. Centuries of human drive work in her; human
ecstasy of achievement; satisfaction deeper and more fundamental than
sex. *I can do, I use my powers; I! I!*" (132). Most of the critics have
interpreted this passage as a return, after so much misery, to Olsen's
belief in the individual's will to prevail and triumph over the restrictions of poverty and servitude in spite of almost unconscionable odds.

But Olsen writes, "Reader, it was not to have ended here" (133). According to various critics, Jim was to be involved in a failed strike at the packinghouse. He would eventually desert the family, and Anna would die from a self-induced abortion during her sixth pregnancy. Mazie, as one might expect, would grow up to become a writer. But no legitimate critic can discuss what is only supposition. According to Olsen, she had already written—in 16 pages and alternate drafts—both the abortion scene and the death scene; lacking was a "bridge piece" between the two accounts (Werlock interview, 1990).

What seems more central is that Olsen's work, which she defines by "what might have been" and "what never will be now" (133), is a testament to what is. The word *yonnondio* means "a lament for the lost," for those people who are "unlimn'd" will "disappear," and indeed this novel is that testament. But because *Yonnondio* exists, even in a fragmentary form, the Holbrooks and their compatriots are not "unlimn'd" as Olsen feared, and they have not and will not "disappear."

Chapter Four

"I Stand Here Ironing"

Tillie Olsen has expressed her concern that even on today's campuses students are given far too little literature devoted to "human work" or "women" or "children."[1] Lamenting that "so much is covered over about the human past and the human genius" embodied in the stories of working-class people, Olsen voices her admiration for what Robert Coles has called the "amazing strong children" and the "amazing strong parents" of those in desperate circumstances. One of the "great characteristics of the human race," Olsen says, and one of the "secrets least explored" is that "we do not remain in degrading circumstances forever" (Pearlman interview). And, speaking directly of *Tell Me a Riddle*—on which she spent two additional years because initially "not everything" in it was "publishable"—she praises "manual work," particularly that done by mothers. All four stories contain hard-working mothers whose images culminate in the depiction of the dying Eva, as the "stained words" become "stainless" when uttered through her "working lips" (112).

The four stories in *Tell Me a Riddle*, dedicated to Olsen's mother (1885–1956), are linked by more than the mothers and other family members who appear in three (and possibly all) of them.[2] Numbered consecutively, indicating the specific order in which each should be read, the stories are tied together by their portrayal of the aching hardship of poverty and the themes of exile or exclusion. These themes result from characters belonging to the wrong (working) class or wrong (nonwhite) race. Illness and disease, too, overshadow each story, as do "lost" children, nightmares, guilty or harrowing memories, and prolonged individual silences. Relentlessly Olsen presents us with the inexorable riddle of human existence: it paradoxically comprises not merely the endurance of poverty, bigotry, illness, and pain but the ultimate ability to transcend these. As Olsen's characters rise above their debilitating circumstances, they draw ever closer to the "loftier race" alluded to in the hymn "These Things Shall Be," which is also the subheading of the title story at the end of the collection. Because her literary style is dictated by the "material that I'm trying to convey" (Pearlman interview), Olsen firmly denies that she spends much time thinking about technique, but hardly any critic can resist commenting on the way in which she expresses her ideas in each of the stories. Richard M. Elman calls Olsen's style "experimental" and "individual," and Marilyn Yalom speaks of its "dense richness."[3] Olsen employs imagistic language, meaningful refrains, innovative structure, and a variety of monologues, dialogues and narrative interruptions to convey the components of her themes, her characters, and her "riddles."

Although Olsen refers to "I Stand Here Ironing" as "re-beginning writing," she also says that "I wish I could write directly, simply, as I did in 'I Stand Here Ironing'" (Pearlman interview). The statement is not only the title but also the opening clause of the first story. Its seeming simplicity, however, bespeaks the complexity of the subject: the unnamed mother stands now, in the present, at her ironing board, but her thoughts range back through the years as she attempts to discover the truth about her relationship with her daughter. Nor is this relationship a new interest for Tillie Olsen: Olsen asserts that she has "always been interested in the hardest of all jobs in this society—having to raise kids on your own" (Pearlman interview). Certainly this theme is prevalent from *Yonnondio* (begun in the 1930s) through the stories in *Tell Me a Riddle* (written between 1954 and 1960) to *Mother to Daughter, Daughter to Mother* (edited in 1984), in which Olsen includes the poem by Kay Keeshan Hamod with the central mystique of "the mother secret from you" (Kay Keeshan Hamod, quoted in *Mother to Daughter*, 15). Although she affirms that the story, while not autobiographical, is "somewhat close to my own life" (quoted in Martin, 23), and that she wrote it from 1953 to 1954 during the Stockholm peace initiative urging an end to nuclear proliferation and the cold war (Orr, 38, n. 38), the story is primarily concerned with the mother-daughter relationship.

The unnamed first-person narrator is the mother of a 19-year-old daughter, Emily, about whom the mother has just had a call from a school official (whether teacher or guidance counselor is not clear).[4] In an effort to respond to the official's assertion that Emily "needs help" (1), the mother's thoughts flow back to key moments in Emily's life—and her own. In Sally H. Johnson's words, "Olsen moves our attention back and forth in the ironing rhythm" as the mother ponders her life with Emily.[5] Her recollections take the form of an apparent dialogue with "you," the school official—and you, the reader, and perhaps also

with another part of herself. The story is actually a long interior mon-
ologue in which the mother reminisces, accuses herself, admits mistakes, and asks as many questions as she answers. Indeed, in a text of
12 pages, she asks a total of 13 questions, many of which implicitly
define the helplessness of the mother in response to circumstance and
explicitly point to the astonishing ways human beings—in this case
both mothers and daughters—survive and prevail.

In the opinion of Elizabeth Fisher, an early reviewer, Olsen's accom-
plishment is to show that this mother is like all parents who have tried
to do their "best" and at some point realize that they have done their
"worst."[6] Yet according to both Helen Pike Bauer and Joanne S. Frye,
part of the power of Olsen's depiction is that the mother never saddles
herself with "the burden of excessive guilt"[7] and never "self lacerate[s]"
(Frye, 290), for she is a realist and a survivor. Nonetheless the mother
pays a price for her tenacity and indomitability, for an emotional coldness emerges in her self-portrait as mother during the troubled years
of Emily's early childhood. Even now, some 10–17 years after the
events she recollects, a curiously flat tone inheres in the mother's rem-
iniscences; perhaps this results from the armor that not only enabled
her to survive but that protected her from being overwhelmed by guilt.
Unquestionably, as Bauer points out, neither the mother nor her
daughter Emily ever "give up" (Bauer, 37), whereas Emily's father
"could no longer endure" the realities of poverty and the responsibilities of wife and baby daughter and had simply disappeared one day (2).

As the school official's question "moves tormented back and forth
with the iron" (1), the mother is naturally on the defensive, protesting
that she cannot help whatever has happened, that she and her daughter
are two separate individuals. She has no time to summarize or to draw
conclusions because interruptions will doubtless occur—just as they
have throughout her life and Emily's. The mother's life has been interrupted by childbirth, desertion, poverty, numerous jobs, childcare, re-
marriage, frequent relocations, and five children. "Time," according
to Bauer, "is the first casualty of poverty," and the lack of both time
and money "constitute the dimensions of the mother's powerlessness"
(Bauer, 36). So, clearly, "time" is a key word here, for it is precisely
time that the mother did not have for Emily when Emily was
younger—until it was "too late," a phrase recurring, choruslike, in this
story punctuated by references to clocks, specific moments, lengths of
separations. But as she irons, the mother does take the time to recollect
her memories of Emily, and although she thinks she "will never total

it all" (12), she not only implicitly defines the riddle of her relationship with her daughter but also articulates a solution of sorts.

As her thoughts move back in time, the mother reveals that Emily, born during the depression, had been a "beautiful baby." A source of awe to the young mother, the baby Emily evinces the same bright potential so obvious in baby Bess of *Yonnondio*: "She blew shining bubbles of sound. She loved motion, loved light, loved color and music and textures. She would lie on the floor in her blue overalls patting the surface so hard in ecstasy her hands and feet would blur. She was a miracle to me" (2). The wonder and potential of babies is poignantly articulated here, but time and circumstances cruelly intervene in the relative luxury of caring for the baby: Emily's father abandoned them both when Emily was eight months old, giving the mother no choice but to go to work and leave the "miracle" of a baby daughter with a woman for whom Emily "was no miracle at all" (2).

This was the first in a series of separations from Emily. Although the mother had tried her best, even switching to night shifts so that she could be with Emily during the day, she is fooling only herself when she says the change had made things "better": clearly things were not better, for necessity then forced her to send Emily to her father's family. When Emily returned at the age of two years, "thin" and weak from a recent bout with chicken pox, the mother not only "hardly" knew her (2), but clearly felt some repugnance as she noticed (and reiterates) Emily's resemblance to her father. Pockmarked and shoddily dressed, Emily, who even walked "quick and nervous" as her father had, was no longer a miracle to the mother who observes that "all the baby loveliness" had disappeared (3).

She then sent Emily to nursery school—which the mature and retrospective mother belatedly recognizes as one of many children's "parking places" maintained by unsympathetic harried teachers (3). But that the mother herself had been unsympathetic and harried in those days is evident in the comment made at the time by one of the tenants in her apartment building: "You should smile at Emily more when you look at her" (4). Guiltily the mother now acknowledges that she smiled only later at the other children. She sent Emily a second time to the father's family. Again she protests that things were "better" when Emily returned because she had a "new daddy" to love, when in fact the new interest in her mother's life must have been difficult for Emily. Having suffered abandonment, poverty, and the consequent inability to cope with a young child, the mother had been captive to the demands of a new love and a new marriage—and quite possibly the "merciless physical drives" she later hopes will be delayed for the adolescent Emily (9).

Thus, although Emily had come home to live, separations from her mother continued to recur. In particular, the mother recalls that she and her new husband, Bill, had gone out at night, leaving Emily and telling themselves that "she was old enough" (4). Emily's pitiful fear of being left alone, if only for a while, is evident in her throwing the clock out in the hall so she would not hear the "loud" sound of its voice that so frightened her (5). In a seeming allusion to the biblical account of Christ's abandonment and betrayal, the mother recalls Emily's telling her that three times she had called for her mother. Three times, however, she received no answer, and when her mother and Bill finally arrived home Emily was "rigid awake" (5).

Shortly afterwards the mother had left Emily again, for a week, this time, to have her second baby, Susan, and again she recalls that Emily said the "clock talked loud" (5). Not only did she leave Emily to go to the hospital but, on her return, she had to isolate Emily because Emily had contracted red measles. (The story takes place in the preinoculation days of chicken pox and measles.) Emily then suffered from nightmares for which her mother had little time or sympathy—although she did have time to get up to tend to Susan. In fact, after all these years, the mother's awareness of her preference for Susan is embodied in her specific recollection: "twice, only twice when I had to get up for Susan anyhow," did she go to sit with Emily (5). The repetition of the word "twice" clearly indicates the mother's repressed but accurate memories of particular moments when she neglected her daughter.

Seven-year-old Emily was again sent away, this time for eight months to a "convalescent home" where she was not allowed to keep letters; where she formed one friendship with a little girl who disappeared; and where, deprived of both her friend and her mother's letters, Emily shouted out, "They don't like you to love anyone here" (6). The mother recalls during her visits an "invisible wall" bearing an imaginary sign reading "Not To Be Contaminated by Parental Germs of Physical Affection" (6). This metaphoric wall, suggests Frye, underscores their "inevitable separateness" (Frye, 289)—itself healthy in a mature mother-daughter relationship, but at this point just one more difference between the mother's troubled relationship with Emily and her warmer one with the younger children.

Apparently this eight-month separation had lasting effects on Emily. When her mother tried to "hold and love her" on her return, Emily stiffened and turned away. The refrain "too late," although it does not appear at this specific point, reverberates with increasing intensity. Emily's relationship with her younger sister Susan became competitive, resentful, and hostile, not only because Susan seemed to have usurped Emily's place during Emily's virtual exile, but because Susan had those blonde chubby "Shirley Temple" looks her mother implicitly prefers to Emily's thinness and darkness, which, as mentioned, are unpleasant reminders of the man who abandoned both mother and daughter. Indeed, the mother admits that she has "edged away" from "that poisonous feeling between [Emily and Susan], that terrible balancing of hurts and needs I had to do between the two, and did so badly, those earlier years" (8). Even at the end of the story, she admits that Susan seemed to her to be "all that [Emily] was not" (12).

Emily's numerous illnesses—chicken pox, measles, asthma—are emblematic of her emotional neglect, as well as of the other more overt impoverishments of her early years. Moreover, just as her thinness and weakness contrast with the robust health of her siblings, so too does her "unnatural goodness" contrast with their more natural youthful behavior: Emily's mother realizes with a shock that Emily had never rebelled, never had tantrums the way her "normal" children did. Surely Emily's fear of further abandonment occasioned her pathetic attempts to please her mother and to behave as a model child.

During those days Emily developed a voracious appetite. Whereas she had eschewed the repulsive food of the convalescent home, partly because she was too ill to eat, she devoured food ravenously when she came home to stay, partly to assure herself of the tentative security and comfort of home that she had missed so desperately during all those separations and forced absences from her mother.

Emily is the first of the "lost" children portrayed in the stories in *Tell Me a Riddle*—"she was lost, she was a drop" in the big school where she suffered a lack of confidence. Now her mother, standing over her ironing board, her fifth and last baby almost out of infancy, recalls that "I was working, there were four smaller ones . . . there was not time for her. She had to help be a mother, and housekeeper, and shopper" (10). Not only did the mother have little time herself, but she assigned Emily numerous household and childcare responsibilities, frequently allowing her to be absent from school. As a result Emily has had little time for homework, and what she has submitted is often ill prepared or damaged. Now, as the mother interrupts her ironing to change her youngest child, her time for Ronnie is imagistically juxtaposed to the lack of time she had for Emily. In Bauer's words, the mother's "quiet sitting, looking outward peacefully, holding the baby in her arms until he falls asleep, contrasts forcefully with the one scene we have of Emily's infancy" (Bauer, 36), the scene that still haunts the mother with the sound of Emily's continuous weeping at the babysitter's apartment.

The mother recalls three specific times in 17 years when Emily had cried. The first occurred when, with the "fierce rigidity" of the inexperienced mother, she had breast-fed Emily only when the "clock decreed" (2). The cries of the hungry baby haunt her still; she recalls that they "battered me to trembling" (2). Her worry that she may have hurt Emily is shown as she asks herself, "Why do I put that first? I do not even know if it matters, or if it explains anything" (2). Again, although she had fed Emily only at prescribed times, she admits that she has discontinued this rigid schedule with the other children, instead feeding them whenever they are hungry. Second, the mother is also haunted by the times she had fetched Emily from the babysitter, and Emily, still under a year old, "would break into a clogged weeping that could not be comforted, a weeping I can hear yet" (3).

These first two memories of Emily's tears have to do with the young mother's inexperience and dogged attempts to survive as a single parent. The third, however, is fairly recent: as a teenager, Emily auditioned for the talent show and won. One morning she phoned her mother at work to tell her the news, her voice nearly unintelligible through the tears: "Mother, I did it. I won, I won; they gave me first prize; they clapped and clapped and wouldn't let me go" (10)—as her mother had repeatedly done. Surely these tears, seemingly of happiness, are related to those of the child Emily, who—repeatedly abandoned and excluded from a rapidly changing family by a mother who seemed not to care whether she stayed—has wooed an entire audience. This audience, Emily tell us, "clapped and clapped and wouldn't let me go" (10)—they are a "roaring, stamping audience, unwilling to let this rare and precious laughter out of their lives" (11). Emily, seemingly so unwanted as a child, is suddenly in demand. Her triumph is the inexplicable victory against the odds that Olsen continually celebrates.

Emily's darkness may be seen as a paradox: it may signify a lack of fashionable beauty, an average performance in school, a difference from her peers and her sister, but it may also represent the mysterious artistic depths from which her theatrical talent rises. Ultimately, however, this ability—initially developed to ward off her fear of desertion and feeling of being unloved—is a strength rather than a defense and a gift she can give to others. Having seen the dark side of life, she has developed a brilliant talent to brighten her life and the lives of others. Significantly, Emily's is no dark tragic genius but a comic one.

No doubt her talent for pantomime, for strikingly accurate portrayals, is born of her years of solitary observation of others. Indeed, the very nature of pantomime derives from its wordlessness, its dependence on silence. And certainly a notable silence surrounds the mother-daughter relationship, which clearly, even now, lacks overt involvement and warmth. Of Emily's triumph, the mother can only vaguely say that she "think[s]" she had suggested that Emily audition for the amateur show (10). She cannot recall specifically, even now when the exigencies of acute poverty and single parenthood are past memories. Further, in describing the time when she first saw Emily onstage, the mother reiterates her reaction to the toddler who had returned from staying with her father's parents: just as then she "hardly knew" the thin, homely two-year-old, now she barely recognizes her teenaged daughter: "Was this Emily?" (11), she asks.

In another writer's hands a mother who has exiled or excluded her child during her formative years might be seen as a reprehensible figure—but this is not Tillie Olsen's point. The honesty of this mother is almost painful: haunted by her memories of Emily's cries and weeping, she admits that as a new mother she had demanded too much. She was young and inexperienced. When she was the same age Emily is now, she was not a relatively carefree student but a young mother abandoned by her husband, forced to find work in the "pre-relief, pre-WPA world of the depression" (2). She did the best she could, working hard at whatever jobs she could find, paying for care for Emily. We feel her pain as she remembers Emily's cries and rejection of her caresses, just as we feel pain in her admissions that she did not smile at Emily and that she was partially to blame for Emily's marginal academic achievements. As she recalls Emily's goodness and compares it to the normal demands and explosions of her other children, she remarks abruptly, "I feel suddenly ill. I put the iron down. What in me demanded that goodness in her? And what was the cost, the cost to her of such goodness?" (4). The cost to Emily has been significant, as evidenced in her stiffness, her quietness, her trouble at school. The positive effect, however, is that she has experienced and thus understands suffering. Perhaps because Emily lacked affection as a child, she invents the word "shoogily," meaning "comfort" (9),[8] which is adopted into the family vocabulary and movingly murmured by her brother

Ronnie, a happy, loved, and contented baby. Emily extends her ability to bring happiness beyond the family to strangers who need the humor, the entertainment, the warmth she is able to provide them. The mother, as she irons, realizes that Emily has indeed made a special mark, set her individual "seal" (10).

The mother makes a final admission—that she and her husband are powerless to further Emily's talents. Having neither means nor contacts, they simply leave Emily's gift to her. At this moment in the narrative Emily runs in from school. Her step is "light" as she takes the stairs two at a time, raids the icebox, and teases her mother (11).

Here we reach the paradox, or perhaps the riddle. Despite the difficulties of her life, Emily is not doomed any more than her mother is doomed. The mother's strength has in fact been handed down to her daughter. Emily—although exiled or excluded, sometimes "lost," suffering nightmares and long periods of silent solitude, believing herself to be unloved during the dark days—has also worked beside her mother and entertained her when her spirits might otherwise have flagged. She illustrates the enigma of human life: it contains poverty and tragedy and pain but also some fulfilling of potential, a desire to survive. Moreover, according to Frye, toward the end of the narrative there is a growing emphasis on Emily's "separateness" (Frye, 240).

Emily's last remark, tossed glibly over her shoulder—that "we'll all be atom-dead" in a few years (11)—refers to the bomb and the fact that, as her mother points out, she is a child "of depression, of war, of fear" (12). But the mother, too, is a product of those times. She remembers that while she was writing V-mail to Bill during World War II, or while she was ironing or tending the baby, Emily would do humorous imitations that made her mother laugh. Emily probably did so both to lighten her despair and to help her mother (10). Now, in a joking reference to Whistler's mother, Emily acknowledges the ceaseless work that her mother has always had to perform inside the home, for five children, as well as in her job outside the home. Unlike Whistler, however, Emily says she will just have to paint her mother "standing over an ironing board" (11). In addition to her theatrical talents, Emily seems to have some knowledge of painting—and she also has a sense of humor, which her mother pointedly lacks. Emily's imaginative way of approaching life is a gift she can give to her loving but more prosaic mother.

As Emily disappears upstairs, the mother ends her soliloquy—ostensibly to the school official, but actually to a larger audience, including herself. Her remarks constitute a plea, even a prayer for her daughter[9]:

"Only help her to know—help make it so there is cause for her to know—that she is more than this dress on the ironing board, helpless before the iron" (12).

The feminine image of the dress is coupled with that of the iron, suggesting the harsh oppressive molding reality of society and circumstance and its effect on women. Yet neither the mother nor Emily has succumbed. In fact, the mother's last act is to control the iron. Even if the iron has sometimes enslaved her—and even if she, the ironing mother, has sometimes unwittingly oppressed Emily with the way she has molded her life—both women emerge as survivors as well as victims.

Finally, the mother seems the more pessimistic of the two. Ending her catalog of significant events in her life with Emily, the mother in a world-weary somewhat distant manner admits that her "wisdom came too late," that Emily has "much to her and probably little will come of it" (12). Indeed, Vicki L. Sommer believes that the mother's failure to see the "guidance counselor" or to ensure that Emily study for her exam replicates her earlier "pattern of parental neglect" (Sommer, 85). Change is impossible for this conscience-stricken but realistic and enduring woman.

Emily, despite her offhand reference to the bomb, seems confident of herself. In fact, Emily's last act is to kiss her mother and to control her own life: gifted and unencumbered by the hardships her mother had endured at the exact same age, Emily decides she is going to sleep late in the morning, no matter what her mother says. Her wit, talent, and sensitivity to others' needs suggest that Emily, a warmer woman than her mother, intends to avoid the grim life mirrored in the image of the mother at the ironing board.

Chapter Five
"Hey Sailor, What Ship?"

The title of Olsen's first story, "I Stand Here Ironing," is an intriguing declarative statement that invites us to enter the thoughts of the ironing mother, but the title of the second, "Hey Sailor, What Ship?" is a question. Actually a common form of greeting among seafarers, the question was originally intended to establish the identity of the listener. The seafarer's answer affirmed an affiliation with a particular ship, from which he derived an individual identity.

Having posed the question, with its implication that an answer will be forthcoming in the story, Olsen repeatedly uses the phrase to illustrate the dilemma posed by the two personae of Michael (Whitey) Jackson, the main character, who frequently refers to himself as M. Norbert Jacklebaum. Whitey, an aging and alcoholic merchant seaman, desperately vacillates between his old youthful personality ("Whitey") and his tough, defensive one ("M. Norbert Jacklebaum"). He is torn between two ways of life: the itinerant life of the sailor and the settled, "respectable" life of his friends Lennie, Helen, and their three children. These two choices constitute the major refrains of the story: running alternately through Whitey's head are the phrases, *"Hey Sailor, what ship?"* and *"Lennie and Helen and the kids."*

The action in "I Stand Here Ironing" occurs in one brief section, but in "Hey Sailor, What Ship?" the action is divided into four parts, all written in the present tense. The first three sections, spanning a period of about twelve hours, introduce Whitey and reveal his thoughts as he interacts with his old and dear friends Helen, Lennie, and their three daughters, Jeannie, Carol, and Allie. We learn that Whitey is ill, lonely, and alcoholic, and that he is attracted both to his wandering seafaring life and the settled domestic life of his friends. Olsen uses numerous refrains or leitmotivs, nearly always set off in italics or enclosed in parentheses. These refrains, keys to the gradual revelations of Whitey's character, reach a crescendo in the fourth section when, five days later, Whitey decides "what ship"—which life—he will embrace.

Although Olsen maintains that this story is only "somewhat different" in technique from the earlier "I Stand Here Ironing" (Pearlman interview), certainly it is experimental and complex by comparison. The story's technique is reminiscent of Virginia Woolf's *The Waves* (1931), a novel whose "musical writing" Olsen admires (Pearlman interview). Similar to *The Waves* in its use of six characters and their relationships to one another, "Hey Sailor, What Ship?" concentrates on the central personality of Whitey (an ironically knightlike or heroic figure) just as Woolf concentrates on the character of Percival. The rhythmic movements of the story, with its cadences, its tidelike swellings and recedings, and the ebbing and flowing of Whitey's ceaseless thoughts, are also reminiscent of those in Matthew Arnold's "Dover Beach," with its "tremulous cadence slow," bringing "the eternal note of sadness in." Indeed, the story is notable in that Olsen appears to depart from her customary handling of predominantly autobiographical material. Here, she moves in a direction of modernist literary allusions and observed life that she handles with great skill, but, for reasons she has not discussed, she has never returned to these techniques. That she has not pursued them in her later fiction isolates "Hey Sailor, What Ship?" from the body of her work and may help to explain why Olsen critics have virtually neglected the tale.

From the beginning of the story with its insistent question, iterated and reiterated, the story is in many ways classic and mythic in its suggestive allusions. Whitey's dilemma echoes that of numerous seafaring heroes such as Alfred, Lord Tennyson's Ulysses, who returns from his 20 years of adventurous exotic wanderings to a home that no longer suits him. Whitey is "home" as in Robert Louis Stevenson's poem "Requiem": "Home is the sailor, home from sea. And the hunter home from the hill." And John Donne's famous equation of man to both land and sea, to the "continent" and the "main," is suggested here. Whitey is not only the "sailor" but the "hunter," the seeker, the quester, the erstwhile heroic or knightly figure, as he attempts to come to terms with both his past identity and his present and future. The story is drenched in allusions to water, with all its mythic implications of wandering and life-giving force. But all twentieth-century readers know that water can also be polluted, as T. S. Eliot demonstrates in his river that "sweats oil and tar."[1] Indeed, Whitey seems very much a seagoing character from *The Waste Land,* or the hesitant, unsure Prufrock figure from the Eliot poem "The Love Song of J. Alfred Prufrock."[2] The name M. Norbert Jacklebaum echoes the name J. Alfred Prufrock, but with a decidedly less refined ring—its odd mixture suggests both French and German sounds, an upper-class affectation or the French use of "M." for "monsieur," as well as the seemingly incongruous elemental words "baum" (tree) and jackal (animal). The name suggests a cosmopolitan but hard-headed traveller similar to the many faced narrator questing through *The Waste Land*.

Rain is falling as the story opens. Whitey stands in a grimy San Francisco waterfront bar. Whitey is drunk and lonesome. In addition to the two refrains—*"Hey Sailor, what ship?"* and *"Lennie and Helen and the kids,"* Olsen introduces the themes of friendship, illness, time, money, and identity. The author indicates clearly that Whitey has developed the habit of paying for companionship—for a stranger's drinks at the bar or a prostitute at "Pearl's" in San Francisco or at "Marie's" in Managua (15,14). His trembling hands denote his illness: Whitey is obviously alcoholic; in fact, his last visit to San Francisco included a five-week stay in the Marine hospital (19). The contents of his pockets, shipping tokens and tickets from the Philippines and Nicaragua, suggest his traveling, rootless life.

Like the mother-narrator in "I Stand Here Ironing," Whitey asks numerous questions. The first is "Wha's it so quiet for?" suggesting his discomfort with silence and need for noise. The second is "Wha time's it anyway?" (13), emphasizing both the importance of time and his difficulty in distinguishing between past and present. Another significant question soon follows: "Where'd it all go?" (14). The "it" refers to time and to money, both of which slip through the aging sailor's fingers. As Whitey rummages through his pockets he mentally "lurches through the past" (14). His illness, his identity crisis, and his emphasis on money, which Helen says is "the only power he has" (33), all surface in his drunken recollection of his departure from the ship four days ago. The paymaster had refused him his wages because Whitey was "too stewed" to sign his name to the voucher (14–15). When Whitey attempts to mimic the accent of the Scandinavian paymaster (14), the humor falls flat. Obviously Whitey is at a crossroads in his life: he wanders between his two identities just as he travels back and forth between east and west, between Manila and Managua, and between visiting Pearl's brothel and the home of his old friends in San Francisco.

Other refrains indicating Whitey's dilemmas are introduced in this section. On the first page he personifies and dismisses the ship, muttering "Hell with ship. . . . hell with your friends" (13). He repeats the same condemning phrases a few moments later (whether to the

barman or the former bar owner is unclear): "hell with you. . . . hell
with your friends" (15). This refrain, hurled later at Lennie in only
slightly altered form (36), indicates Whitey's defensive rejection of
those who no longer understand him or sympathize with the identity
he is trying to acknowledge. His need to fill up the silence with music
is introduced here, too (13). Silences, variously indicative of loneliness,
exhaustion, or illness, are familiar to any reader of Olsen's work.

Whitey's disorientation is underscored when he asks the barkeeper
for an advance against his paycheck. This man, a stranger, refuses, and
Whitey asks to see his old friend Bell, the bar owner. But Bell has
given up this seedy waterfront life, sold the liquor business, and
"moved to Petaluma to raise chickens" (15). Both friends mentioned
in this section are absent: Deeck, his best friend from the ship, and
Bell, whom he has known throughout his seafaring life. Whitey assures
the barman that "Bell knows me. Get Bell. Been drinkin' here twenty-
three years, every time hit Frisco. Ask Bell. . . . But Bell sold" (15).
The repetition of "Bell" suggests Donne's statement that "no man is
an island"; each is simultaneously part of the earth and of the sea. If
any part is washed away, including "thy friend's" or "thine own," the
whole is lessened: "Any man's death diminishes me because I am involved in mankind, and therefore never send to know for whom the
bell tolls; it tolls for thee."

Whitey's sense of security, community, and friendship seems to be
dissolving. Bell has made his decision to leave the waterfront, opting
for a more conventional domestic life in which he works with animals
and the land. Now Whitey will have to make his decision. As the
"bell" sounds in Whitey's consciousness, the reader expects the barten-
der, like the pub keeper in Eliot's *The Waste Land*, to say, "Hurry up
please, it's time." Whitey's precarious future is further suggested in
the numerous "cards" in his pockets, including calling cards and "trip
cards"; the several references to cards recall Eliot's Madame Sosostris,
the "lady of situations," and her "wicked pack of cards" from which
she selects the "drowned Phoenician Sailor" (*WL*, ll. 43–47).

Like Eliot's drowned sailor whose eyes have washed away in the current of the sea, Whitey begins his walk to Pearl's, recalling Eliot's line
"(Those are pearls that were his eyes. Look!)" (*WL*, l. 48). Like Eliot's
Prufrock, Whitey views women—in this case the women at Pearl's—
in only a "visual, not physical" way (15). Whitey lacks both the physical desire and perhaps the capability to articulate his yearnings, and,
like Prufrock, he wanders through the cheap waterfront bars "toward

some overwhelming question" ("Prufrock," l. 10). Both characters seem completely disoriented, although in Whitey's case the sense of unreality stems also from his inebriation.

The first section of the story concludes as the drunken M. Norbert Jacklebaum, feeling increasingly ill, stumbles out under the "bile green" of the Bulkhead sign (15) and weaves his way across the screeching brakes of rush-hour traffic, only to be recognized as Whitey and rescued by his old friend Lennie. Despite Whitey's protests, and his memories of a brighter past, he is now helpless; he needs protecting. This reunion will not be the happy one of the past, for Whitey, half-blind with drink, hardly recognizes Lennie. Noting dimly a "worn likeness" (15) of the friend in the car beside him, Whitey feels only his own "sickness," which, like an animal, "crouches underneath, waiting to spring" (16). His thoughts are muddled, but he hears the refrain of *"Lennie and Helen and the kids"* propelling him toward Lennie's home. The uncertain nature of the homecoming is clear. Its potential salvation for Whitey is undercut by the final refrain *"Hey Sailor, what ship?,"* the incessant question that ends the section.

In *The Waste Land* Eliot links the mythical narrator figure Tiresias with the lines from Robert Louis Stevenson's "Requiem": the blind old man awaits "the evening hour that strives Homeward, and brings the sailor home from the sea" (*WL,* ll. 218–21). Like the blind Tiresias, "throbbing between two lives," Whitey vacillates between his two identities as he reaches the home of Lennie and Helen. Their old peaked hilltop house represents the love, warmth, and security that have sustained him throughout his travels and uncertain life. Whether on board ship, "in flophouses and jails," or at "union meetings," Whitey "has imaged and entered [the house] over and over again in a thousand various places a thousand various times" (16). But now Whitey senses that it is "too late" (16): time is running out for Whitey, and that fact is underscored when he barely "makes it to the top" of the "innumerable" stairs (16). The domestic life is nearly beyond him, and when he reaches the top, as Tennyson's Ulysses found waiting for him "an agèd wife," Whitey is appalled to find Helen so "grayed" (16).

Although quick to see signs of aging in Helen and Lennie, Whitey is blind to his own battered, worn face and body. Yet the effects of time are clearly evident to Helen, who takes one look at him and bursts into tears. But Whitey simply asks "Whassmatter Helen?" (17). Recalling Poe's Helen, whose "hyacinth hair" and "classic face" brought "home" the "weary, way-worn" wandering sailor, Olsen's Helen has been an ideal for Lennie. Probably half in love with her himself, Whitey recalls her telling him "how she really was and what was really happening, sometimes things she wouldn't even tell Lennie" (20). Like *The Waste Land* narrator who repeatedly refers to the "Unreal City" through which he passes, Whitey wonders, "*Who is real and who is not?*" (16) and again, "is he really here?" (17).

The two younger daughters Carol, age ten, and Allie, age six, greet him enthusiastically, but 15-year-old Jeannie stands aloof, watching him suspiciously. Indeed, twice in this section Whitey compares Jeannie to her mother, Helen, the first time noting that she is taller (16), the second time actually confusing the two: "Is that Helen? No, it is Jeannie, so much like Helen of years ago, suddenly there under the hall light, looking in at them all, her cheeks glistening from the rain" (22). Like *The Waste Land* hyacinth girl—her "arms full" and her "hair wet"—with whom Eliot's narrator cannot communicate (l. 38), Jeannie becomes more and more alienated from Whitey as the story progresses. Her arms are full not of flowers but of books; Whitey sees her illuminated by the light but can say nothing, just as *The Waste Land* narrator admits,

> I could not
> Speak, and my eyes failed, I was neither
> Living nor dead, and I knew nothing,
> Looking into the heart of light, the silence. (*WL*, ll. 38–41).

That he has a new scar on his face, a serious one, is underscored by his and the children's repeated allusions to it (17, 19, 22, 31). Like Prufrock, who worries that friends will comment on the thinness of his arms and legs and about his aging appearance in general, Whitey has arms described as "lean" and "scarred," and he refers defensively to his "new" nose, which replaced the recently broken one (19); he anxiously changes the subject whenever the girls ask him about his new scar. Briefly he feels that the house is a center of warmth and protectiveness, hiding "the city, the bay, the ships" (18). But the feeling does not last, and he is unable to "sing a song" (17). Whitey's "sickness springs at last and consumes him" (18): he passes out.

Alarmed, Lennie and Helen call a doctor, Whitey's old friend Chris. Again Olsen hints that Whitey's past is a more heroic and romantic one than seems possible for the battered seaman she portrays. As a boy, Chris had worshiped Whitey as a "he-ro" (19), even wanting to travel with him. Now, as a doctor, Chris can only gaze on the diminished hero the way *The Waste Land* narrator gazes on "the king my brother's wreck" (*WL*, 1. 191); Jeannie's view is that Helen, Lennie, and Whitey are all "peaceful wrecks" (22).

When he recovers, Whitey momentarily basks in the warmth of the fire. Lennie and Helen are holding hands and asking him questions, and six-year-old Allie falls asleep on his lap. But although he strokes her hair, "it is destroying, dissolving him utterly, this helpless warmth against him, this feel of a child—lost country to him and unattainable" (20). The sense of lost time is stressed again, for not only can Whitey never recapture the lost innocence of his youth, but he will never have a child of his own to love, shelter, and protect. As Allie recalls her nightmare in which she "was losted," Whitey remembers the children he has encountered in Korea and the Philippines (20–21), and he tells Helen and Lennie of his concern for these "begging children and the lost, the thieving children and the children who were sold" (21). Wanting to shield these children, Whitey "strokes Allie's soft hair as if the strokes would solidify, dense into a protection" (21). He speaks of a "kid," a shipmate named Howie Adams whom he has befriended and tried to protect. He is the "best kid" Whitey wants to introduce to this family—the "best people"—and Helen tells him he is "probably the best man" on board his ship (22). But this sense of familial community is fraying around the edges. No longer can Whitey help in the kitchen, stack wood, play with the children, or protect anyone. Almost an invalid himself, he tells stories—but they are not the heroic ones the children remember, instead they are drunken tales of pointless violence.

This scene by the family fire is the last one for Whitey, for he, like Allie, is a lost child. But unlike Allie who has a family to protect her, Whitey is now a homeless outsider to this group. Whitey watches as Lennie's shadow cradles Allie when he takes her upstairs to bed. On one hand Whitey seems to long to be in Lennie's position, protecting and caring for a young child. On the other hand, he seems to need such protection himself. Yet a still stronger instinct tells him that he wants to be alone; he "endures" the family's goodnight embraces and kisses. As the family ascends the stairs to an upper region where Whitey cannot follow, he remains in lonely exile, aware of the rain "beseechingly" moving on the windows, "like seeking fingers of the blind" (23). Olsen emphasizes that Whitey's is a lonely quest by references here and elsewhere (31, 38), to "seeking" and "blindness." In-

sistently, the section ends with the refrain, *"Hey sailor, what ship?"*:
that Whitey must answer the question becomes increasingly clear.

The third section opens the next morning with Whitey, who has
been moaning in his sleep. Like Emily of "I Stand Here Ironing" or
like Allie who dreamed she was lost, he has had bad dreams. Although
a 40-year-old seaman, he is similar to Emily not only in his nightmares, but in his illnesses, his scars (Orr, 90), his fearful awareness of
passing time, and his sense of exclusion from a warm family group.
He awakens to the disturbing silence of the empty house. The loud
seagoing life is his reality: he does not belong in this quiet house where
his friends have hidden the bottle he desperately needs. Just as Emily,
when left alone by her mother and stepfather, feared the clock that
"talked loud," Whitey abhors the loud silence broken only by the
"whisper of the clock," which orders this house now as everyone has
punctually departed for work and school. In the old days when he
chopped wood or painted furniture or cleaned the house, he felt needed
and valued for his contributions, but now he feels useless, alone, lost.
He is accustomed to "various voices of the sea" (23) and shipmates
whose lives are "as senseless as one's own" (24).

Walking out into the yard, he sees that the rain, associated with his
ceaseless searching, his "watery shiftings" (36), has stopped and his
feet are wet. Although he has the "old vision" of his formerly knightlike self, Whitey again seems a wandering figure from Eliot's *The Waste
Land,* longing for security and identity. He disobeys Helen's note with
its motherly injunction, "don't go down to the front" (24). Instead,
like Prufrock, he turns back "and descend[s] the stair" ("Prufrock,"
l. 39). Like Prufrock, strangely "etherised," Whitey seems compelled
to follow streets that insistently lead him "to an overwhelming question" ("Prufrock," l. 10). That overwhelming question for Whitey is
"Hey sailor, what ship?" Deliberately turning his back on *"Lennie and
Helen and the kids,"* Whitey walks away from the house, hearing only
the question.

The fourth and final section opens five days later as the drunken
Whitey bursts in on the family dinner, swearing like the proverbial
sailor and bearing food and gifts. Here Whitey seems an ironic Christ
figure—Carol has earlier asked why he was not with them for Christmas (17). Moreover, like the hunter suggested earlier, he brings home
the meat: "Whatever you're eating, throw it out," he orders, because
he has brought "steak" (25). But this liquor-induced bravado produces
only a hollow echo of the "old vision" he attempts to reenact here—
the vision of providing for this family he has loved for many years.

Olsen's technique in this fourth section is richly complex. Additional refrains appear, adding to the ceaseless but insistent movement of the narration. The muddled motifs and refrains in Whitey's head ebb and flow over the narrative, approaching a crescendo. The counterpointing of *"Lennie and Helen and the kids"* against *"Hey sailor, what ship?"* throughout the first three sections is clearly unsettling to Whitey, Lennie, and Helen, all of whom evoke a sense of "disequilibrium" (Orr, 87). As Lennie and Helen move into separate rooms, the "kids," like the women in "Prufrock" who "come and go, talking of Michelangelo" ("Prufrock," ll. 35–36), move back and forth, talking to Michael Jackson. Arguments occur between both Lennie and Whitey and Helen and Jeannie. Internal arguments occur as M. Norbert Jacklebaum wars more openly with Michael Jackson.

Replacing the author's limited omniscient view of and through Whitey's consciousness, an intrusive and sympathetic narrator moves back and forth between the living room (where Whitey and Lennie are speaking) to the kitchen (where Helen and Jeannie are speaking), revealing the history of the friendship. The narrator intercedes as Whitey becomes increasingly unable to articulate his thoughts and demonstrates the mounting tension and differences between the life of *"Lennie and Helen and the kids,"* and that of the *"sailor."*

Both Lennie and Helen criticize Whitey, as does the increasingly grown-up Jeannie, who by graduating from junior high school surpasses Whitey, who did not. All three ask him to curtail his swearing and his drinking and to stop throwing his money around (26, 29). In fact, Lennie and Helen treat him as one of their children. Irritated at Whitey's inebriated interruption of supper, Lennie "explodes," "Sit down, kids. Sit down, Whitey," and Helen adds, "Watch the language, Whitey, there's a gentlemen present. . . . Finish your plate, Allie" (26). And disregarding the strong, proud, generous image that Whitey tries hopelessly to project, Lennie tells him that by throwing his money around he is acting like a sailor "down on the front" (29). Whitey retaliates against the "adults"—Lennie, Helen, and even Jeannie—as, drunk and offended, Whitey tells Lennie that he and Helen look as if they have "been through the meat grinder" (30). Since Whitey wants to evade the silence he so abhors, he asks Jeannie to play a marimba recording, but Lennie asks him to slow down his drinking and then takes away his bottle. Whitey pulls out a spare from his jacket pocket.

Nor is this discipline new to Whitey. We learn that he has also been chastised by the "old man" (notably named Blackie) who started out as

Whitey's equal long ago, but now commands the ship. In childish fashion, Whitey sees all life in terms of black and white: Whitey is good, the man Blackie is evil. As another illustration of Olsen's proclivity for paired opposites, the black-white dichotomy here is ironic, for Whitey has clearly lost much of his earlier goodness. Blackie, also the "old man" or father, metaphorically joins forces with parents Lennie and Helen who must discipline their children and also the childlike Whitey. Similarly Chris, the impressionable 17-year-old "kid" who wanted to ship out with Whitey 14 years ago, is now a doctor who administers vitamin B shots and dispenses medical advice. Whitey alone seems to have resisted the move to adulthood, responsibility, and domesticity. His cavalier but childish rejection of those he senses are criticizing him or—worse—abandoning him, culminates in the words "Screw you" (29) when, like his other friends, Lennie seems to betray him.

In typically adolescent fashion Jeannie is embarrassed at the thought of any of her friends seeing Whitey in his drunk condition or hearing his rough language, and her attitude is perfectly understandable since she lacks the insight into the family's past relationship with Whitey that would make her more compassionate. To Jeannie Whitey is a "Howard Street wino." She is unable to pity the Whitey who is like a kid himself, a lost child. Instead she prefers the sedate alcoholism of a respectable neighbor who has "quiet drunks" (34). Jeannie has much to learn of Whitey's former goodness and heroism. She is merely irritated when Whitey lovingly recalls her as the child in whom he took the utmost interest and pride. In this final section the earlier hints about Whitey's more heroic past are validated by both Helen and the narrator. Although she shares Jeannie's distaste for Whitey's rough language, Helen tries to make Jeannie see that she can still "learn from him" (34). In short, Helen tries to make her daughter "understand"— and this verb is echoed by the narrator, who directly tells the readers that we too must "understand": understand that their friendship dates back to 1934 when Whitey saved Lennie's life in a dock strike, that they served together and fought fascism during World War II, and that they all admired the Filipino Jose Rizal, who had died a hero's death. In his earlier years Whitey was, in fact, a hero who saved the helpless, battled evil, was himself the object of hero worship for at least one young man, and even now identifies with the Philippine hero Jose Rizal.

The narrator emphasizes that Whitey went from youth and idealism to *"memories to forget, dreams to be stifled, hopes to be murdered"* (34, 37), a new refrain that frames the narrator's background information. Nor is this repression and despair a recent development: although he has spent 23 years as a sailor, the decline started at least 13 years ago, and we are witnessing its dénouement. The narrator tells us that Whitey, Lennie, and Helen had all been young together once; Helen and Lennie had believed in Whitey's potential, "had believed in his salvation, once" (37). They supported him when he was sober, but as he increasingly retreated into alcoholism, they have had to tell him that for the children's sake he is unwelcome when he is drunk (37).

We also learn through the intrusive narrator that the young Whitey had started to drink because, reminiscent of Prufrock, he could not go to a prostitute unless he was drunk (34, 37). Indeed, given Whitey's similarities to the effeminate Prufrock and his despairing "Love Song," Whitey's dilemma can be interpreted as a sexual one: he may have been wavering between the homosexual and the heterosexual life, or the bisexual and the heterosexual. Whitey's life has been lived almost entirely among men; his only friends are male; his repeated references to his "new nose" and his "new scar" have phallic implications, as do the allusions to his "loss" and "blindness." Moreover, in the fourth section we learn that he has rented an apartment with his friend Deeck ("Dick"?).[3]

The measure of the changes in Whitey is enormous. The heroic and chivalrous battles he once waged have become pointless and physically disfiguring brawls. Whitey's idealism has suffered not only from age, but from change—even American ports now seem the same as the foreign ones, and he is no longer welcome in the "respectable" parts of town. Whitey is an outsider, excluded from the lives of the more prosperous. In his head echoes the restriction, *"only so far shall you go and no further, uptown forbidden, not your language, not your people, not your country"* (36). Even the union, which presumably staged the 1934 dock strike, has changed. Whitey drunkenly admits to Lennie that recently the union fined him for trying to stand up for the rights of his young friend Howie (35), just as Blackie had punished him for trying to improve the food on board ship.

Whitey's inability to reconcile his youthful promise with the scarred and broken alcoholic he has become is poignantly demonstrated when Carol brings her scrap book containing a picture of him in the flush of youth—only a year or two older than Jeannie—when he was joyous and full of hope. The pitted, scarred face of the present Whitey confronts the photograph of the youthful Whitey: "Under the joyful sun, proud sea, proud ship as background, the proud young man, glistening hair and eyes, joyful body, face open to life, unlined. Sixteen? Seventeen?" (31). Rejecting the picture, he denies that he is Whitey: "M. Norbert Jacklebaum never saw the guy" (31). Recalling earlier references to searching, sightlessness, and touch, with blind, "seeking" fingers he traces *"the scars, the pits and lines, the battered nose"* of his face—the face of M. Norbert Jacklebaum (31). He has betrayed his earlier promise, denied his youthful idealistic self. He seems to be rechristening himself as "M. Norbert Jacklebaum," but his former beauty is suggested in the description of the seafaring narrator of *The Waste Land,* "who was once handsome and tall as you" (*WL,* l. 321).

Whitey, once handsome and brave in his courageous fight for a better world, now sits for the second time in five days in Lennie and Helen's living room. This time, though, the family is divided and dispersed and arguing; no one thinks to light a welcoming fire. The idea of the greeting *"Hey sailor, what ship?"* moves ever closer to Jose Rizal's "El Ultimo Adiós," which the children have been begging Whitey to recite. Again, one thinks of Robert Louis Stevenson's "Requiem" for the dead sailor-hunter. Apparently "Crown 'n Deep," the title of Rizal's piece, with its implications of ascent and descent, of rising and falling, had been the acme of Whitey's past performances. As Orr notes, Whitey is similar to the ironing mother's daughter Emily in his gift for mimicry; now, like Emily, he can perform before a willing audience (Orr, 86).

He begins with the wrong poem, quoting the line *"When there is November in my soul."* Recovering, he takes "the old proud stance" and points out that he learned "El Ultimo Adiós" when he was young (32)—but in his explanation he confuses Carol with Jeannie, just as he has earlier confused Jeannie with Helen. After the false start, he repeats the title, "The Valedictory," written by Jose Rizal just before he faced the firing squad. It begins, "Land I adore, farewell" and moves on to Rizal's "joyous" sacrifice of his "sad life" in order that "the vision may rise to fulfillment." Even if his life were "Young or rose-strewn," he would still relinquish it. And even if he is forgotten, he knows *"I shall be speech in thy ears, fragrance and color, / Light and shout and loved song. . . ."* But Whitey's voice becomes inaudible, then trails off on the line, *"I am leaving all with thee, my friends, my love, / Where I go are no tyrants. . . ."* (32–33); then he ceases altogether.

The "forfeited garden of Eden" he addresses parallels Whitey's own earlier love for his comrades and his romantic idealism, but instead of resulting in a youthful death for a heroic cause, Whitey's idealism and his experience with socialism has culminated in what the narrator describes as *"the death of the brotherhood"* (35): now, "more and more of them [are] winos" (36). And although Helen and Lennie have consistently tried to instill in their children a respect for the Whitey of the past, the inescapable fact is that the past is over and cannot be recalled any more than Whitey can recall the rest of the poem.

At best, the lines he does manage to recite stay with Lennie and Helen and the kids, and with us. Whitey leaves with us some of the fragrance and color and brightness of youth, before he became the drunken, faltering, middle-aged sailor. In the words of Kathleen McCormack, by juxtaposing his "decaying body" against "the song that still sings within him"[4] Olsen portrays him even in failure as a symbol of the human ability to hope and to dream. Yet in the postwar fifties Whitey is a relic. While others—Lennie, Chris, Blackie, even Jeannie—have struggled forward, Whitey has joined the ranks of the seafaring winos. To this extent, at least, Jeannie is right: What in fact can she learn from Whitey? Too drunk to articulate even his most meaningful memories, Whitey, like Prufrock, is ineffectual and bumbling, an object of derision to young women like Jeannie.

As Donne affirms that the loss of even a small "clod" of the continent dispels the sense of human connectedness and interdependence, so Lennie protests to Whitey, "you're a chunk of our lives." But Whitey's unsentimental response is, "Shove it, Lennie. So you're a chunk of my life. So?" (36). Although he does not vocalize his earlier refrain, we can imagine it: "hell with you, hell with your friends." Whitey believes he will be happier with sailing men like his friend Deeck who will let him make noise and will look at him "without reproach or pity or anguish" (38).

The water imagery completes the tidelike motion of the story as, no longer vacillating, he makes his decision. As he walks away from the hilltop house the fog lifts and he sees the city below him. He walks away, seeing behind him the house on the crest of a wave, a hill, one of the many in "wave after wave" of his own journey (38). Now it is the "myriad [houses] that stare at him so blindly"—his own vision is clear. Whitey's end is sad but inevitable.

As "he goes down," the recurrence of the refrain *"Hey sailor, what ship?"* is supplemented by another, *"Hey Marinero, what ship?"* (38). The use of a Spanish name—especially in conjunction with the German and French implications of Whitey's adopted name M. Norbert Jacklebaum—suggests the universality of Whitey's situation. Erika Duncan reminds us that because the 1930s evoked "a rush of internationalism," many people sympathetic to the Left felt a "connection" to "struggles the world over, in Africa, in the Philippines, in Guatamala, San Salvador, Chile and Asia" (Duncan 1982, 211). Notably, the addition of the Spanish word "marinero" not only recalls the opening references to Manila and Managua, Whitey's love of the marimba, and to "El Ultimo Adiós"—dedicated to Philippine hero Jose Rizal with memories of Helen and Lennie and the kids—but also serves to connect him with the dead hero. Finally, to underscore still further these references to both American and Spanish-speaking heroes, the story's dedication at its close is "For Jack Eggan, Seaman. Volunteer, Abraham Lincoln Brigade," an American sailor who died trying to protect the Spanish against Franco during the Spanish Civil War. Although both Rizal and Eggan gave their lives for noble if lost causes (the Philippine independence movement, the Spanish Civil War), Whitey, in his own mind at least, resumes his heroic status.

The reality of the present has intervened in Whitey's relationships with his friends of the past as they have retreated behind the "front" lines into domesticity, but the aging sailor makes his decision. Like Emily of "I Stand Here Ironing," with whom he shares so many similarities, Whitey asserts his independence at the end, refusing to allow others to dictate his future for him. As Martin notes, his potentialities, like Emily's, may never be realized (Martin, 25). He returns to the farthest westward tip of the North American continent, presumably poised on the brink of further adventure. Realistically, one can hardly believe that he has either the strength or the health to sail again; indeed, Blackie has probably assured that he will not. Nonetheless, like Tennyson's Ulysses, who, having rejected his aged "family," vows to "sail beyond the sunset . . . until I die," Whitey "goes down" the hill to the fate that awaits him. A certain essential dignity inheres in Olsen's final image of Whitey, a dignity that cannot be diminished by the encroaching thought of his imminent death.

Chapter Six
"O Yes"

At the end of "Hey Sailor, What Ship?" Whitey disappears into his own version of home and self, but Lennie and Helen, Carol and Jeannie reappear in the third story, "O Yes." The white family is counterbalanced by a black family, Mrs. Alva Phillips and her three children, Parialee (Parry), Lucinda (Lucy), and Buford (Bubbie). "O Yes" takes place two years after the episode with Whitey and focuses on the 12-year-old Carol and her metaphorical baptism into the riddle of life. As she hovers on the threshold of womanhood, she wavers between her natural feelings of love for her black friend Parry and the social reality of white prejudice against blacks and middle-class condescension toward the working class.

"O Yes" is divided into two sections. The first, narrated in the present tense, occurs at a black storefront church as Helen and Carol join the Phillips family at Parry's baptism ceremony. The second, told largely in the past tense, takes place at Carol's home during the next few days and months. The first sentence of the story depicts Carol, clutching tightly with one hand to her mother, and resting her other hand lightly on her friend Parry, an image that suggests two major themes. First, the story is very much concerned with racial prejudice. Although Olsen wrote "O Yes" "just before Little Rock," she agrees that it is still "very current" (Pearlman interview). Second, it is a "story of mothering" (Lyons, 99), and Olsen's emphasis on the black and white mothers and their daughters indicates that this is very much a women's story. The story focuses on the two mothers, Alva and Helen, the two daughters, Carol and Parry, and the mother-daughter linkages between Alva and Parry, Helen and Jeannie, and Helen and Carol. In fact, as Orr has pointed out, we are "not sure" whose story it is (Orr, 94), for the relationships are fluid and intermingled. "O Yes" is profitably viewed as a story of women encountering the painful dichotomies of black and white, wealth and poverty, faith and denial, illness and health, affirmation and negation, rising and falling, past and present.

The central metaphor of the baptism, ironic on several levels, refers not only to Parry's literal baptism, but to Carol's immersion in the harsh realities of adulthood—and womanhood—and then her instinctive resistance to them. Carol's unpleasant awakening, for instance, is lyrically reinforced by music and water imagery. Although in the previous story Whitey called several times for music to fill up silences, only "singing his song" as a valedictory at the end, in "O Yes" music saturates the pages from the beginning. Paradoxically, as both Carol (and her grandmother Eva in "Tell Me a Riddle") know, music results from imposed order on conflicting, "struggling" sounds. The black church music evokes an inherently contradictory image, because it represents not only the indefatigability of black religious faith and the potential oneness of humanity but also the troubled disharmony of Carol and Parry's friendship. Carol is profoundly disturbed by the inner turmoil that the music sets in motion. In each section, the same piece of music, a black hymn of encouragement and affirmation, engenders Carol's awareness of the difficulties inherent in her friendship with Parry.

Both Carol and the reader are quickly immersed in the words and sounds of the black hymns, the frequent refrain *"Oh yes"*[1] reiterated as numerous members of the congregation testify to their faith in the Lord. This refrain becomes a leitmotiv echoing within the minds of the characters and the readers. Rose Yalow Kamel points out that the refrain suggests "how the power of the word militates against silence" (Kamel 1988, 98). The words are both affirming and optimistic, and they allude to the admirable aspects of family, community, and religious faith. Concomitantly, the words *"O yes"* also allude to the black struggle for freedom from racial and class prejudice. At the story's end, however, both Helen and Carol agonize over this seeming contradiction, and Olsen implies that Carol, like her mother, will try to resist it.

In all her stories Olsen employs repetition and refrain to convey her characters' experiences. But unlike "Hey Sailor, What Ship?," which opens in the loneliness of rain, "O Yes" opens in sunlight and warmth, which, like the music, suggests both the loving nature of Carol's youthful friendship with Parry and the black religious experience. Whereas Whitey's story is almost entirely colorless, sketched in drab misty greys or stark blacks and whites, Carol and Parry's is painted in bright colors—intense blues, yellows, purples, reds.

Throughout the first part of the story the golden light streams into the church through a "window of curtained sunblaze" (41); a painting of God depicts Him standing in the blue waters of the River of Jordan, embracing a brown man and pointing to letters of gold: "REJOICE; GOD IS LOVE; I AM THE WAY, THE TRUTH, THE LIFE" (40). At first Carol instinctively joins in with the rhythm surrounding her, tapping along with the singing of the black youth choir. Dressed in "robes of wine, of blue, of red," they sing of the land of freedom and promise, the congregation affirming with the chorus *"Yes, O Yes"* (40). But just as Carol begins to feel at one with the black congregation, she notices Eddie Garlin, a black classmate, and she becomes rigid: her social consciousness intrudes on her instinctive sense of oneness with the congregation. She "stiffens" and grows anxious, and although the sun still blazes warmly into the room and the rhythm still sounds like "one glad rhythm," Carol begins to wonder how to "untwine the intertwined voices" (41), to divide them, to analyze them. Dimly beginning to separate her whiteness from the surrounding blackness, Carol worries about the consequences of her white presence in this black church: What if Eddie "said something" or actually "talked to her right in front of somebody at school" (41)? In her anxiety Carol is like her older sister Jeannie in "Hey Sailor," who was acutely concerned about her friends' reactions should they meet the drunken, foul-mouthed Whitey. As Carol points out Eddie Garlin to Parry, their difficulty in communicating is suggested in the different speech patterns of the two girls:

> "Parry, look. Somebody from school."
> "Once more once," says Parialee, in the new way she likes to talk now.
> "Eddie Garlin's up there. He's in my math."
> "Couple cats from Franklin Jr. chirps in the choir. No harm or alarm." (40)

But the widening gap between the two friends has not yet surfaced in Carol's consciousness; at this point she is aware only of the joyous closeness of humanity as the mixed choir sings *"Ezekiel saw that wheel of time / Every spoke was of humankind . . ."* (42).

While the preacher talks of God, Carol daydreams, recalling childhood memories of her friendship with Parry during elementary school. The "sun fired" barrette in Parry's hair "strikes a long rail of light" (42), and Carol can feel Parry's "warm" arm, which recalls their ele-

mentary school days when they played together "drenched in sun and
dimness and dream" (42): "And as the preacher's voice spins happy and
free, it is the used-to-be play-yard. Tag. Thump of the volley ball.
Ecstasy of the jump rope. Parry, do pepper. Carol, do pepper. Parry's
bettern Carol, Carol's bettern Parry" (43). The past warmth and closeness of these two girls, black and white, is further emphasized during
the service as Carol returns to their old game, tapping the rhythm of
a song on Parry's warm arm, urging her to "guess" the song (42). The
old game suggests the shared rhythms of childhood, before the awareness of social and racial difference.

Carol, a product of white culture, is unprepared for the black congregation's emotional response to the preacher's exhortations. Suddenly
her contented state is interrupted again, this time not by the sight of
a face but by the sound of a voice—the fearsome and unaccustomed
noise of a woman screaming. Now the sun "no longer blare[s] through
the windows" and the scene becomes void of color. Carol notices only
the white-gloved hands of the ushers and the "ladies in white dresses
like nurses or waitresses wear" (43). The chorus of "O Yes" intensifies
to a moaning chant and Carol reaches for a fan; she weakens, yet the
preacher still has the power to fascinate her. As he speaks of "Dizzy"
and "Muggsy" and "Satchmo" his "voice com[es] out like a trumpet,"
prompting Carol to whisper, "Oh Parry, he's so good" (43).

She becomes caught up in motion again, tapping and chanting
"Great Day" with Lucy and Bubbie as the preacher speaks of Adam
awakening Eve, yelling, "Great Day, woman, don't you know it's the
Great Day?" (44). Numerous repetitions of "Great Day" emphasize the
importance of the moment. But now Carol sees as well as hears a "little
woman . . . screaming and shaking" (44–45), engendering "an awful
thrumming sound . . . like feet and hands thrashing around, like a
giant jumping of a rope" (44). Although Orr views the rope simile as
a perversion of the "childhood memory" (Orr, 96), it expands the image of Carol's youthful game with Parry to include this small black
woman who is "not much taller" than Carol (45); further, it implies
the twining of human lives, particularly those of women. The chorus
of "Yes . . . O Yes" resounds, as does a "trembling wavering scream"
(45, 46) and a loud and unified response, "Shout, brother, shout / We
won't have to die no more!" (47). The sounds reach a crescendo:

A single exultant lunge of shriek. Then the thrashing. All around a clapping.
Shouts with it. The piano whipping, whipping air to a froth. Singing now.

I once was lost who now am found
Was blind who now can see.
(47)

The singing of the spiritual "Amazing Grace" alludes to ideas of loss
and blindness, recalling not only the imagery used to convey Whitey's
predicament but also the lost children who permeate so much of Olsen's fiction. Like the screaming woman, Carol hears the preacher say
that their burden will not last forever. Carol also feels the shaking
inside her (45) and identifies with the small black woman, but she
consciously denies any similarities between herself and the black
woman. Indeed, Carol's resistance to new and disturbing insights fore-
shadows the loss of her friendship with Parry and her willed blindness
to the struggles of others. She resists the implications of the sounds
and tries to imagine herself in another place where she has the power
to control the noise. Earlier she has tried to imagine the singing as a
record (41), which she can examine intellectually, separating and identifying the various strands that make up the whole. Now she imagines
her fan is a protective wall behind which she could reduce the sound
"into a record small and round," making it "all tiny (but never any
screaming)" (47). Carol shuts both her eyes and her ears to the meaning
and begs for the first of many times, "Mother, let's go home" (47). But
her mother, Helen, clutches Carol as tightly as Carol clutched her at
the beginning of the story. Alva, "strong Alva," rocks and chants beside Carol, saying "*O Yes*" while inside Carol's head her own voice says
"No" (47). Helen may be communicating her own needs to Carol as
she grips her hand, but Carol, resisting both mothers, knows only that
she wishes to escape the frightening scene.

The music "leaps and prowls" and the shrieks become "ladders of
screamings" (47). The affirmative and harmonious singing becomes
unadulterated terrifying noise. As the imagery of ascent intensifies
("*Come on my brethren it's time to go higher*" (48), Olsen introduces powerful water imagery: "*wade wade in the water*" (47) sings the congregation, their "voices in great humming waves . . . [everyone] moving
like in slow waves and singing, and up where Eddie is, a new cry, wild
and open, 'O help me, Jesus'" (48). This time the voice "up" in the
choir is not that of a nameless little woman, but that of Carol's black
classmate (her name is Vicky, but Carol does not identify her until the
end of the story). As she continues to resist identification with the
black girl and the small black woman, the effort overpowers Carol.

Now "the rhinestones in Parry's hair glitter wicked" (48) and the sounds are of swelling water and thunder. In a near faint, Carol "is drowned under the sluice of the slow singing and the sway" (48).

Languorous in the "deep cool green" of the waves, Carol, now semi-conscious, imagines herself with a black woman; this time it is Parry's mother Alva. In her underwater dream Carol recalls her trip to Alva's workplace, Hostess Foods, and, reminiscent of Alice in Lewis Carroll's *Alice in Wonderland,* envisions Alva swimming strongly beside her, competently starting the machinery with a touch of her hand and surrounded by wheels of cheese and barrels of pickles. Alva, godlike, calm, and in control of both the machinery and the food, suddenly appears in a blaze of light as Carol dimly hears Alva asking her to drink from a cup she proffers. Her mother echoes Alva: "DRINK IT" (49). At this point the seeming allusion to Lewis Carroll's Alice and her fantasy of the bottle labeled "Drink Me" merges with a more spiritual one: both the black mother Alva and the white mother Helen urge Carol to drink, as from a communion cup. The two women friends seem to be baptizing Carol, initiating her into a communion of love. But just as Carol denies her connection with the tiny black woman and her black classmate Vicky, she now actively resists both Alva and Parry: backed by her recent initiation into bigoted and stultifying schoolgirl social codes, Carol returns to consciousness, repeats to her mother her desire to "go home" (46, 49), and apologizes to Parry for having to miss her baptism.

This is a crucial scene in the relationship between Carol and Parry. Throughout this section the narrator has hinted that despite their mothers' loving attempts to keep them together, the two girls have been growing apart. Parry, who earlier displayed her newly acquired "jivetalk" (53) in such phrases as "no harm or alarm" and "no need to cuss and fuss" (49), forgoes her rhymes and faces Carol with utter seriousness: "Don't feel sorry. I'll feel better you not there to watch. It was our mommas wanted you to be there, not me" (50). The beginnings of the rift are now undeniable. And in fact Parry is right—the "mommas" are trying to shore up their daughters' friendship—but their common efforts crumble against the ugly truth of the social and peer pressures Carol and Parry are experiencing. Thus instead of seeing the church baptism of Parry, we see the immersion of both girls in the relentless reality of their racial differences.

Like Helen in "Hey Sailor, What Ship?," Alva wants very much to have Carol "understand" the importance of this ritual to Parry. But her efforts, for the moment at least, are useless. As with Jeannie's refusal to comprehend the goodness behind Whitey's drunkenness, Carol refuses to listen to Alva or to learn the value of "people letting go that way" (50) or to "hear" the music that evokes strong feelings and comforts burdened people. Alva explains that to many black people "church is home" (51), a place where they can be themselves. To Carol, however, this church is not home; it is a terrifying place filled with the noise and emotional testaments of both pain and faith. To Carol, home is the familiar place where she can retreat with her family and people of her own kind. Unlike Whitey who needs noise to fill up the soundless void of his "senseless" life, Carol in her refusal to listen adumbrates her grandmother Eva's tendency to shut out noise in "Tell Me a Riddle."

Significantly, this section concludes not with Carol's departure with Helen, but with Alva's eloquent descriptions of the origins of her religious faith, her sense of self-worth, and her identity as a mother. Like the words of the black hymns, Alva's words are italicized, suggesting a parallel between the church songs and Alva's "song." She vividly describes her pregnancy with Parry at age 15 after the child's father abandoned her. Alone at the delivery clinic, she had a fiery vision of hell and heard agonized screaming, her own included. But then she heard the voice of God. He spoke to her through "*a small little child*" who led her "*upward,*" calling, "*Mama Mama you must help carry the world*" (51–52). Naomi N. Jacobs notes that Alva's vision is pointedly similar to the process of childbirth.[2] Certainly Alva implies that she is reborn or baptized as, with the help of her own mother, she and her baby emerge from darkness into a world of light where "*multitudes*" are "*singing,*" and where she feels "*free, free*" (52). Lyons sees the vision or song as one of "classic death and rebirth," suggesting that "nurturing is thus the road and the rule" (Lyons, 100). Additionally, Jacobs points out the conflation of the images of Alva as teenager with Alva as mother, and the conflation of the emerging child with Alva's own mother. Ultimately, says Jacobs, "Alva becomes her mother" (Jacobs 1986, 7).

The intermingling of these mother-child images implies the universal bond among women as mothers replicate themselves in their daughters—thereby, as the ironing mother would say, making their marks or leaving their seals. Taking as her cue the Christian assertion that God gave us "a little child to love" and to believe in, Alva rejoices in her identity as mother. The repetition of "*Mama, Mama,*" "*Alva,*"

Alva," and *"Free, free,"* implies that Alva's strength is rooted in her sense of herself as mother, as woman, and as independent individual accepting and affirming her role in the human community. The meaning of Alva's song informs the rest of the story in which Carol and Helen as daughter and mother discuss the human propensity to "care" about others.

In the next section of this story, which takes place at Lennie and Helen's house, Olsen traces the events of two different times: the hours following Parry's baptism and—several months later—the two days when Carol is confined at home with the mumps. During the hours following the baptism, Helen tells Lennie and Jeannie (now 17) of Carol's emotional reaction to the church service. Clearly, Helen is at least as upset as Carol had been. Whereas Jeannie seems mature and cynical in her attempts to explain reality to her mother, Helen seems more like a daughter than a mother: in fact, three times in this section she or Lennie or the narrator note Helen's resemblance to Carol (55, 56, 62). Lennie, on the other hand, plays a role as mediator, speaking to Helen more as a daughter, Jeannie more as an equal. Notably, Carol is absent: her crisis is the catalyst for the anxieties and conflicts of Helen and Jeannie.

Jeannie listens closely, but she refrains from voicing her reactions to her mother's bewildered account of the afternoon—an account she finds irritatingly naïve. Finally she says aloud, "Grow up, Mother" (53), and begins to instruct her parents about the "sorting process" that takes place in junior high school. As Jeannie speaks, Helen recalls the way girls are encouraged to believe in the "correct" way to dress and to behave—and to shun those who do not fit the mold. Suddenly she remembers Carol's "self-righteous" voice as she told her mother of a teacher who attempted to wipe "forbidden lipstick" from a girl's face: Helen is unaware that this girl is Vicky from church, but she hears "a mute cry of violated dignity" in Carol's description of the way Vicky had resisted the white teacher's rules by fighting with and cursing her (54–55). In this scene Vicky is like Whitey who never graduated from junior high school and who remembers the voices that said, "only so far shall you go and no further."

Both Vicky and Parry are victims of this sorting process. Jeannie tells her parents that Parry's teachers "treat her like a dummy and white kids . . . treat her like dirt" (53). Carol, too, is a victim, as Jeannie explains. She accuses her parents of "tearing Carol apart": they teach her to treat everyone equally, but they send her to a school that denies equality and encourages the racial, cultural, and economic sorting process. Helen realizes suddenly that Jeannie is talking about herself as much as she is talking about Carol. So as Carol's identity fuses with that of Vicky and of Parry, and as Helen's identity fuses with that of Carol, Jeannie, too, becomes entwined in this shifting image of frustrated, violated female individuality in ceaseless conflict with the system.

Certainly Jeannie reacts to Carol's crisis by voicing her own concerns with paradox—with the distance between the way life should be and the way life is. She tells her parents that they hardly noticed when, in a similar way, she and her best friend Ginger sorted themselves out and parted ways; that is, they hardly noticed because Ginger is white. The principle, she seems to be arguing, is the same: Ginger was sorted out because she was not planning to go to college; she quit school and has "two kids now" (52–53). In "Hey Sailor, What Ship?" Jeannie, 15, was typically judgmental and one-sided: she could pity the refined neighbor who drank because he talked "intelligent" and lived in a "nice house" and had "quiet drunks," but she condemned Whitey whom she termed a bum, a "wino." Now, two years later, Jeannie has matured. She recognizes the paradox of wanting to care for people regardless of their class but of being allied to the social and cultural norms that teach children to stay with their own kind. Jeannie's angry frustration recalls Emily's during her stay at the convalescent home: "They don't like you to love anyone here." When Jeannie's father voices the idea that Carol and Parry could be friends despite school pressures, Jeannie responds, "They can't. They can't. They don't let you" (54). In frustration she blames her parents: "What do you want of that poor kid anyway? Make up your mind. Stay friends with Parry—but be one of the kids. Sure. Be a brain—but not a square. Rise on up, college prep, but don't get separated. Yes, stay one of the kids but . . ." (55). Jeannie's anger is invoked by Carol's experience because the eldest daughter understands the dichotomy between her parents' lessons in human equality, caring, and responsibility and society's lessons in inequality and upward (white) mobility.

Helen learns from Jeannie's outburst. Obviously a good-hearted, liberal woman, she is committed to her friendship with Alva. The two mothers are devoted to each other, but they need to be reminded of their daughters' separate experiences and of the significant amount that the daughters, "secret from" the mothers, withhold from them. During Jeannie's angry outburst, Helen is as disoriented as Carol had been at the church service: she has trouble listening and comprehending. Gradually, however, the truth of Jeannie's words penetrates her brain and "a foreboding comprehension whirl[s] through Helen" (54). Like Carol, she temporarily resists it, admitting to Jeannie that she "wasn't listening" (56). Similar to the ironing mother, Helen tries to make sense of the myriad implications of her life and the lives of her daughters, and those of Alva and Parry. She realizes she has not really been listening to Carol's tales of junior high school, and she literally cannot listen to all that Jeannie is saying. The mother's dilemma is universal.

Lennie, who does listen, agrees with Helen and reiterates to the children that just because society decrees this sorting process does not mean the process cannot be overcome. Yet although he is loving and rational, Lennie, like Alva, is somehow removed from the emotional crises besetting his wife, his daughters, and the women and girls who are their friends. Lennie believes, in fact, that they have all had enough for one day and tells Helen, "You look about ready to pull a Carol" (56). He calls their attention to Carol and Parry who, as he speaks, are outside playing again together, "leaping, bouncing, hallooing, tugging the kites of spring" (56). Like the black congregation and its chorus of "O Yes," Lennie sees only the possibilities of the scene: "And now Parry jumps on her pogo stick (the last time), Carol shadowing her, and Bubbie, arching his body in a semicircle of joy, bounding after them, high, higher, higher" (56). The use of the present tense implies an image of possibility, of affirmation, of the way life could or should be—and yet, as the parentheses suggest, the scene has a tenuous sense of fragility and finality.

The joyous moment of "high, higher, higher"—a physical reenactment of the phrase "O Yes" and its limitless potential—does not last. Alva and Helen remain friends, shopping together and visiting in each other's homes, but Parry no longer accompanies her mother on these outings. The friendship between Helen and Alva contrasts with the isolation of the ironing mother who seemed to have no time for women friends, who had no one to sustain her and therefore had little time to instill humanistic values in her daughter. That mother exemplifies Olsen's concern with parents who "worked so hard that there wasn't much of [them] left" (Pearlman interview). Yet Helen and Alva, both working mothers, seem to draw strength from each other, exemplifying the other part of Olsen's riddle—that it "is not the nature of human beings to just lay [sic] down and be victims" (Pearlman interview).

A brief midsection describes the next few months when Carol and Parry rarely "walk the hill together" (56). Increasingly, not only race but class differences become apparent because Lennie and Helen's family has two incomes and Alva's has only one. Inevitably, Carol goes with her new friend Melanie to their clubs, to the skating rink, and to their friends' homes, but Parry must go home after school to take care of her siblings while her mother works the afternoon-to-midnight shift at Hostess Foods. Parry's responsibilities at home, like Emily's in "I Stand Here Ironing," leave her little time or incentive for homework. And like Jeannie's friend Ginger, Parry has no time, no space, and seemingly no reason to study.

Then Carol contracts mumps. As so often happens in Olsen's stories, a physical illness becomes a metaphor for a deep emotional problem. Here Carol's sickness, like Emily's and Whitey's in the previous stories, signifies her loneliness and her struggle for self-definition. For the "mommas," the illness represents another chance to bring the two girls together. The scene opens as Helen stays home from work, realizing that for this day at least Carol will need her. Carol will in fact need her mother less because of her illness than because of her emotional upheaval following Parry's visit the day before, when Parry brought Carol the homework she had collected from Carol's teachers. Parry's visit to Carol is pivotal, as signalled by Olsen's use of indentation to indicate a number of flashbacks and a narrator who lets the reader into Parry's thoughts.

Glancing only once at Carol, Parry seems a blur of nervous self-conscious movement as she maintains a constant stream of talk: "Hey frail, lookahere and wail, your momma askin for homework, what she got against YOU? . . . looking quickly once then not looking again and talking fast. . . . Hey, you bloomed. You gonna be your own pumpkin, hallowe'en?" (57). Again, as at the baptism, Olsen uses speech patterns to emphasize Parry's difference from the white girls. Parry's speech and movement are in direct opposition to the bedridden Carol's immobility and speechlessness. A sense of the fifties era is evoked as Parry, in italicized parentheses, sings lines from Jerry Lee Lewis's *Whole lotta shakin goin on* (57, 58)—and in fact her presence is shaking Carol's life to its very core. Speaking quickly of "Miss Rockface," apparently the school principal, Parry tells Carol only that the principal did not believe Parry could successfully deliver Carol's homework.

But Parry is silent about the truth. In a further indented passage (within the already indented one), the narrator informs us of incidents Parry has withheld from Carol: Miss Campbell assumed that Parry's mother was Helen's maid, not her friend; Miss Campbell assumed Parry was stupid; Miss Campbell feared Parry would steal from Carol's locker; Miss Campbell did not trust Parry to go directly to Carol's house with the assignments. Miss Campbell personifies Jeannie's generalization about teachers who treat Parry "like a dummy." Although the two mothers had meant well, doubtless hoping again to bring the girls together, they had failed to understand the pain they would unwittingly inflict on Parry.

Returning from the doubly indented to the singly indented scene, Parry speaks admiringly of Miss Fernandez. In contrast to Miss Campbell, Miss Fernandez is a good-hearted teacher who tells Parry that she admires her for taking care of her friend and that Carol's only assignment is to get well. Notably Miss Fernandez is a kindly, nurturing figure who means the "most" to Parry; her Hispanic surname suggests her minority status and her humanity offsets the suspicious bigotry of Miss Campbell. The kindly Miss Fernandez thus takes her place alongside the white Helen and the black Alva. But Parry, carefully guarding her emotions, understands that she has been "sorted" or "labeled," separated from the accelerated, presumably white, college-bound students, and she yearns hopelessly to enroll in Miss Fernandez's classes. Yet Parry understands that Miss Fernandez teaches only girls like Carol, not girls like herself: "Wish I could get her but she only teaches 'celerated" (58).

In an indirect way, however, Parry does tell her unvoiced story to Carol. Parry moves quickly to the news that Vicky, the girl whose cries during the church service triggered Carol's fainting spell—and who defiantly wears lipstick—will probably be suspended for telling Miss (Campbell) Rockface not to give her "no more bad shit" (58). Vicky has more courage and honesty than either Parry or Carol because she lashes out against unjust treatment and affronts to her self-worth and dignity. Her earlier rebellion in the lipstick incident demonstrates Vicky's spirit. The significance of this information becomes clear when we recall that Carol understands, if unconsciously, that Vicky, too, is a victim of the sorting process. Vicky's loud and demonstrative protests verbalize the unhappiness that the more inhibited Parry and Carol suffer. In Parry's voiceless frustration she draws "lipstick faces—bemused or mocking or amazed"—on each of Carol's bookcovers (59). These images on the outside of Carol's books provide the life lessons of this story.

The arm-in-arm picture of the two girls stares mockingly at them from Carol's mirror, reminding them that only one year has passed since Carol and Parry's graduation from elementary school. But the innocent girlhood world of dolls and Katy Keane comic books has been irreparably shaken since that graduation. Silently, wordlessly communicating with Carol—despite her constant chatter—Parry literally turns their graduation picture upside down and shakes up the entire room full of memories of their love and friendship. As she leaves, even the mobiles and kites are still "twirling and rocking" (59). Parry's behavior recalls that of the little black woman whose shaking Carol could feel. In a parting shot, Parry tells Carol that the next time she is sick, her "buddybud Melanie" should collect her assignments (58).

Carol's precarious position between childhood and adulthood is demonstrated by her "just budding breast" as she reaches for her "childhood pillow," a plush stuffed animal (59). In comparison, Parry seems more mature both physically and emotionally. Parry takes pride in what Kamel calls her "budding sexuality" (Kamel 1985, 64) and in the alluring colorful clothes she wears—the springtime pinks, lavenders, and purples. Parry seems more like Jeannie and less like Carol in her frustrated understanding of reality. In contrast, Carol seems one of Olsen's "lost children" who suffer from nightmares. Disoriented just as she was after Parry's baptism, Carol, in her feverish delirium, tries to talk to the lipstick faces and stand on her head to face the upside-down picture. As Annette Bennington McElhiney notes, this regression to chaos in her nightmare is similar to the experience of "novices prior to initiation" (McElhiney, 79). Carol is reaping the results of the "Great Day," her own baptism into the confusing clash of black and white, right and wrong.

Ill, feverish, filled with troubled visions of Parry and lipstick faces, Carol awakens the next morning to her mother's radio, which blares the same song she heard before fainting at the church service: *Come on my brethern we've got to go higher / Wade, wade . . .* (60). Again the sounds intrude on her willed silence, just as Parry's motion and "shaking" had intruded the day before. Carol races to the radio to quell the noise, yanking off the dial in her urgency. Here Olsen conflates all the major motifs of the story—the music, the imagery of water and ascent, the "sorting process" of whites and blacks that denies their liking for and natural similarities to each other. Carol sobs against her mother, confessing, "I hear it all the time" (60). The "it" refers to the sound of black voices, singing of freedom and home—and the "different" voices of Parry and Vicky. The song, suggests McCormack, with its "images of intertwined voices" indicates that Carol will be healed "through the possibility which her mother offers" in her friendship with Alva (McCormack, 64).

Carol confesses that she and Parry are no longer really friends; further, she finally speaks of Vicky—the one "who got that way" when Carol fainted, the one who is "always in trouble" and may be expelled from school: "She acts so awful outside but I remember how she was in church and whenever I see her now I have to wonder. And hear . . . like I'm her, Mother, like I'm her" (61). Carol, once "lost" and "blind," at last sees the commonality among the shaking of the little black woman who is "not much bigger" than she, the brave rebellion of Vicky and the silent one of Parry, and the denial of racial hostilities in the persistent friendship of Alva and Helen. This daughter has begun her *"baptism into the seas of humankind"* (61); the girl's "baptism" or coming-of-age is no mere awareness of her changing body but an awareness of inequality and bigotry. Kamel views Helen's metaphor of the "seas of humankind" as "reminiscent of Anna's sailing song in *Yonnondio*, remind[ing] us as well how landlocked are the Annas, Emilys and Parrys existing in an exploitative system offering them little bread and no roses" (Kamel 1988, 102).

Helen's decision to withhold an explanation is interesting here. Resisting her earlier futile attempt to explain to Jeannie the reasons why she should not condescend to Whitey ("Hey Sailor, What Ship?"), in "O Yes" Helen thinks of various explanations—familial, historical, emotional, religious (60–61)—and then rejects them all, choosing instead, like Alva, to "rock" and to "hold" her daughter. Helen again demonstrates her merged identity with Carol as she echoes her daughter's words: *"Why is it like it is? . . . And why do I have to care?"* Yet as Olsen points out, Helen knows more than Carol: she understands that she lacks the ties that bind Alva to her world, and she "hungers" for a similar sense of community (Werlock interview, 1990) (61–62). In this final image of Helen, Selma Burkom and Margaret Williams see a link among "I Stand Here Ironing," "Hey Sailor, What Ship?" and "O Yes": "all three stories reiterate Olsen's awareness that the ideal human community is never achieved, but neither is the dream destroyed" (Burkom and Williams, 75). Like Emily's mother in "I Stand Here Ironing," Helen knows that she can embrace but not really protect her daughter from the realities of the world; and "she mourn[s] the illusion of the embrace" (62). According to McElhiney, Helen may not always have "done as much as she intended, but she hopes, like the [ironing mother], that her daughter will find a place of strength and will be able to do more for others than she has done" (McElhiney, 80). Nonetheless, she and her husband, Lennie, have instilled in their children enough hope and idealism so that they may make a difference in their community. Carol and Parry may yet be friends, Helen tells her daughter, "as Alva and I" are friends. The title "O Yes" begins as an affirmation in the black church, retreats paradoxically to a weary "Oh yes" which acknowledges the reality of unfairness, and at the end signifies a vision of a brighter future where people will question injustice and act affirmatively because they do indeed feel the need to care about others.

Chapter Seven
"Tell Me a Riddle"

"Tell Me a Riddle," subtitled "These Things Shall Be," is the fourth and final story of the collection, and it addresses some of the riddles and paradoxes posed in the earlier ones. It has been called "one of the most moving of all American short stories" (Turan, 56), "the most artistic of her works" (Yalom, 62), and it has been praised for its economy: "what a world is here compressed!" (Fisher, 474). Olsen herself says that "In 'Tell Me a Riddle,' it's all there. . . . People read it for the 20th time and they weep" (quoted in Mills, 3).

Olsen says that she began "Tell Me a Riddle" to "celebrate a generation of revolutionaries" (quoted in Lyons, 91), and indeed the story is dedicated to both her mother and her father and to "Seevya and Genya," two "infinite, dauntless, incorruptible" women (116). According to Rosenfelt, the real-life models for Eva were Olsen's mother and Genya Gorelick, a socialist revolutionary and gifted public orator. Further, Rosenfelt states that Eva is a "composite" of several women: both Anna of *Yonnondio* and Eva are "extensions and demystifications, . . . renderings of the essentially heroic lives which circumstances did not allow to blossom into public deeds, art, and fame" (Rosenfelt 1981, 400). As with all of Olsen's work, motherhood is again thematically central to the story (Johnson, 35).

The chief characters are David and Eva, Russian immigrant grandparents of Jeannie, Carol, and Allie, and parents of seven children—Clara, Hannah, Lennie, Vivi, Max, Paul, and Davy, who had been killed in World War II. At the urging of her family who knows that she is dying, Eva—the only one ignorant of the cancer that riddles her body—reluctantly embarks with David on a physical journey that brings into her conscious memory the past events that will contribute to her understanding of her own life.

The themes of home, solitude, and death predominate here. Orr points out that although David and Eva's story occurs last in the collection, the two are "actually first"—as the parents and grandparents of a host of characters in *Tell Me a Riddle*. Like the ironing mother, Eva is unnamed throughout her story. Only a few pages before the end do we learn her name, which, of course, suggests the first woman, the mother of us all (Orr, 103). Mary K. DeShazer sees tremendous power and suggestiveness in the name, claiming that Eva is not only Eve but also Everywoman, and the Sphinx: she believes that for Olsen "it is woman, Sphinxlike, who understands the oracular paradox."[1]

Perhaps because of the importance of the past to the major characters, this story, unlike the others, is written in the past rather than the present tense. Although written chronologically and divided into four sections, much of the narrative is in pieces and fragments because the dying woman is fighting with her memories and their relation to the present. Johnson notes that, in true Olsen style, a "consistent rhythmic shift of focus" impels the narrative movement between inseparable opposites: silence and song, solitude and community, bitterness and faith (Johnson, 33). In fact, according to DeShazer, the story can be understood in terms of paired opposites: present and past, noise and silence, motion and stillness, others and self, life and death (DeShazer, 21). Here Olsen extensively uses the technique of indentation that she uses only sparingly in "O Yes" and not at all in "I Stand Here Ironing" or "Hey Sailor, What Ship?"[2] The technique facilitates and highlights specific flashbacks, thoughts, and memories. In DeShazer's words, it produces "a visual echo" (DeShazer, 25) and illuminates the reasons for Eva's suffering. Primary to Olsen's technique here is, as always, the use of repetition and refrain to portray the mental journeying of the characters.

Although Olsen uses song extensively in "Hey Sailor, What Ship?" and "O Yes," in no other work does music assume such central, metaphoric significance as it does in "Tell Me a Riddle," partially because music so clearly evokes the human potential for both harmony and discord. Eva's whole journey may be viewed as a voyage toward the music and song long buried within her. As Johnson observes, "No other dialogue with the other characters seems possible until the grandmother can hear the 'song' of the child within her" (Johnson, 33). Both Lyons and McCormack believe that song represents hope, possibility, human potentiality; in McCormack's words, song is Eva's own "triumphant metaphor" (Lyons, 101; McCormack, 68).

The first section opens near the end of Eva's life but at the beginning of a new phase of her 47-year marriage to David. Now that all their children have left, they no longer have to tend to others' needs and can reopen old quarrels and disagreements. Numerous critics, Sara McAlpin, for example, comment on the fairness with which Olsen

presents these two old people, assigning blame to neither David nor
Eva. Despite their inability to communicate clearly and to compro-
mise, "the reasons for their stubborn, sometimes helpless, inability,
are revealed not only with sympathy, but with remarkable understanding."[3] Their argument as the story opens regards where and how they
will live out their remaining years. David wishes to go to the Haven,
a retirement community where he would be "*care*free" and utterly without responsibility (64). David's idea of a safe harbor, a paradise filled
with people, is drastically different from his wife's (Rosenfelt 1980,
19). Eva believes she has earned the right to live exactly as she wishes.
Her adamant refusal to sell the house—which David thinks is too
big—is a key to her development. Indeed, her frequent voicing of her
attachment to her home becomes a refrain, one that grows in meaning
as she journeys away from it: "She would not exchange her solitude for
anything. *Never again to be forced to move to the rhythms of others*" (68).
Closely allied to the house motif is her reason for wanting to keep it:
soon enough, she reminds David, they can move to a closet, that is, a
"coffin"—but she is not yet ready. The coffin motif also echoes
throughout the narrative.

Exile and solitude are other related images. Eva believes that her
hard life in both Russia and the United States, for many years marked
by extreme poverty and a large family, has earned her the solitude in
which "she had won to a reconciled peace" (68, 69). Variations of this
refrain occur frequently during the first half of the story. We learn
through David that in Eva's youth, during the Russian Revolution of
1905, she had been sentenced to one year of solitary exile in Siberia
and confined to a room that doubtless calls forth her dislike of "closets"
and "coffins."

Eva's difficult life with David is alternately presented as familiar and
comical, poignant and painful. As the story opens they are arguing
with each other: he yells at her over the noise of the vacuum, and she
turns down her hearing aid so that she will not have to listen. She calls
him "Mr. Importantbusy," and he calls her numerous names, among
them "Mrs. Enlightened," "Mrs. Cultured," and "Mrs. Unpleasant."
When he suspects that she is ill, he seizes the opportunity to extol the
virtues of the Haven: "'At the Haven,' he could not resist pointing
out, 'a doctor is *not* bills. He lives beside you. You start to sneeze, he
is there before you open up a Kleenex. You can be sick there for free,
all you want.' . . . 'Diarrhea of the mouth, is there a doctor to make

you dumb?'" (71). Buried within the comedy of their bickering is the more serious intimation that David refuses to acknowledge the serious nature of her sickness. As she grows increasingly weak during this section, even her "tongue lashing" of David ceases. Eva listens to David, her son Paul, his skeptical wife Nancy, and the doctor to whom they send her. None of them sees her illness, but she thinks, "I am not really sick, the doctor said it, then why do I feel so sick?" (74).

Frequently the comic overtones of their dialogue are interrupted by Eva's painful memories of 18-hour work days and the "humiliations and terrors" of having to beg of the butcher bones "for-the-dog" so that she could feed her husband and children (67). Her bitterness is apparent when, recalling all the years when she went nowhere and saw no one but the children, she tells David, "You trained me well. I do not need others to enjoy" (66). Her refusal to respond to others now is emphasized in an indented scene of compressed examples of David's unsuccessful attempts to make her convivial:

"They won't come back. People you need, the doctor said. Your own cousins I asked; they were willing to come and make peace as if nothing had happened. . . ."
"No more crushers of people, pushers, hypocrites, around me. No more in *my* house. You go to them if you like."
"Kind he is to visit. And you, like ice."
"A babbler. All my life around babblers. Enough!" (73)

David's attempts to socialize Eva are frustratingly ineffective because at this stage in her life Eva has no patience with others, refusing their company and preferring the solitude of her house. She declares that she is accustomed to it; since the birth of her first babies nearly five decades ago she has had no time for socializing.

An especially memorable image is that of Eva as a young mother trying to hold two babies and read Chekhov in the only "spare" time she had—and then David returning from his night out and urging her to put away the book so that they can make love (67). Although we do not learn until later the magnitude of her passion for reading, the impact of the scene is unmistakable. Eva, a woman who in her youth loved books and music, is now half-blind and half-deaf and has to satisfy herself with recalling memorized passages from books. Although no longer able to read, she can still use a magnifying glass to look at pictures, and when David is away, she can turn up the phonograph to listen to the music she so loves with its antithetical "ordered sounds" that blend with "the struggling" (68).

Despite their bickering and genuine resentments of each other, however, Eva's proclaimed wish for solitude is uneven. One night when she feels especially ill and despondent she asks David not to go out but to stay with her. When he refuses, accusing her of eschewing company every time he has offered it, she unexpectedly bursts into tears, screaming, "Go, go. All your life you have gone without me" (74). At his retreating figure she sobs and utters "curses he had not heard in years, old-country curses from their childhood" (74). Again, Olsen demonstrates that the couple has lost the habit of communicating their real feelings to each other. Sommer suggests that because of Eva's "inability or unwillingness to formulate mutually fulfilling relationships" either in the home or in the community, "she actually helped to create the very real isolation" in which she now exists (Sommer, 80). Naomi Jacobs, too, notes that parallel to her mental journeys back to her Russian prison is Eva's creation of her "self-imposed" prison.[4] In this scene David leaves to meet his cronies, and Eva exiles herself to the porch. One night after she has been sleeping alone for a week, David suddenly awakens to find her singing "a Russian love song of fifty years ago" (75). Her restless movement between her desire for solitude and her desire for companionship is thus introduced here, as well as her love of the songs of her youth and her memories of her Russian past and her girlhood village of Olshana. These memories will multiply and intensify in the next sections of the story, and David will experience a more profound awakening than the physical one depicted here.

Meanwhile, Eva's confusion is mirrored in an all-too-common but nonetheless excruciatingly real paradox. She tells her daughter Vivi that she lived all her life "between people" and no longer wants to live with them, as David urges her to do at the Haven. "Different things we need," she explains, shattering Vivi's image of her mother as one who lived all her life "*for* people" (76). Eva then suffers "doubly" because, by telling the truth, she hurts her children whom she genuinely loves (76). Here, again, Olsen points to the mothers' dilemma, which is a microcosm of the larger human riddle of the conflicting demands of self and others. The section ends abruptly as the nature of Eva's illness is discovered and disseminated to everyone but her: the "cancer [is] everywhere. . . . at best she has a year" (77).

The second section opens after the surgery as Eva, believing that she has recovered, begins to feel "happy" again: her children have visited her, she turns up her hearing aid, and she is surrounded by flowers (although she comments that they remind her of a funeral) (78). Age and youth are conflated in her "gnome's face pressed happily into the flowers" (78). Recuperating from the operation at Hannah and her doctor-husband Phil's house in Connecticut, Eva seems bent on using all her senses, noticing the colors of flowers and smelling the scents of autumn. The ironic mingling of life and death permeates these passages: as the "gladioli" are emphasized against the "autumn air," David notes *"How happy she looks, poor creature,"* and the narrator intrudes, asking, "Why are you so happy, dying woman?" (79). Yet despite her relative happiness, Eva yearns for the solitude and the silence she can find at home; hence her new refrain: like her granddaughter Carol in "O Yes" who wishes to escape unpleasant revelations, Eva continually pleads, "Let us go home."

In fact, now that Eva no longer isolates herself behind the protective wall of her failed vision and hearing, her sharpened senses aid her in beginning a journey through memory into her past. Still at Hannah's, Eva reacts nervously and angrily to any mention of religion. In another indented passage, she is furious to learn that the rabbi visited her after the surgery because she was on the "Jewish list" at the hospital. Eva orders Hannah to alter the list: "Tell them to write: Race, human; Religion, none" (80). She disapproves of Hannah's lighting the candles of benediction as part of her wish to give her children a sense of "heritage" and "tradition" (81). Eva is appalled that her daughter honors a religion, she tells David, that dictates candles be bought when bread is needed, "[a] religion that stifled and said: in Paradise, woman, you will be the footstool of your husband, and in life—poor chosen Jew—ground under, despised, trembling in cellars. And cremated. And cremated." (81). Pointing out Eva's similarity to Helen in "O Yes," Lyons comments that the Jewish faith and that of the "Negro church" prove "equally impossible solutions" for these women (Lyons, 94). Eva's bitterness at the oppressive, meaningless restrictions of organized religion appears in her humanist convictions: Parents should teach their children that ghettos must be outlawed, "learned books" must be read (81).

But in an echo of the ironing mother, Eva realizes that despite her philosophic idealism, she had in fact been too busy to teach these lessons to her children, particularly her daughters Hannah, Vivi, and Clara (81, 88, 107). Her anguish is the greater because obviously someone had taken the time to teach her to read, to teach her the humanist values and rhetorical skills that made her, in David's words, "an orator of the 1905 revolution" (81). Eva's confusion is magnified in her repetition of the phrases "to teach," a duty she clearly espouses, and of "not to go back, not to go back"—to the dark days of ignorance, but also to the remembered past. The latter meaning of the phrase temporarily prevails, and Eva retreats into her vow "not to travel" (82), suggesting her denial of the need to embark on either physical or mental journeys.

Her paradoxical wish to "go home" but "not to go back" remains in limbo as she and David begin their westward journey away from home but toward their children and grandchildren, toward the past, toward Eva's death. It begins as a physical journey. After visiting their nearby children in the East (Max and Sammy probably live in New York or New Jersey; Hannah and Phil live in Connecticut), David and Eva plan a western itinerary to see Vivi in Ohio, Clara somewhere between Ohio and California, and Lennie in San Francisco. Eva goes only at David's urging, unaware that he needs to escape not only the house but the reality of her imminent death. Their children also wish to spend as much time as possible with her.

During the plane trip to Ohio, the small round airplane window evokes Eva's first confused, disoriented flashback, with its bewildering relation to the present. The memories then form in disjointed circular images as she rides her "steerage ship of memory that shook across a great, circular sea" (82–83). These references recall Anna's "sailing ships," Whitey's voyages, and Helen's metaphor for Carol's embarkation on the "seas of life." Eva thinks of her escape from Russia in the steerage ship through whose portholes she could see the ocean, circular apertures that remind her of the sun, the moon, the round thatched roofs of her girlhood village Olshana—and the "smaller window" of her "solitary year of exile when only her eyes could travel, and no voice spoke" (83). The silence of plane travel "stilled of clamor" (84) echoes the utter silence of her enforced isolation and the protective solitude to which she desperately clings.

As her mind journeys on her "ship of memory," across the sea, the water imagery expands to include her feelings for her children whom she had loved dearly:

The love—the passion of tending—had risen with the need like a torrent; and like a torrent drowned and immolated all else. . . . On that torrent she had borne them to their own lives, and the riverbed was desert long years now. . . . Surely that was not all, surely there was more. Still the springs, the springs were in her seeking. Somewhere an older power that beat for life. Somewhere coherence, transport, meaning. If they would but leave her in the air now stilled of clamor, in the reconciled solitude, to journey on. (83–84)

Inherent in these images is a mother's silent plea that her life have meaning outside family concerns. Eva is still an individual "seeking" and "beating" with a passion to live, and she concludes she must journey on alone, without her children and their babies. Vivi's baby evokes such conflicting memories that Eva actually sweats and trembles as it is placed in her lap. Again reminiscent of her granddaughter Carol who "drowned" and swooned at Parry's baptism, Eva helplessly reimmerses herself in the "long drunkenness; the drowning into needing and being needed" (84). The memory is so vivid, she will not hold the baby for the rest of the visit (85). Eva had loved her babies, had nearly suffocated in the "torrent" of "the love—the passion of tending" and, like her daughter-in-law Helen and the ironing mother, she still suffers over the lives of the adult children that she "could no longer hold nor help" (83). For the remainder of their time with Vivi Eva volunteers to cook and clean, but she will not feed or tend to anyone's needs.

Numerous critics have commented on Eva's response to motherhood. Jacqueline Mintz, for instance, claims that Eva's experience in this story represents "the death of the ideal of Mother Love" and "the myth of the all-giving and all-loving mother."[5] Likewise McAlpin, speaking of Eva in particular and of Olsen's mothers in general, asserts, "even though they are tirelessly responsive and responsible, constantly interruptible and available to their children, they experience little satisfaction and no triumph at the end of long years" of self-sacrifice (McAlpin, 50). Johnson perceives that Eva has been unable to respond to the "self-nurturing instinct" in herself although she has been able to nurture her children (Johnson, 37). Yet Kamel points out that Eva's husband and children provide a "source of bonding as well as bondage" (Kamel 1988, 104), underscoring the paradox that within the drowning image she is also aware that the "springs were in her seeking. Somewhere an older power that beat for life" (84).

Eva refuses to tell riddles to her grandchildren, despite their eager requests. Speculating on this scene, DeShazer suggests that "traditionally woman has been unable to riddle, for she has lacked the power to name her own experience," and, further, she knows that "the riddle remains insoluble" (DeShazer, 21). Although Eva maintains that she knows "no riddles," she is in fact increasingly preoccupied with her own. In an italicized scene she recoils from the loving but demanding children: the "crowded noisy house" becomes like a great ear listening for her, insisting, *"let me in, let me in. . . . How was it that soft reaching tendrils also became blows that knocked?"* (86). The mixed metaphor is another forceful indication of the contradictions that mystify Eva. As she repeatedly asks to "go home" where she can enjoy "reconciled solitude" (86), the children and the noisy house illuminate the riddle of her dilemma: How does one balance one's individual needs with the responsibility of caring for others?

Not only the grandchildren but Vivi, too, clamor for Eva's attention. Because Vivi wants to reclaim a happy childhood when her mother tended lovingly to all her needs, Vivi's recollections depict her mother sewing, washing, nursing, reading to the children—and they are true for her. Vivi recalls memories that Eva in her unhappiness has repressed—memories of her mother dancing to Sammy's harmonica with Davy in her arms (88) or her mother calling to her children to see the sunset (89). The dancing mother who thrilled to beauty is very different from the one Eva keeps calling to mind. Vivi in the "maze of the long, the lovely drunkenness" (87) of young motherhood is linked to her mother who nervously recalls "the turning maze; the long drunkenness; the drowning into needing and being needed" (84). Imagistically the bewildering maze of motherhood connects Eva with Mazie, too.[6] Yet Vivi's bright perhaps romanticized memories cannot define her mother apart from her nurturing role, and thus they merely add to the tumult in Eva's brain and to our sense of the "mother secret from you." Eva's thoughts are at odds with Vivi's tranquil, nostalgic ones when, as with Hannah, she feels anguish at not having given her children "what I intended and did not" (88).

The voices of Vivi and the grandchildren coalesce in the "knocking and knocking" of the house, an insistent, almost ominous refrain. Eva's granddaughter Ann has made her some paper dolls with yarn hair and "great ringed questioning eyes" (86, 89). But Eva avoids these dolls and the questions their little girl eyes are asking. She hides in the girls' closet—small, like a coffin—filled with feminine clothing. Here she hunches next to the girls' dresses, sometimes braiding and unbraiding the sashes, echoing Carol's efforts to twine and untwine the sounds of black song, or her own habit of listening to the phonograph, marveling at the mingling of the "ordered" and the "struggling" sounds.

The image of women in closets—not uncommon in women's literature—combines with the feminine images, the noise of the house, and the screaming of the children to evoke Eva's prison days and the first reference to her girlhood friend Lisa. Eva recalls her "gentle and tender" friend "screaming and screaming" at the prison mate who had betrayed them, "biting at the betrayer's jugular" (90). The significance of Lisa in Eva's life will be clarified only on Eva's deathbed. The significance of this particular scene lies in its images of girls' and women's lives—the dolls with their questioning eyes, the dresses, the girls' closet, the braiding of the dress sashes, and the children's screaming, which echoes Lisa's. Eva must come to terms with the implications of all of them.

Still in the closet, Eva reluctantly confronts the confluence of the old and the new, the past and the present: "Today she had jacks and children under jet trails to forget" (89). Although she tries hard not to remember, she sees herself as a child in Olshana playing jacks with stones; meanwhile her grandchildren play the game as planes roar by above their heads. Her memories, like the children themselves, are insistent. Mingled in her mind are images of the stones: the myth of Sisyphus and his endless, repetitive motion as he pushes his giant stone and the story of David, who slew the giant with a stone. McElhiney suggests that the allusion to the Sisyphus myth underscores the "difficult eternal task" of coping with and understanding life (McElhiney, 83). Jacobs observes that the references to David suggest not only the biblical David who fought Goliath, but also Eva's husband David who helped kill both "the giant of monarchy" and also "Eva herself" (Jacobs 1986, 404). Moreover, the reference to David is one of several references to her son Davy, a pilot who was shot down and killed in World War II. These images of Eva's cultural and personal past nearly overcome her before she is discovered in the closet by one of her grandchildren.

Eva is learning that she can escape neither the physical nor the emotional links between the past and the present. They constantly intermingle not only in her grandchildren and their references to school bomb shelters of the 1950s (87) but also in Eva's 50-year marriage to David and his allusions to the Roosevelts and Jack Dempseys of the 1930s and 1940s. At the end of the section this inescapable relationship between past and present is suggested in the round images of the eyes of her grandchildren Dody, Ann, Morty, Richard, and the unnamed baby: Richard's eyes look like Eva's, Ann's like Tim's, Morty's like the "great-grandmother he will never know," and Dody's like David's—David her "springtide love" (92). The eyes visually echo her memories of the round huts of Olshana, the prison window, the reading circles she had no time to join, the plane windows. The circles are closing in on her as she and David embark on the next segment of their westward journey.

Section 3 takes place in southern California, on the beach, where dwell the "cast-off old." Temporarily, Eva's frequent refrain about her "reconciled" peace and solitude disappears, but the imagery of coffins and water reappears: The sun is "like a tide" that sucks the old out of their boarding houses and then "sweeps them into decaying enclosures once again" (92). Eva finds herself irresistibly drawn to the sea: she runs to it, walks in it, and she scrutinizes the sand with her magnifying glass. Like stones and rocks it is ancient, "the shore that nurtured life as it first crawled toward consciousness millions of years ago" (94). Both Jacobs and Orr see the sand as the connector of all the natural imagery of the story, for it is both the source of life and the dust to which Eva will return (Orr, 110; Jacobs 1986, 404). In Jacobs's words, on the beach "earth, water and air come together in their simplest forms" (Jacobs 1986, 404). As Eva herself will come to realize, everything is both "fragmented and interpenetrating" (Jacobs 1986, 404). But at this point she has not yet, in the words of the ironing mother, "totalled it all." The paradox is everywhere. The water imagery recalls not only the "torrents" of her childbearing years but also her standing in the rain to sing a Russian love song from her childhood (Orr, 111). Life and death, past and present insistently intermingle in the appearance of their granddaughter Jeannie, who is both a link with the past and a bright sign of the future.

Now a visiting nurse, Jeannie has arranged their rooms by the sea. From this temporary home David and Eva take another trip to the past, this time to visit Max and Rose, relatives from the Russia of 50 or 60 years ago. Again Olsen excels at presenting paradox as these aging Russian Jews, revolutionaries in their youth, face each other across the American "Duncan Phyfe table" speaking words ascribed to no one in particular: "*hunger; secret meetings; human rights; spies; betrayals; prison; escape*" (95). Ironically, the significance of the past is both heightened and undercut by the incongruous interruption as the grandchildren of Max and Rose ask for Coke during a television commercial (95).

David and Eva also meet Mrs. Mays, Eva's friend from past days when the children were small. She takes them to her "slab of room" where she has shrunken her life into one room which, says Eva, is "like a coffin" (98), an image used repeatedly to describe the home of this solitary widowed mother of eight. Despite her coffinlike existence, however, Mrs. Mays has not become one of the embittered, one of the lonely, one of the "cast-off old."

To the contrary, she plays a key role in bringing Eva back into life before she dies, insisting that Eva and David attend the weekly community sing. Eva, who has stopped using the magnifying glass to enhance her vision, protests. Once again she turns off her hearing aid to block out the sound, as she would like to block out the sight of the humanity around her and before her. But the music engulfs her as a torrent, and her memories well up in a great chorus of song. The music of a Russian love song burbled through her pain and self-imposed exile on the porch in section 1. Now music recalls the myriad faces and aspects of Eva's past: they become "*chorded into* children-chants, mother-croons, singing of the chained love serenades, Beethoven storms, mad Lucia's scream drunken joy-songs, keens for the dead, work-singing" (96–97). Here Olsen uses synesthesia, itself a metaphor for life's riddle. As the faces evolve into sound, and sound into faces, Eva breaks through, finally, to the youthful image of herself: "*from floor to balcony to dome a bare-footed sore-covered little girl threaded the sound-thronged tumult, danced her ecstasy of grimace to flutes that scratched at a cross-roads village wedding*" (97). And as Eva sees her girlhood, associated with pain and poverty but also with the ecstasy of music, community, and love, she finally realizes what the rest of her family has known all along: she is dying. This image will become the final one toward which she has been struggling. Acknowledging her own illness in Mrs. Mays's coffinlike room, Eva approaches an acceptance of the intertwining of life and death.

The role of music and song in Eva's transformation reaches a crescendo of sorts in this section. The description of the effect of the community sing has been often and deservedly praised. And yet no reader should be surprised at either the image or the message, for both have been central to Olsen's work since she wrote *Yonnondio* in 1932. In fact, McCormack points out the similarities of this scene in "Tell Me a Riddle" to the following passage in *Yonnondio*: "They sang and sang, and a longing, a want undefined, for something lost, for something never known, troubled them all. The separate voices chorded into one great full one, their faces into beauty" (*Yonnondio,* 53). As McCormack notes, the phrase "chorded into" recurs in the community sing that Eva attends, and the image of faces and voices is remarkably similar (McCormack, 59). Like images occur in Whitey's valedictory and in Alva's "song," as well as in the singing of the black spirituals that Carol, like Eva, tries in vain to ignore.

The vision of a sea of humanity singing and harmonizing together could have been the final paragraph of a different story. By now, because of Tillie Olsen's superb employment of language and technique, especially the metaphor of song, readers are attuned to the paradoxes to which Eva must reconcile herself before her death. But Olsen's technique here is suspenseful as well as emotionally moving: a number of times throughout the story Eva draws close to realization—as, for example, when she leaves the hospital and turns up her hearing aid or sniffs the scent of flowers—but each time she retreats. Suspense increases in anticipation of the moment we are sure is imminent, but more revelations and more fragments of song are required to effect Eva's epiphany.

Section 4 opens with the familiar refrain, "Let us go home" (99), but Eva, now that she knows she is dying, understands why David cannot bear the idea of going home. She therefore turns more and more to Jeannie, who instantly understands Eva's need: Home is where one is surrounded by one's own possessions. Notably, none of Eva's children can intuit her needs as Jeannie can. She gives Eva a gift, something to own even in the strange unhomelike rooms of Los Angeles: a cookie in the shape of Rosita, a little Mexican girl who has recently died. In death Rosita is the cause of music and dancing rather than pain; her relatives sing the songs and dance the dances she loved. Her image brings joy to Eva. Similar to the girl paper dolls her other granddaughter Ann gives her—the ones with "great ringed questioning eyes"—the Rosita cookie is a work of art, "shaped like a little girl" with "darling eyelashes"—"something of my own," says Eva (100, 101). This time, though, rather than fleeing the girl image, Eva claims it.

The youth, music, and dancing already implicit in the images of the young dead Rosita and the young dancing Eva—as well as the image of the young mother Eva, as Vivi has reminded her—are reinforced in the young Samoan Marine Jeannie introduces to her grandmother. He performs the songs and dances of his native country, bringing happiness to Eva who continues to try to imitate his sounds and motions long after he has gone. The international and interracial humanity evoked in "Hey Sailor, What Ship?" and "O Yes" recurs here in the images of young people from Russia, Mexico, Samoa, and the United States. Music, youth, and art are associated with Jeannie, too, who brings her grandmother a radio so she can listen to music. Now Eva tries to hear all the music. Rather than turning off her hearing aid, she listens with every remaining nerve; Jeannie actually sketches her grandmother lying by the radio, her body shaped like a huge ear.

Rosita, Jeannie, and Lisa, three young girls who fearlessly associate with both life and death, are central to Eva's transformation. Jeannie not only triggers Eva's memories of her own and Lisa's girlhood, but also personifies for Eva the link among the generations of women. Eva wants Jeannie to know that her great-great-grandmother and great-grandmother "had already buried children" (104) by the time they were her age, but despite their scrawny, poverty-starved bodies, they too danced. A brilliant image of the human snubbing of age and adversity is depicted in Eva's passionate "pulsing red flower" and "yellow skull face" (103). Eva knows the image is incongruous when she looks in the mirror, but she leaves the flower in her hair and lets it "burn" (103).

Light, as Jacobs observes, plays an increasing part in the story (Jacobs 1986, 405). The brightness of the candles lit for Rosita has its counterpart in the radiance and lightness of Jeannie (101, 106). As she sums up her life, Eva increasingly associates Jeannie with the young Lisa. Eva whispers to Lennie and Helen when they visit, "Like Lisa, she is, your Jeannie" (103). Now we learn the full significance of Lisa, Eva's Tolstoyan friend. Lisa, a young Russian noblewoman, taught 16-year-old Eva, the peasant, to read. Despite the beatings her father inflicted on her, Eva braved whirling snowstorms and howling "terrible" dogs to meet Lisa in secret for their reading lessons. To Lisa, associated with Thuban, the Egyptian polestar, "life was holy, knowledge was holy" (103). The light of the revolutionary Lisa's "holiness" contrasts with Hannah's traditional burning of the candles of the patriarchal Jewish benediction that Eva has resisted. To Lisa's bright image Eva would travel through the darkness of Russian winters and the darkness of her own illiteracy. Even the young Lisa, however, paradoxically blends her life-affirming image with a life-denying one: this young woman to whom life was sacred killed another, one who had betrayed them all in the prison, and "they hung her" (103).

Critics view Lisa as either betrayer or avenger. Edward L. Niehus and Teresa Jackson see Lisa's "betrayal" as devastating to Eva: "the shock of disillusionment for the youthful Eva must have seemed comparable to the discovery that something as fixed and eternal as the pole star could be subject to change."[7] Kamel, on the other hand, seems to applaud Lisa's "revenge on those that would stultify ideas of human liberation" (Kamel 1985, 69). Certainly Lisa represents human nature in its glory and its horror, its nobility and its savagery: "There is so much blood in a human being," Eva says, but, sounding like Helen or Alva, she adds, "All that happens, one must try to understand" (104). The blood-red images seem to return her to the passion of her youth. No longer silent now, as she lies dying Eva speaks "incessantly" (103).

Lisa's great friendship and contribution to Eva's education is nowhere more apparent than in Eva's love of books. Despite her failed vision and hearing, Eva's memory proves true, and she quotes passages from some of her favorite authors such as the revolutionary Victor Hugo. The fragments issuing from her lips recall those reeling through Whitey's brain in "Hey Sailor, What Ship?," including the phrases *"The bell . . . summon . . . what enables"* and *"No man one . . . except through others"* (108, 109), which echo Donne's "Meditation 17." To David, astonished that she remembers so much, it seems "that for seventy years she had hidden a tape recorder, infinitely microscopic, within her, that it had coiled infinite mile on mile, trapping every song, every melody, every word read, heard, and spoken" (109).

But Eva's intellectual passion also brings pain to David as he learns that the dying Eva has little to say of him and the children. As David protests, "sturdily," then "bitterly," that their life contained "joy" as well as pain, she seemingly ignores him and bursts into a song calling up her own passionate girlhood images. After singing parts of the uplifting socialist hymn "These Things Shall Be" (Jacobs 1986, 410), Eva speaks of the family only in terms of their desperate poverty and her frustration at being unable to give the children all they wish: "One pound soup meat . . . Bread, day-old. . . . The thread, hah, the thread breaks. Cheap thread" (114). She recalls telling Hannah she needs help with the household and children and telling Clara that she cannot give her what she does not have (114).

This aspect of a mother's life is strikingly illustrated by the visit from Clara, the eldest, the least frequently mentioned of all the children. We know where all of them live except Clara, who lives somewhere west of Ohio. Could she be the mother of Emily in "I Stand Here Ironing"? Although numerous critics have noticed the similarity between Clara and the ironing mother, no one has suggested that they may be one and the same.[8]

Notably, at the end of "Tell Me a Riddle," although all the children but Vivi (busy with her children) come to visit their mother, Olsen portrays the thoughts of only two of Eva's children in any detail: Clara and Lennie. But Olsen's handwritten manuscript depicting this scene specifically features Hannah, not Clara, in the bedside scene with her mother.[9] Why did Olsen change Hannah to Clara? Could she have wanted a character more like herself to play this scene? Did she intend to link "I Stand Here Ironing," the only story unlinked by family, with the other three? Certainly, "I Stand Here Ironing" has elements of autobiography, likely drawing on Olsen's early experiences as a single mother, and on her relationship with her eldest daughter Karla (a Russian word meaning "strong"). The similar names are suggestive; Clara could be an anagram of Karla. And if Tillie Olsen is to some extent fictionalizing herself and Karla in the ironing mother and Emily, she may also be fictionalizing Karla, herself, and her own mother, to whom "Tell Me a Riddle" is dedicated. Eva bears notable similarities to Ida Beber Lerner, whom Olsen describes in "Dream Vision": "my mother—so much of whose waking life had been a nightmare, that common everyday nightmare of hardship, limitation, longing, of baffling struggle to raise six children in a world hostile to human unfolding—my mother, dying of cancer, had beautiful dream visions—in color" (in *Mother to Daughter*, 261). If in fact the dying Eva is mother to the ironing mother and grandmother to Emily, paralleling Ida, Tillie, and Karla Olsen, then Olsen has subtly tied together all the characters in the four stories of *Tell Me a Riddle*. Moreover, if Clara is in fact the ironing mother, her relationship with her mother Eva helps explain why Clara also treats her eldest daughter coldly. Both the ironing mother and Eva are warmer with their younger children than with their eldest daughters, who were born during times of extreme economic hardship.

Clara's visit to her dying mother appears in the last of the indented scenes that have charted Eva's past. Clara "clenche[s]," and her words, a lament of the eldest daughter, the bereft daughter seeking her missing mother, echo Emily's: "*Pay me back, Mother, pay me back for all you took from me. Those others you crowded into your heart. The hands I needed to be for you, the heaviness, the responsibility*" (107). She softens, however, as hearing Eva's singing, she is reminded of "*that singing from childhood*," and she wonders, "*Where did we lose each other, first mother, singing mother?"* (107). Her anger evaporates as she looks down at her dying mother and realizes, *"I do not know you, Mother. Mother, I never knew you"* (107). Typical of all Olsen mother-daughter relationships, the mother is "secret from" the daughter. Clara cannot understand her own mother any more than the ironing mother understands Emily.

Lennie, the other child whose visit is described, also echoes the thoughts of the ironing mother—possibly his sister—as he suffers "for that in her which never lived [and] for that which in him might never come to live" (107). He says goodbye to the mother who "taught [him] to mother [himself]" (108). The double entendre is probably intentional: Olsen may mean that Lennie can take care of himself; she may also mean that he has learned how to care for others, as when he carries Allie up the stairs in "Hey Sailor, What Ship?" or listens carefully to Helen and Jeannie in "O Yes."

Undoubtedly, both Lennie and Helen have the ability to mother, and their lessons reach fruition in their eldest daughter. Jeannie, having passed through the painful often thoughtless stages of girlhood and adolescence, has emerged as a young woman who does not question the rightness of her feelings (102). Jeannie resigns her job as visiting nurse because, she realizes, "I let myself feel things," and she knows she cannot be "professional enough" (102). Drawn close to Rosita's Mexican family, the young Samoan Marine, and above all else her "darling Granny" (106, 107), Jeannie devotes all her time to Eva, her face lighted with "the pure overwhelming joy from being with her grandmother" (107). Like Emily, Jeannie undoubtedly has artistic talent and perhaps, when she has time to think over her options, she will attend art school. Now, however, absorbed with her grandmother, Jeannie blends her love for Eva with her love for art.

She sketches two pictures of Eva—one when Eva is curled in the shape of an ear, silently listening to voices, to music, to the ideals of her youth; and the other as she and David reach out for each other and hold hands. This silent form of communication is more effective than their attempts to communicate with words, wherein they invariably fail to understand each other. The drawings depict Eva as individual and Eva as part of a family relationship. Jeannie, who seems to understand Eva in both capacities, is instrumental in David's awakening to the nonmaternal, nonwifely aspects of Eva's life. "She needs you," Jeannie tells David. "Isn't that what they call love?" David is moved by Jeannie's own love for Eva.

The first sign that he has reawakened to Eva not as mother, not as grandmother, occurs after he hears her cracked voice singing, *"These things shall be,"* a hymn that predicts the coming of *"a loftier race"* in whose souls will burn the *"flame of freedom"* and in whose eyes will be reflected the *"light of knowledge"* (110–11). The word "race" here appears to connote not ethnicity but a future generation: after the horrors of the revolution of 1905, and World Wars I and II, David and Eva's grandchildren stand "a head taller than their grandparents . . . beautiful skins, straight backs, clear straightforward eyes" (112). "Yes, you in Olshana," says David to the village he had left 60 years ago, "they would look nobility to you" (112). These magnificent grandchildren are the hope of the future.

As Eva in her broken voice affirms that *"every life shall be a song,"* he recalls the dark treacherous disease-ridden days of their youth and realizes that while he has retreated, she still believes in their old ideals: "Eva!" he whispers and it is here, three pages before the end, that he first uses her name (113). DeShazer believes that by naming neither David nor Eva until the end, "Olsen attaches to the act of naming a sense of affirmation, an almost metaphysical significance" (DeShazer, 27). As he utters the name of his wife, David, like all Olsen's major characters, begins to ask questions in order to understand. Sommer, calling the questioning and understanding process a "positive, useful and nourishing philosophy," sees it as central to Olsen's work (Sommer, 82). In David's case, the questions help him to recognize how he has turned away from the cause for which they had both fought so passionately in their youth.

When Eva sings another song whose words recall her shorn braids while in prison, the meaning of her "exile" to Vivi's daughters' closet finally becomes clear. Reenacting her time in solitary confinement, she "braids and unbraids" the sashes of the dresses that evoke the long-ago loss of her hair and her individual feminine identity. The words prompt David to delve further into his memory, "past the mother treading at the sewing machine, singing with the children; past the girl in her wrinkled prison dress, hiding her hair with scarred hands," and he finally recognizes her: "Eva!" (114–15). This is the last word he speaks, signalling the end of Eva's life and the end of the story, but also valorizing the woman Eva had been and has tried to be. David enunciates not only the name of his wife, his first love, but of the "first mother, singing mother" to whom Clara alludes and of Eve, mother of us all.

He has seen the girl he loved during their youth, has realized that she had not always wished for solitude, has recalled "a girl's voice of eloquence that spoke their holiest dreams" (110). As Olsen herself says of David's revelation, "Eva gives back to her guy a sense of what was important in his life" (Pearlman interview).

The final images, both literally and figuratively, are articulated not by David but by Jeannie. When David lies down on the bed, holding his wife's hand, Jeannie sketches the two of them clasping each other, her artist's hand rendering the image fixed and timeless. The next day, Jeannie tells him that Eva has confided in her and that his wife knows exactly where she is going: she is returning to Olshana, the place where she had first heard music; she will become again the little barefoot girl—this time without sores or pain—dancing to the fluted music of a village wedding. As Jeannie frames our final image of her grandmother, we realize that Eva's most constant refrain has been neither about solitude nor about coffins, but about "going home." We realize that the word "home" refers not only to the house Eva has so obstinately refused to sell but to the thatched hut in Olshana, the source of her girlhood happiness. Eva's concept of "home" merges with her images of youth, girlhood, dance, and song.

At the end, with Eva's songs, all the riddles and paradoxes are twined and braided into one giant song, which is the overriding metaphor of the book. Although, like the ironing mother, Eva is not a particularly warm or likable character, she embodies Olsen's understanding of life as the commingling of hope with pain. Grandmother and mother, Eva is linked with all of Olsen's women, both in this book and in *Yonnondio*. Nor are we surprised to see that the warm likable women in Olsen's work are the young ones, of whom Jeannie seems to be the archetype. The possibilities for a more fortunate generation seem especially to belong to young women, in this case, Jeannie.

Jeannie's development in the last three stories of *Tell Me a Riddle* is notable. From "Hey Sailor, What Ship?" to "O Yes" to "Tell Me a Riddle," Olsen has presented her in various stages of confusion and understanding, darkness and light. Our view of her at the end of "Hey Sailor" is in the darkness of rain and night; Jeannie is not yet able to comprehend or accept the myriad complexities of the human condition. We see her in the afternoon light in "O Yes," midway on her journey to understanding, sympathetic to the plight of her younger sister Carol and her black friend Parry, angry and frustrated in her newly acquired comprehension of injustice. At the end of "Tell Me a

Riddle" Jeannie appears in the morning sunlight, a confident young woman who voluntarily participates in the paradoxical rituals of love and death. Individualistic but not narcissistic, she emerges as independent, educated, and self-assured, a young woman aligned with youth, art, and life, respectful of the complexities of human life.

As Eva realizes at the end, one must understand, continue to believe, and hope—and Eva has surely left her mark on her granddaughter. Because Jeannie can build on the strength handed down to her by her great-great-grandmother and her grandmother Eva, she has become the most recent link in a chain of strong, resilient, and compassionate women who apparently will fulfill the promise of the earlier Mazie and Emily. That Jeannie has the last word in the final story is itself a fulfillment of Eva's belief that *"these things shall be"*: daughter of Eva and David's son Lennie, Jeannie is indeed a member of a *"loftier race,"* one with the light of love and knowledge in her eyes, the embodiment of David and Eva's dream "come true in ways undreamed" (112).

Chapter Eight

"Requa"

"Requa," originally published in the *Iowa Review,* is, like Olsen's other four stories, a chronicle of both despair and recovery, this time during the depression year of 1932. The central character, 14-year-old Stevie,[1] loses his only tie to security and affection when his mother dies.[2] His uncle, Wes, who scrounges out a barebones living through part-time work in a junkyard in the Klamath Valley of northern California, arrives in San Francisco to take this nephew north, back to the rooming house where Wes lives among the strangers who constitute his family.[3] Stevie is emotionally shaken and understandably disturbed by his mother's death, and these emotions are exacerbated by the well-meaning gruffness of his bachelor uncle, who has had little or no experience in addressing a child's pain in productive ways. In fact, Wes has seen so many families on the brink of collapse, has watched them sell their most treasured possessions ("Even guns and fishin gear, and thats get-by when nobodys workin"[4]) for traveling and food money, that he lives in his own limited cocoon, one that includes very little space for pity or succor. Wes is not a brutal or abusive man; in fact, as Olsen says, "he knows a lot" (Pearlman interview), but all that he knows about the world of men is of little use initially to this pained and troubled boy.

Stevie responds to his mother's death and to Wes's offhand affection by withdrawing into a self-healing sleep state, often rolled up, "curling and curling" (55) in the peacock quilt, "rocking, scratching, snuffling" (65), hand flung over his eyes, like an overgrown fetus, on a used army cot. This is an enervated, exhausted Stevie who shares a "gaunt room" (57) with Wes—a room that is suffused with his private ghosts: "Was that his mother . . . sagged there in the weight of weariness?" (58). And there is a marked change from the boy who "stay[ed] up to take care of his mother, afraid to lie down even if she was quiet, 'cause he might fall asleep and not hear her if she needed him" (54). Now, Olsen writes, he "lay down on a cot with the bundles stocked around him and went into a dream" (55). Every orifice betrays him; he spends days "heaving," "puk[ing]," "swallowing snot," "his nose bubbling blood" as if the body of the once stoical boy, mature and responsible, is itself on sick leave.

What might draw Stevie out of this disconnected state is, of course, a connection to someone or something, but it is that empowering link which Stevie does not have and does not initially want; he "jumps up," literally and figuratively, to "re-close the door" on any intruder (including Wes) into the protected space of his room. Stevie also refuses to go to school—perhaps seeing school as just one more separation from the new and fragile link to Wes—and he lights out from the school bus stop at which Wes unceremoniously dumps him, much as Wes's customers dump their unwanted belongings at his junkyard. Underlying this sense of sadness and dislocation are other images of separation: Stevie, the city boy who did not even have time to "say goodbye to the lamppost that he could hug and swing himself round and round" (54), "who has rocked his nights high on a tree of noise, his traffic city" (56), is thrust into the world of hunters, fishermen, trappers—an indoors boy in an outdoors world. It is clear that the other males perceive him as an incomplete ghost of a boy: "Would you believe it? He's never been fishin never been huntin never held a gun never been in a boat" (57).

His only parent, a woman "twisting from the pain: face contorted, mouth fallen open fixed to the look on her dying dead face," (70) has been replaced by a tired but hearty man with a full appetite for work and women and a loose lip when it comes to describing Stevie: "looney," "skinny little shrimp," "ghostboy" (five times), "miserable kid," "ending up in the dummy or looney house, for sure," "snot," "firebug nut." That uncle is, moreover, offended by Stevie's lassitude and physical ineptness almost as if Stevie's apparent weakness poses a threat to the uncle's masculinity, his strength.

More dichotomies surface when Stevie's mother's meager possessions, brought from San Francisco, betray her as a woman with an unlettered lust for beauty: "kewpie doll green glass vase . . . plush candy box . . . pincushion doll . . . china deer miniature" (60). Those keepsakes reveal both her financial impoverishment and her emotional richness, but Wes says they are junk: "Jesus, what junk" (60). Wes scatters and tosses what is left of his sister's life into various piles, flagrantly and unthinkingly giving away the mother's symbolic possessions of light and time—the lamp to Bo and the clock to Highpockets. This underscores again Stevie's precarious position in a world in which one person's treasure is another person's junk, where people and lives and futures are disposable, disposed of, junked, and where Stevie himself is, in a way, extraneous. Olsen's language mirrors this sense of fragmentation. The words run together: "everywhich," "bad-dream," "bumproad," "doremi," "thinghillocks," as do Stevie's past and present, his bad days and worse nights. And the phrases fall apart: "Being places he had never been. Waiting moving sliding trying" (54). "All he wanted was to lie down" (54). What is happening, in fact, is what Olsen calls "disorder twining with order" (65).

Intertwined with the images of disorder, uprooting, fragmentation, are the scenes where Wes's affection for ordering is displayed. He tries to teach Stevie to "sort outa the bins into these here washboilers: like, pipe fittins: brass here copper there: elbows flanges unions couplings bends tees. Check out the drawers, see just what belongs is in 'em; get acquainted: like this row: wing nuts castellated slotted quarter inch *Pay attention!*" (64). Stevie continues to function only in a half-hearted fashion, like a "ghostboy," a shadow, unable to sort out the flanges or his emotions, neither of which he understands. Instead he swaddles himself in Wes's coverlet or rocks back and forth in a "filthy ragquilt" that he finds in the junkyard, the scrapheap of deserted dreams. Words like "apparition," "spectral shapes," "swathed forms floated," "dark and things that can get me," "stupor . . . lostness . . . torpor," "*the dead things, pulling him into attention, consciousness*" (65), emphasize his shadowy, fragile state. They allude too to the message in all of Olsen's work: sustenence and the means for existence are hard won for the majority of society, who are defeated more by circumstance than by lack of will, and that life can use up the best spiritual and physical and emotional resources of the working population, leaving them, in essence, bereft, ghostlike, exhausted. Stevie, like most of Olsen's characters, does have emotional resources, but, because of the events of his short life, those resources have been exhausted almost past the point of replenishment. Olsen is suggesting, then, that circumstance—orphanhood, poverty, loneliness—not character has turned Stevie into a "ghostboy."

"Waste and depression" and the waste of both people and objects, which Blanche Gelfant says are Olsen's subjects here (Gelfant 1984, 61), reverberate, and this sense of loss and deprivation is responsible for an emotional collapse on the part of the boy: "Easier to just lie there roll into the poncho shrink into the coat cry . . . *Not all there*"

(69), "and the head on his pillow bulging, though still he is having to hold it up somewhere And the round and round slipping sliding jolting moved to inside him, so he has to begin to rock his body; rock the cot gently, down and back" (56). The reader senses that Stevie, like a wasted family, political system, or social structure, must collapse before he can be rebuilt in a better form and that he must see the trees outside as "red, like blood that oozed out of old meat" (54) before he can see the greening leaves. As Gelfant notes, "Olsen can describe such recoveries because she has a strong sense of history as both a personal past which gives one a continuous identity and a social legacy that links generations" (Gelfant 1984, 65). Recovery is also suggested by several allusions to Stevie's developing sexuality, including an unexpected erection when he is pumping gas at the junkyard for a girl who is "so close he can smell her" (67) and another when he realizes, later in the story, that Wes is at a whorehouse: "Gently he began to rock. The hardness had gone down by itself" (70).

As he moves toward recovery, Stevie begs Wes for a "learn job" at the junkyard "by you" and seems to be following some inner directive to connect with someone, something, some work, to link up against the potential devastation of aloneness. He tells his Uncle Wes, "You said: I'll help you, Steve. You said it. [Evans] don't have to pay me. You hurt me, Wes. A learn job. By you. You promised. Not school Never Forever" (63). His repeated refusal to go to school provokes one of the few physical assaults by Wes, despite his often-cited annoyance with the boy: "O my God, you dummy. How'm I goin to explain *this* one to Evans" (66). But the issue of recovery remains central to the story and the transformation of Stevie, the ghostboy, has its genesis in what Gelfant calls "the salvaging effect of work, even the work of salvaging" (Gelfant 1984, 67) and in Wes's insistence that "I got so much to learn you" (64).

That potential for growth and wholeness, crucial to Olsen's vision, is the idea encoded in the scraps and tatters of these lives, but it is also expressed in the mother-daughter relationship in "I Stand Here Ironing," where, as in "Requa," two people are both apart and together and the need on both sides is visible, frangible. The need is contained within the drunken sailor in "Hey Sailor, What Ship?," a story about affection and disaffection. It surfaces through the memories of the dying, anguished mother in "Tell Me a Riddle." What is different in "Requa" is that Olsen's other stories, despite their expressions of alien-

ation, at least contain intact families of some configuration. This time
Olsen pairs a motherless child with a man who is himself pained and
needy and unmothered. Wes and Stevie become a family because Stevie
sees the "face of his mother. *His* face. Family face" (71) in the face of
his drunken uncle, and Wes clearly acknowledges, even welcomes, the
connection: "I'll tell you this, though, [Stevie's] not goin through what
me and Sis did: kicked round one place after another, not havin nobody. Nobody" (56).

In Tillie Olsen's fiction the idea of family usually means "human
family," but here, as elsewhere, the linkages between "despised peoples" are the most valuable and instructive. Ironically, Stevie moves
closer to recovery in the scenes where Wes is drunk, incoherent or
"peddlin hooch . . . just when it's goin to get legal" (69), or when
Stevie is waiting for Wes to return from an unsatisfactory visit to "Annie Marines. She sells it. . . . I've had better imagines" (70). It is in
this scene, when Wes feels "lower than whale shit," that Stevie moves
from the blanket of his own pain to an awareness of Wes's loneliness
and anger. The boardinghouse occupants—Mrs. Edler (the landlady),
Yee (the cook), Highpockets ("who stuck his hand out at supper and
said 'Shake, meet the wife'" [56]), Bo (a roomer), and Evans (of the
junkyard)—are part of Stevie's evolution. It is Mrs. Edler who urges
Wes to "let [Steve] be a while" (57), and it is she who offers Stevie a
trip "upriver with her tomorrow to the deer or jumpdance or some
such Indian thing they're having up at Terwer" (59), and takes him to
church and to visit the cemeteries on Memorial Day where "if you were
a dead soldier, you got a flag" (73). There the ghost images reoccur
but in a changed fashion. These are the buried ghosts, the harmless
apparitions: "dead fly in the hymn book" (73), "the Requiescat in Pace
gate" (73) at the cemetery, the grave of "Leo Jordan, 1859–1911, 'He
is Not Dead but Sleeping'" (74), the baby girl buried beneath a marble
lamb, that allow Stevie to finally bury his own ghosts.

While he is waiting for Mrs. Edler to put flowers on the graves,
Stevie alternately stands "in the tall blowing weeds" (74) with the attendant biblical implications of the motherless Moses about to be rescued by the surrogate mother, or he stays in the car, another safe space.
When he returns to the boardinghouse that night, he is "frisky as a
puppy" (74), not, as Wes expects, "near dead, bad as in the beginning"
(74), and although Stevie again curls up and falls asleep, he is now
"stealthily secretly reclaiming" (74), the last words of the story. Now
it is Wes who escapes into sleep and Stevie, previously afraid of the

dark, who is finally "glad to turn off the light and have the shutting darkness" (71). Stevie is, in effect, letting down "his low little walls," the piles of "boxes and bundles" (57) that had previously surrounded his bed; he is, as Wes has wished, "catch[ing] hold," letting go of despair, continuing, and recovering—as Olsen's characters are wont to do—in this ironically named town of Requa, a Native American word for "broken in body and spirit" (Gelfant 1984, 62).

Chapter Nine
Silences

At first glance *Silences* (1978) seems an odd book. It is a collection of several essays and talks (given between 1962 and 1972) that, in part, restates Olsen's most important and influential views on the position of women as writers, most of which were well known by the time of its publication in 1978. The volume is also her most detailed statement on her relationship to writing, and to the vast silences that have surrounded her life as a "worker-mother-writer." Finally, *Silences* is an explanation—a "lamentation," an "apologia" (Kamel 1985, 55) for the relatively small number of women writers, and it is Olsen's prescription for redressing the balance.

The laudatory reviews of the book are legion. Annie Gottlieb joins the consensus when she says, "Probably she is not the first, but to me Tillie Olsen *feels* like the first, both to extend 'universal' human experience to females and to dignify uniquely female experience as a source of human knowledge."[1] Dillon notes that because several of the essays were written in the 1960s, "before the women's movement was really underway," they seem "a bit dated" (Dillon, 106), but Alix Kates Shulman believes that although much of the information in *Silences* is familiar, nevertheless the book remains "moving and important."[2] Atwood agrees, adding, "We've heard a lot of this before, but it's invigorating to see its first expressions by women coming new to the problems" of lack of confidence, the hardships of mothering, female timidity in the male world (Atwood, 27). Shulman also calls it a "classic of feminist literature" by a "perceptive, learned, and generous artist" whose work has encouraged "an entire generation of women writers" (Shulman, 528, 529), and Dillon adds that "what remains fresh and compelling is Tillie Olsen herself" (Dillon, 106).

Shelley Fishkin and Sally Cuneen, among others, credit Olsen with developing a reading list that is widely used in women's studies courses across the United States.[3] Largely because of Olsen's influence, out-of-print works by women have been reissued and are now readily available—for instance, Rebecca Harding Davis's *Life in the Iron Mills,* Agnes Smedley's *Daughter of Earth,* and Charlotte Perkins Gilman's *The*

Yellow Wallpaper. In spite of these accomplishments, Olsen regularly tells audiences that she is a "survivor": "one who must bear witness for those who foundered" (39, n.). Most readers and writers, however, particularly women, assert that it is Olsen's faith in the "human ability to survive" and the "dignity and wonder" of human life that she communicates so powerfully to each of us (Cuneen, 570). Ellen Cronan Rose, too, speaks of Olsen's "galvanic effect" on students—"mostly women"—whenever she utters her famous words from *Silences:* "We who write are survivors, 'onlys.' One—out of twelve" (Rose, 3).

The book, divided into three major parts, opens with acknowledgments to "my mother and my father" and to "Genya Gorelick, Jack Eggan" and "Jack Olsen" among others, all familiar names to readers of *Tell Me a Riddle*. In an introductory note Olsen explains, "These are not natural silences, that necessary time for renewal, lying fallow, gestation, in the natural cycle of creation. The silences I speak of here are unnatural; the unnatural thwarting of what struggles to come into being, but cannot. In the old, the obvious parallels: when the seed strikes stone; the soil will not sustain; the spring is false; the time is drought or blight or infestation; the frost comes premature" (*Silences*, xi). She attests to the "passion and purpose" with which she wrote the book, as well as to her extreme feelings of both love and hatred—"love for my incomparable medium, literature; hatred for all that, societally rooted, unnecessarily lessens and denies it; slows, impairs, silences writers" (xi). Her purpose, she says, is to "rededicate and encourage" (xi). This introductory passage is framed by quotations from Thomas Hardy and André Gide.

Part 1: The Silenced Writers

Part 1 begins with the essay "Silences" and its eloquent opening line: "Literary history and the present are dark with silences." For Olsen these are "unnatural silences," and she illustrates these darkly blank periods with four examples of "the great in achievement" who have known such silences—Thomas Hardy, Herman Melville, Arthur Rimbaud, and Gerard Manley Hopkins (6–7). Having established the general definition of literary silences, Olsen then defines them as specific sorts of inactivity: "hidden silences," the agonies of which readers never know because they see only the work that "does not come to fruition" (8); "censorship silences," an extreme form of silences imposed by governments and sometimes followed by imprisonment (9); "one-book silences," when writers fail to follow their first publications with others (9); a ceasing of the ability to create real literature, despite frequent publication of books (9–10); and, most serious of all, the "mute inglorious Miltons," those who may have had the talent, but never the conditions necessary to enable them to produce literature (10).

Quoting Joseph Conrad and Henry James, Olsen suggests that the essential requirements of those who wish to write include hard work and unconfined solitude—"the even flow of daily life made easy and noiseless" and "the old, old lesson in the art of meditation" (12). A few may benefit from the fabled poverty of life in the garret; a very few need the inspiration and experience of going out to do paid work. But for the majority, "the actuality testifies: substantial creative work demands time, and with rare exceptions only full-time workers have achieved it" (13).

Olsen then discusses the subject of women writers in particular and addresses the sexist notion that marriage and motherhood are incompatible with writing. She points out that of the women whose literary achievements "endure for us," few ever married—Jane Austen, Emily Brontë, Christina Rosetti, Emily Dickinson, Louisa May Alcott, Sarah Orne Jewett, for example—or they married late. Of those who married and had children as young women, she highlights only four writers in the text—George Sand, Harriet Beecher Stowe, Helen Hunt Jackson, and Elizabeth Gaskell (18). Our own century, she argues, is not significantly different: most women writers either have not married or have remained childless (16). But as this book goes to press, the situation of women writers is markedly improved, unquestionably due in some part to the efforts of women like Olsen.

Olsen asserts vigorously that motherhood and writing are mutually engaging. She believes that "in intelligent passionate motherhood there are similarities" to the talents that contribute to writing, "in more than the toil and patience. The calling upon total capacities; the reliving and new using of the past; the comprehensions; the fascination, absorption, intensity. All almost certain death to creation—(so far)" (18). To make her point she quotes H. H. Richardson, who observed, "There are enough women to do the childbearing and childrearing. I know of none who can write my books." Olsen recalls herself thinking rebelliously, "yes, and I know of none who can bear and rear my children either" (19). But Olsen is the first to admit that "literary history is on [Richardson's] side. Almost no mothers—as almost no part-time, part-self persons—have created enduring literature . . . so far" (19). Again Olsen points out that "so far" this has been true for an obvious but insistent reason: "More than in any other human relationship, overwhelmingly more, motherhood means being instantly interruptible, responsive, responsible" (18). Ironically, then, qualities antithetical to writing become the norm in motherhood: "interruption, not continuity, spasmodic, not constant toil" (19). At this point Olsen becomes almost apologetic as she speaks of her "own silences," which she believes appear "presumptuous after what has been told here," but she thinks that telling of her "individual experience" may add weight to her argument (19).

During 20 years of raising children and working, she testifies, "the simplest circumstances for creation did not exist" (19). After her youngest entered school, Olsen, at that time a transcriber in a dairy equipment company, carried her writing with her on the bus, at work, at night, during and after housework: no wonder, she says, that the "first work I considered publishable began: 'I stand here ironing'" (19). Olsen tells her story—of how she applied for and was awarded eight months' writing time, of how, despite the fact that she still had family responsibilities, she was enabled to spend three days a week writing— and then had to return to work where she took jobs as "Kelly girl" and "Western Agency girl." She became, in her words, "like a woman made frigid. When again I had to leave the writing, I lost consciousness. A time of anesthesia" (20). Thus the award of a Ford grant, though gratefully received, "came almost too late" (21). For a long while, she admits, she was like an "emaciated survivor trembling on the beach, unable to rise and walk" (21), for now a toll was being extracted, a "cost to our family life, to my own participation in life as a human being" (21). The result was that, having begun yet again to write, she "had to leave work at the flood to return to the Time-Master, to businessese and legalese. This most harmful of all my silences has ended, but I am not yet recovered," she says, and "may still be a one-book silence" (21). Her situation, Olsen believes, is not at all unique. She is convinced that "we are in a time of more and more hidden and foreground silences, women *and* men. Unnatural silences" (21).

Olsen notes that when she gave the talk (at the 1971 Modern Language Association Forum "Women Writers in the Twentieth Century") reprinted in part 1 as "'One Out of Twelve': Writers Who Are Women in this Century," only one book by a woman existed for every four to five books by men (24). She speaks of the "little accorded recognition" for women writers and asks one of her central questions: "Why?" (25).

Before answering the question, she says, one must see the "punitive differences" between the genders. Here is Olsen at her best. Although women have been called upon to do the most onerous sorts of physical labor, in most of the world they have been considered

Unclean; taboo. The Devil's Gateway. The three steps behind; the girl babies drowned in the river; the baby strapped to the back. Buried alive with the lord, burned alive on the funeral pyre, burned as witch at the stake. Stoned to death for adultery. Beaten, raped, Bartered. Bought and sold. Concubinage, prostitution, white slavery. The hunt, the sexual prey, "I am a lost creature, O the poor Clarissa." Purdah, the veil of Islam, domestic confinement. Illiterate. Denied vision. Excluded, excluded, excluded from council, ritual, activity, learning, language, when there was neither biological nor economic reason to be excluded. (26)

Acknowledging that all writers must be convinced of the importance of their ideas, she points out that this self-confidence is difficult for the working classes and for men not born into the privileged classes, but it is "almost impossible for a girl, a woman" (27).

Olsen angrily denounces "the acceptance—against one's experienced reality—of the sexist notion that the act of creation is not as inherently natural to a woman as to a man, but rooted instead in unnatural aggression, rivalry, envy, or thwarted sexuality" (30). She quotes Elizabeth Mann Borghese, Thomas Mann's daughter, who, when told she must decide between art and "fulfillment as a woman," replied, "Why? Why must I choose?" (31). Why indeed. This is the focal point of Tillie Olsen's book. She believes that women should not have to choose; each should be able to be a "worker-mother-writer" (262). She believes that we may have lost Shakespeares, "mute inglorious Miltons," because so many potential women writers have been unable to find the time or the right conditions in which to write. When the talk was published as an article in *College English* in 1972, Olsen, citing the "stunningly documented" findings of Elaine Showalter's "Women and the Literary Curriculum," averred that there were "313 males, 17 women" taught in college texts.

Perhaps, says Olsen, there were "other marvels" (32)—but we will never know how many women writers were silenced before they even had a chance to begin. Women have had to battle not only the "angel in the house" of Coventry Patmore and Virginia Woolf, but what Olsen terms the "essential angel" (34) who lives in men's and male writers' houses and makes sure that daily life functions smoothly and pleasantly

(34). It is this essential angel, necessary to the survival and comfort of the husband and family, who prevents women from fulfilling their potential as writers; often when they do write, their books are not as good as they could be because the writer, stealing precious time from her essential angel duties, can work only part-time (36). Olsen then names the major problems: the devaluation of women, condescending (male) critical attitudes, coolness to women in literary circles, restricted women's access to travel, education, and wider social circles, constriction of women into stereotypical roles, the myth of the Bold New Woman (she is really not at all New) (40). Olsen's prescriptions for the devaluation of, condescension to, and constriction of women is clear, as is her goal: women should teach and read women writers, develop their critical faculties, support other women, and help create new women writers. The goal is to have an equal number of women writers—not just one out of twelve—by the end of this century (44–46).

Assessment of Rebecca Harding Davis

Also included in part 1 is a reprint of Olsen's afterword to Rebecca Harding Davis's *Life in the Iron Mills*. Extremely well written (free of the footnotes and repetition that some critics find either unnecessary or annoying in the rest of Olsen's book), it is Olsen's attempt to piece together the life of Davis and to pay tribute to her as a talented, influential nineteenth-century American woman writer. Despite her birth into a fairly wealthy upper-middle-class family, Davis interests Olsen because Olsen sees parallels between their interests and their artistic talents.

From Olsen's passionate reading of Davis's works, she gives us her version of the life and achievement of Rebecca Harding Davis. Davis was born in 1831 in Wheeling, Virginia (now West Virginia), to a father who was a successful businessman and an Anglophile. Davis was an intelligent young woman who graduated as valedictorian of the Female Seminary in Washington, Pennsylvania. Although she enjoyed the "loving bonds" of a "peaceful home," Olsen suggests that Davis lived a narrow somewhat "cramped" life; however, she had a room of her own and "secret longings" that found an outlet in her writing talent (50–59). Davis, who tried for a time to write about "heroines in white dresses that never needed washing," soon realized the futility of the endeavor, admitting that she herself lived "in the commonplace" (61).

How, then, did she learn about the poverty and squalid existence of the mill hands she would feature in her books? Olsen surmises that as Davis saw these people trudging by her window, she must have utilized what Olsen calls "trespass vision" (62), that is, intelligent, imaginative reconstruction of a reality barred to her because of her class and gender. When, at age 30, Davis submitted her novella "Life in the Iron Mills" to the *Atlantic Monthly* and it was accepted, it caused an instant "sensation" and was recognized as a "literary landmark" (64–66). Her next work, however, eventually published as *Margaret Howth: A Story of Today,* an account of life among textile mill workers, was accepted only after Davis agreed to make the story less depressing (67). Nonetheless, as Olsen adds in a footnote (which in fact belongs squarely in the text), Margaret Howth is the first "working girl" heroine in American fiction (68).

Davis's writings brought her fame and an eventual invitation to visit Hawthorne in New England. On the trip she met and conversed with Oliver Wendell Holmes, Ralph Waldo Emerson, and Bronson Alcott (and briefly met Louisa May Alcott). Davis disliked Bronson Alcott, who talked a great deal about things he had never seen firsthand, and she was disappointed to see Emerson so obviously servile to Alcott. Apparently Emerson, though impeccable in his courtesy to Davis, looked at her, she reported, as an "entymologist" would look at a "beetle" (79). But she and Hawthorne admired each other a good deal. Although the excerpts Olsen quotes contain interesting bits of literary history and gossip, Davis, well received by the men of Concord, nevertheless found all of them but Hawthorne strangers to the twin realities of war and poverty, realities that she, the "commonplace" person, believed she understood in far greater depth.

From New England Rebecca went to Philadelphia where she became engaged to L. Clarke Davis, a young man four years her junior, a student of law, and a *Peterson's* magazine employee with whom she had been corresponding for several years (82). Olsen believes that Clarke liked Rebecca for "what would have made most men shun her: her very achievement, seriousness, power; her directness and sardonic eye for sham; the evidence of a rich secret life" (81). Writing to her good friend Annie Fields, wife of the *Atlantic's* editor and good friend of Sarah Orne Jewitt, Davis exclaimed, "O Annie, my summer days are coming now" (quoted on p. 84). The couple was married in 1863. Davis was 32. Having already achieved acclaim as a talented writer, she would now have the rest of what life had to offer.

The remainder of the narrative deals with Davis's marriage to Clarke. Davis, according to Olsen, now had no room of her own, and both she and her husband found marriage an adjustment from the relatively tranquil single lives they had been living. Davis suffered a breakdown that Olsen surmises resulted from Clarke's negligible earnings and their need to live in rather crowded circumstances with Clarke's sister and her family. Moreover, Davis was pregnant. They moved to their own home in the fall of 1864, a few months after she gave birth to Richard Harding in April. A second son, Charles, was born in 1866, and a daughter, Nora, was born 10 years later (94, 95). Meanwhile, Rebecca continued to write voluminously. Olsen analyzes in detail "The Wife's Story," in which the wife realizes that the happiness of being a wife and mother is superior to that of the independent woman writer (89–93), and speculates on its autobiographical qualities. Davis was doubtless torn between the responsibilities of wife- and motherhood, on the one hand, and her need to write, on the other. Significantly, however, during this period she published numerous novels and articles; she became an associate editor for the *New York Herald,* and her husband gave up the law to become an editor for the *Philadelphia Enquirer.*

Her novels address such volatile issues as slavery, insanity, and government corruption: Davis became known, as one reviewer said in 1867, as "the poet of the poor people" (quoted on p. 99) and was so prolific that Olsen claims several years are necessary to read and study all of her work, including the critical and popular success, *Silhouettes of American Life* (1892). Olsen offers a detailed analysis of Davis's "Anne," the story of a woman in her sixties who runs away from home and later realizes the folly of the adventure but wonders at the end, "Is she dead?" (quoted on p. 111). Olsen makes the point that Davis lived to see her son, Richard Harding Davis, become a famous writer and journalist before she died at age 80.

Clearly Olsen acknowledges—and owes—a great debt to Davis. In her fiction Davis was consistently committed to life as it "might—but never can be" as long as horrific conditions proliferate among the poor (Davis, quoted on p. 50). Olsen was reading those ideas at 15. Always beneath the surface of her text is the "secret," the "Hope," words that suggest the potential of human beings, a theme of regeneration common to both Davis and Olsen (50, 63). *Life in the Iron Mills* ends optimistically, as Olsen notes, with the "promise of Dawn," just as "Tell Me a Riddle" ends in the morning. Olsen not only embraces

Davis's major ideas in her fiction but also uses them as one of the refrains in *Silences*.

Familiar to Olsen's readers at the beginning of her narrative is her tendency to use paired opposites to describe Davis's life: "All [Davis's] growing years, the slave South, the free North, the industrial future, the agrarian present, the wilderness that was once all the past—were uniquely commingled here" (51). Moreover, as Olsen points out, Davis was both a southerner and an abolitionist—although, because the state that would become West Virginia generally shared her antislavery views, Davis's abolitionist stance was not as anomalous as it would have been in one of the states in the Deep South. Olsen can identify with the youthful Davis's "hunger to know" (63), her "secret" longing to write, and her successful use of her "trespass vision" (62). She further sees a kindred spirit in Davis because by 1860 one in every seven Americans was a mill hand (65)—and Davis demonstrates in *Life in the Iron Mills* that she was fully cognizant of their plight.

Davis found on her trip to New England that while Alcott and Emerson "thought they were guiding the real world, they stood outside of it, and never would see it as it was" and that these idealistic men moved in a vacuum, "always apart from humanity" (quoted on p. 78). Olsen, of course, like Davis, writes not of intellectuals, but of real, working men and women. Kamel believes that the Korl Woman, a sculpture of a woman created in pig iron, the central metaphor in *Life in the Iron Mills*, "symbolizes nearly all Olsen's narrator-personae, from Anna to Eva" (Kamel 1985, 59). Furthermore, although when Olsen was writing *Yonnondio* she had read only *Life in the Iron Mills*, Davis's next novel, *Margaret Howth*, could have served equally well as a basis for Olsen's novel "From the Thirties." The similarities between Olsen's and Davis's poor working-class characters is illustrated in Olsen's excerpts from Davis's work, wherein the black peddler Lo describes her childhood labor in the mills: "like I was part o' th' engines, somehow. Th' air used to be thick in my mouth, black wi' smoke 'n wool 'n' smells. In them years I got dazed in my head, I think. 'T was th' air 'n' th' work. . . . 'T got so that th' noise of the looms went in my head night 'n' day—allus thud, thud. 'N' hot days, when th' hands was chaffin' 'n' singin', th' black wheels 'n' rollers was alive, starin' down at me, 'n' the shadders o' th' looms was like snakes creepin'— creepin' anear all th' time" (quoted on p. 70). In a strikingly similar manner, *Yonnondio*'s young Mazie Holbrook, lying "between the out- house and the garbage dump," describes her life: "Men and daddy goin' in like the day, and comin out black. Earth black, and pop's face and hands black, and he spits from his mouth black. Night comes and it is black. Coal is black—it makes a fire. . . . Day comes and night comes and the whistle blows and payday comes. Like the flats runnin on the tipple they come—one right a-followen the other. Mebbe I am black inside too. . . . The bowels of earth. . . . The things I know but am not knowen. . . . Sun on me and bowels of earth under" (*Yonnondio*, 5–6; Olsen's ellipses).

Olsen discovered the identity of the author of *Life in the Iron Mills* in 1958, at about the time she was writing "Tell Me a Riddle," but, as she says in *Silences* (118), she had no chance to read Davis's other works until 1962. Nonetheless, remarkable resonances occur in Olsen's work. For example, the woman character Audrey in Olsen's excerpt from Davis's *Earthen Pitchers* (serialized in *Scribner's Monthly*, 1873–74) sounds much like the mother in "I Stand Here Ironing" and Eva in "Tell Me a Riddle." Audrey had been a musician—singer, violinist, composer—and then she married a man blinded in a train accident. Years later, on the beach, she rocks her child and sings a "little cradle song." Her husband, Kit, comments to her that her voice, which used to be so pretty ("You were going to teach the whole world by your songs" [quoted on p. 106]), is now "quite gone" because of the music lessons she has given to earn money. Olsen quotes the following passage from *Earthen Pitchers*: "For one brief moment the tossing waves, the sand dunes, the marshes put on their dear old familiar faces. Old meanings, old voices came close to her as ghosts in the sunlight. The blood rushed to her face, her blue eyes lighted. She buried her hands in the warm white sand. She held the long salt grass to her cheeks. She seemed to have come home to them again. 'Child,' they said to her . . . 'where hast thou stayed so long?'" (quoted on p. 106).

Audrey's likeness to Eva in "Tell Me a Riddle" is easily discernible in her love of the beach, her touching of the sand and salt grass, which is echoed by Eva's running into the sea and lovingly examining the grains of sand. Further similarities occur in Audrey's singing in a "cracked voice," her husband's failure to understand the bitter distance between present reality and past talents and aspirations, and in her leaving her "child." Audrey, aware of her "discordant" voice, suddenly "knew that whatever power she might have had was . . . wasted and gone. She would never hear again the voice that once had called to her" (quoted on p. 106). Similarly Eva, her "throat bubbling, straining," recalls a "melody, ghost-thin," and David remembers that "before the hoarse voice" there had been "a girl's voice of eloquence" (109–10).

Kit, sensing that Audrey is upset, asks if she is sorry that she has nothing to leave the world "but that little song": "'I leave my child,' said Audrey; repeating after awhile, 'I leave my child'" (quoted on p. 106). This sense of continuity from one generation of daughters to another is likewise suggested when Eva, knowing that she is dying, takes comfort and pride in the granddaughter Jeannie who will remain after she is gone. *Earthen Pitchers* concludes with the narrator's ironic comment that "the husband, at least, was sure that she made no moan over that which might have been and was not" (quoted on p. 107). Like Audrey's husband Kit, Eva's husband, David, throughout "Tell Me a Riddle" misunderstands his wife. At the end, however, he finally comprehends her disillusionment with her thwarted idealism and potential and her simultaneous faith that "these things shall be": the future may validate the ideals for which she worked in her youth.

What are we to make of Olsen's assessment of Davis's work? While a number of the perceived parallels between the lives of the two women are illuminating, some seem invented. Olsen has been unwaveringly adamant about divided loyalties and responsibilities—and the cost of these to women who write. But Davis never seems to have suffered from lack of money, after those first few years of marriage. She wrote consistently even in the years when she had babies and young children. By 1870 she and Clarke had moved into a large house that Olsen says Clarke bought with his wife's earnings from her writings. In that same year Davis, certainly neither weak nor retiring, was freed of domestic chores through the services of a live-in maid named Annie (101); Davis, meanwhile, managed the household and wrote numerous articles. The novels continued to pour out: *Waiting for the Verdict* (completed 1868), *Dallas Galbraith* (1868), *Put Her Out of the Way* (1871, arguing in favor of the rights of the insane and influencing changes in the Pennsylvania lunacy laws), *Earthen Pitchers* (1873–74), and *John Andross* (1874, decrying the control of government by special interests). In 1878 a reviewer of *A Law unto Herself* wrote that Davis "succeeds in giving a truer impression of American conditions than any writer we know except Mr. Howells" (quoted on p. 109). The reviewer says that Davis's "grim and powerful etchings" capture "the American atmosphere, its vague excitement, its strife of effort, its varying possibilities," and her books are "individual and interesting if not agreeable" (quoted on p. 109). Far from the image of a dominated, harried housewife, then, Davis seems to have enjoyed a full and challenging existence—and she was still writing, still hammering away at social injustices and inequalities.

Davis considered herself a writer, and that fact is evident in a letter to her son Richard, fledgling journalist and novelist. In the quotation that Olsen chooses, Davis's tone suggests both the loving mother and the experienced writer advising the novice: "I don't say like Papa, stop writing. God forbid. I would almost as soon say stop breathing, for it is pretty much the same thing" (quoted on p. 110). But, she advises, he needs to develop his talents slowly, learning how to dramatize and characterize and display "keen sympathy for all kinds of people"; she tells him, "I've had 30 years experience and I know how much [getting published] depends on the articles suiting the present needs of the magazine, and also on the mood of the editor when he reads it" (quoted on p. 110). She closes by saying, "I had to stop my work to say all this, so goodbye dear old chum" (110).

Davis sounds like neither an anxious mother nor a timid writer; on the contrary, she sounds confident, knowledgeable, and thoroughly professional. Although Olsen contends that Davis "seldom stopped to use her advice" herself (110), the sheer volume and consistency of her output attest to her energies, her talent, and her professionalism. Thus Olsen is not convincing as, apparently attempting to fit Davis into her thesis, she comments, "For all the insights throughout her writings on the narrowness, triviality, drudgery, hurts, restrictions in women's lives—yes, and evidences of capacity within those restrictions—she could not envision women 'as they might be'" (103). Indeed, the reverse appears true: Rebecca Harding Davis, to a far greater extent than most women, actualized the possibilities of her nineteenth-century life: wife, mother, and committed writer.

In fact, Olsen may not completely understand Davis's society and Davis's place in it, particularly as a member of the William Dean Howells set. Davis held a far more respected position in society and in literary circles than Olsen would in the 1930s. The important difference was that Davis was essentially a "reformer" rather than a radical visionary, and she shared Howells's view of the place of the professional writer in society. Moreover, like her son, Davis was essentially a journalist who sought to write for the literate public for both financial and political reasons. Writers, women as well as men, had a social status and respect during Howells's age that no serious writers have today, because they have been exiled into the roles of "outsiders" during the whole modernist period. The academic honors bestowed on them give them no status in the controlling Establishment. Paradoxically, Olsen presents Davis as an "outsider," yet even the evidence Olsen uses tends to make the opposite point: not only was Davis not an "outsider," but she would have been shocked by the idea that she was a "victim" of society, as Olsen actually was, rather than a woman with a duty to work from the inside to make society behave properly.

After all, Davis, as Olsen herself points out, was still writing when she died in 1910. This remarkable fact would have been more evident had Olsen moved into the text her footnote in which she quoted Elizabeth Stuart Lyon Phelps's excellent tribute: Davis wrote, "with an ardor that was human, and a passion that was art" (quoted on p. 115). Nonetheless, Olsen performs a great service in renewing our interest in and paying tribute to this astonishingly strong, talented woman and in energizing the Feminist Press to reissue *Life in the Iron Mills*. Davis left behind a huge body of work, much of which, in Olsen's words, "remains important and virtually alive for our time" (115).

Parts 2 and 3: Women Writers and Criticism

Part 2 of *Silences* has been referred to as a grab-bag or a "patchwork quilt" (Atwood, 27). It consists of quotations that, says Olsen, have been "selectively chosen for maximum significance" (119). Clearly they speak to Olsen directly: we see Thomas Hardy writing of the "sheer drudgery" of editing and cutting his work, of the "tediousness" that made him "weary" (124), or Gerard Manley Hopkins finding his priestly duties "wearying," leaving him "nothing but odds and ends of time" that result in a total of only 26 lines in six months (129). Olsen quotes Melville and Emerson, and includes a brief section on Willa Cather, pointing out that Cather had a "master in Sarah Orne Jewett, who helped her find the courage to resign from her job with *McClure's Magazine* and "write life itself" (quoted on p. 139). Olsen repeats her earlier list of conditions that she finds essential to artistic creation: hard work (quoting Balzac on p. 154), unconfined solitude (quoting Hawthorne on p. 154), and "long subconscious preparation" (quoting Gide on p. 158). She concludes the section by asking whether James "(or Woolf)" or Conrad or Melville could have created their large bodies of work had they been forced to leave regularly for nine-to-five jobs (162).

In the last section of part 2 Olsen returns to an earlier subject: "The Writer-Woman: One Out of Twelve—II." Framing it with words of William Blake and herself, at both beginning and end she quotes Blake's "Blight never does good to a tree" and her own "And yet the tree did bear fruit." She compiles lists of the (horrifying) ratios of men to women in the garnering of such literary prizes as the Nobel and the

Pulitzer (188–89). Returning to the H. H. Richardson line quoted earlier in the book ("There are enough women to do the childbearing and the childrearing. I know of none who can write my books" [200]), Olsen amplifies the gap between childless women writers and those who are mothers. Ellen Glasgow was told to "stop writing and go back to the South and have some babies" (unidentified male critic quoted on p. 197), to which Glasgow responded, "All I ever wanted was to write books. And not ever had I felt the faintest wish to have babies" (quoted on p. 200). Katherine Anne Porter commented that as an artist she had devoted almost all her waking hours to writing; Virginia Woolf, after experiencing a sense of failure over her childlessness, finally, at 48, wrote without qualification, "Children are nothing to this" (quoted on p. 201). Elizabeth Stuart Lyon Phelps and Margaret Walker tried to be both mothers and writers. Phelps's daughter Elizabeth said of her mother, "Her last book and her last baby came together, and they killed her" (quoted on pp. 206–7); Margaret Walker stated firmly that "it is humanly impossible for a woman who is a wife and mother to work a regular teaching job and write" (quoted on p. 209).

Quoting Norman Mailer's infamous observations—his doubts that "there will be a really exciting woman writer until the first whore becomes a call girl and tells her tale," and his conviction that "a good novelist can do without everything but the remnants of his balls" (quoted on p. 238)—Olsen counters with Charlotte Brontë's wonderful line, recalled by Harriet Martineau, "I will show you a heroine as small and as plain as myself who shall be as interesting as any of yours" (quoted on p. 234). But Olsen draws the most critical fire when she takes to task Elizabeth Hardwick and Cynthia Ozick for saying that gender makes no difference to art, that, in Ozick's words, "a writer is a writer" (250–51).

Olsen ends the book by pointing to the emergence in the last century of the sons of working people, black writers, and, in the last decades, writers—including women of color—of working-class origin, perhaps one generation removed. Rarest of all is still the worker-mother-writer whom she believes is "still exceptional: statistically rare" (262). The book concludes with part 3, which contains excerpts from *Life in the Iron Mills, A Note on Clean Haired Yankee Mill Girls,* and, somewhat inexplicably in a book urging improved conditions for women's literature, Baudelaire's *My Heart Laid Bare.*

Although the majority of critics applaud the appearance of *Silences,* there are exceptions, such as Joyce Carol Oates. While affirming that "there is no more powerfully moving" story than Olsen's "Tell Me a Riddle," which bears "repeated readings," Oates finds *Silences* "scattered," comprising "a miscellany of Olsen's speeches, essays and notes" over 15 years.[4] Although Oates believes that Olsen writes "out of passion" and "sympathy," she wishes Olsen had cut down on the "dozens of extremely familiar" Woolf passages and referred more often to her own life and experiences (Oates, 32). She also criticizes the "many, many repetitions" and "inconsequential footnotes" that, she says, could have been incorporated into the text without much trouble; as they stand they "undercut the seriousness of the book" (34). Oates locates the "strengths" of the book in the "polemical passages": "One feels the author's passion, and cannot help but sympathize with it. Certainly women have been more generally 'silenced' than men, in all the arts." On the other hand, Oates considers the book "marred by numerous inconsistencies and questionable statements. . . . Why are men in general the enemy, but some men—perhaps weaker men—welcomed as fellow victims, and their 'unnatural silences' accorded as much dignity as that of women?" (Oates, 33). "Why," she continues, "are men who exploit women criticized on the one hand, and Rilke, who kept himself aloof from responsibilities to his family, admired, on the other hand?" (Oates, 33). Even more damningly, Oates criticizes the underlying assumptions of *Silences:* "We are told that women are not to be trapped into the role of being Women Writers; yet it turns out to be quixotic, and halfway traitorous, to 'proclaim that one's sex has nothing to do with writing'" (Oates, 33). She questions Olsen's dismissal of Elizabeth Hardwick and Cynthia Ozick, suggesting that although "their views differ from mainline feminist views," they "are not, surely, contemptible for that reason." Oates notes that "there is little or no mention of successful women writers of our time" and produces a long list of missing names, including such obvious choices as Eudora Welty and Flannery O'Connor (Oates, 33–34). (One cannot help noting that Oates, one of the most prolific women writers of the century, receives scant mention in *Silences.*) Although she concedes Olsen's generosity in "silencing" her own considerable artistic instincts in order to "reach out" to others who understand her agony, Oates concludes that "the thinking that underlies *Silences* is simply glib and superficial if set in contrast to the imagination that created *Tell Me a Riddle* and *Yonnondio*" (Oates, 34).

Like Oates, Kay Mills comments that "Tillie Olsen is living proof of the death of craft. Harsh, but she readily admits she lacks the facility she once had or could have had" (Mills, part 4:3). Phoebe-Lou Adams believes that Olsen "blames everything except that standard known as writer's block, while quoting the lamentations of a number of writers (mostly men) who suffered no other impediment. The result is a discussion with more eloquence than logic."[5]

Shulman, on the other hand, defends *Silences* as "an eloquent argument presented in a fluid, unorthodox form" and "a case carefully documented and substantiated by testimony from writers spanning time, gender, race, and class, which grows increasingly powerful as the evidence accumulates from topic to topic" (Shulman, 529). Atwood, like Shulman, writes admiringly about *Silences*. To her it is styled like a "scrapbook, a patchwork quilt: bits and pieces joined to form a powerful whole. And despite the condensed and fragmentary quality of this book, the whole is powerful. Even the stylistic breathlessness—the elliptical prose, the footnotes blooming on every page as if the author, reading her own manuscript, belatedly thought of a dozen other things too important to leave out—is reminiscent of a biblical messenger, sole survivor of a relentless and obliterating catastrophe, a witness: 'I only am escaped alone to tell thee'" (Atwood, 27).

In her preface Olsen admonishes the reader, "this book is not an orthodoxly written work of academic scholarship. Do not approach it as such" (iv). Olsen is best when writing about her own experiences, least effective when using random footnotes and techniques better employed in her fiction (for example, repetition, refrain, italics, indentation). Although she lacks the academic resources enjoyed by many of her friends and colleagues, she has said recently, "I am in my way a very true scholar. I am a reading scholar and a writing scholar" (Werlock interview, 1990)—and surely the depth and scope of her knowledge of history and literature attest to the impressive achievements of this remarkable woman. In two interviews shortly after the publication of *Silences,* Olsen demonstrated that she still believes strongly in the contents of the book. In the 1981 interview with Kay Mills, Olsen makes two amendments to her comments in *Silences.* Regarding her well-known statement on survival, she says "But I'm not a survivor. To hell with *just* surviving. Surviving is not enough." And, regarding her use of William Blake's "Blight never does good to a tree," she says, "I didn't say strongly enough in the book, 'And yet the tree did and does bear fruit.'" In her interview with Kenneth Turan Olsen comments, "In all my work, there is that celebration of human beings," a belief that "there is so much more to people than their lives permit them to be. It almost kills you how much is lost and wasted in people who might have been you" (Turan 1978, 59). Although she counts herself "one of the lucky ones, I so nearly didn't write at all," she finds herself "embittered about the whole situation [of silenced women writers], unconsolably, I'm more and more in a rage about it. . . . I'm bitter about all those books that are unpublished or unfinished" (Turan 1978, 59). Rephrasing her famous description of herself as a "destroyed person," she tells the interviewer, "I had destruction happen in me" (Turan 1978, 56).

Silences is Tillie Olsen's own story, "how she joyfully came to writing only to lose the thread for a full twenty years, never to fully recover it, that is among the most affecting of all" (Turan 1978, 56). The impact of Tillie Olsen and the impact of *Silences* on women's studies and on women who write is enormous, for both the author and her work give the lie to the old sexist idea that women, when they write at all, should be childless. Moreover, Olsen's admonition to "teach books by women," is invaluable. Her success can be measured by the number of books by women that are now found in university and women's studies courses and by the number of women to whom Tillie Olsen continues to offer immeasurable encouragement.

As Olsen continues to write into the 1990s, she finds invaluable silent moments of her own. While at the Leighton Arts Colony in Banff, Canada, in September and October of 1990, she spoke in awed and pleasured tones of the early snow falling around her in tiny individual pellets, of the "hundreds of elk" roaming past her cabin window. Immensely responsive to natural beauty, Tillie Olsen still believes that pejorative silences can be transformed into "enabling" silences: "I am still," she says, "a believer in human potentiality" (Werlock interview, 1990).

Notes and References

Introduction

1. Margaret Atwood, "Obstacle Course," *New York Times Book Review*, 30 July 1978, 1; hereafter cited in the text.

2. Tillie Olsen quoted in Shelley Fisher Fishkin, "Reading, Writing and Arithmetic: The Lessons Silences Has Taught Us," panel discussion on "Silences: Ten Years Later," held at the Modern Language Association Convention, December 1988, New Orleans; hereafter cited in the text.

3. Rose Kamel, "Literary Foremothers and Writers; *Silences:* Tillie Olsen's Autobiographical Fiction," *Melus* 12 (Fall 1985): 55; hereafter cited in the text.

4. Tillie Olsen quoted in Kenneth Turan, "Breaking Silence," *New West* 3 (August 1978): 59; hereafter cited in the text.

5. *Silences* (New York: Delacorte Press/Seymour Lawrence, 1978), 6; hereafter cited in text. Also quoted in Catharine Stimpson, "Tillie Olsen: Witness as Servant," *Polit: A Journal for Literature and Politics* 1 (Fall 1977): 10; hereafter cited in the text.

6. Miriam Elaine Neil Orr, *Tillie Olsen and a Feminist Spiritual Vision* (Jackson: University Press of Mississippi, 1987), 135; hereafter cited in the text.

7. Elizabeth A. Meese, "Deconstructing the Sexual Politic: Virginia Woolf and Tillie Olsen," in *Crossing the Double Cross,* ed. Elizabeth A. Meese (Chapel Hill: University of North Carolina Press, 1986), 112; hereafter cited in the text.

8. *Yonnondio: From the Thirties* (New York: Dell Publishing, 1974), 185–91; hereafter cited in the text.

9. Jane Silverman Van Buren, *The Modernist Madonna: Semiotics of the Maternal Metaphor* (Bloomington and Indianapolis: Indiana University Press, 1989), 161; hereafter cited in the text.

10. Fifty years later, Eva still remembers: "there is so much blood in a human being." *Tell Me a Riddle* (New York: Dell Publishing, 1989), 104. The short stories from this text—"I Stand Here Ironing," "Hey Sailor, What Ship?" "O Yes," and "Tell Me a Riddle"—are hereafter cited in the text.

11. Selma Burkom and Margaret Williams, "De-Riddling Tillie Olsen's Writing," *San Jose Studies* 2 (February 1976): 64–83; hereafter cited in the text. Deborah Rosenfelt, "From the Thirties: Tillie Olsen and the Radical Tradition," *Feminist Studies* 7 (Fall 1981): 371–406, and "Divided against Herself: The Life Lived and the Life Suppressed," *Moving On* (April–May

1980): 15–20; both hereafter cited in the text. Stimpson 1977, 1–12. Joanne Frye, "'I Stand Here Ironing': Motherhood as Experience and Metaphor," *Studies in Short Fiction* 18, no. 3 (Summer 1981): 187–92; hereafter cited in the text.

12. For examples see the indices of *Feminist Issues in Literary Scholarship,* ed. Shari Benstock (Bloomington and Indiana: Indiana University Press, 1987); *Mothers, Memories, Dreams and Reflections by Literary Daughters,* ed. Susan Cahill (New York: New American Library, 1988); and Frederick Karl, *American Fictions, 1940–1980* (New York: Harper & Row, 1983), cited by the *Los Angeles Times* as "the best and most comprehensive critical guide to American fiction." Tillie Olsen is not mentioned in either *The Norton Anthology of American Literature,* 3d ed. (New York: W. W. Norton, 1989), or *Benet's Reader's Encyclopedia,* 3d ed. (New York: Harper & Row, 1987).

Chapter One

1. Speech by Tillie Olsen at the 1988 MLA Convention in New Orleans.
2. Blanche H. Gelfant, "After Long Silence: Tillie Olsen's 'Requa,'" in *Women Writing in America* (Hanover, N.H.: University Press of New England, 1984), 62; hereafter cited in the text. Olsen describes her encounter with the judge in "Thousand-Dollar Vagrant," *New Republic,* 29 August 1929, 67–69.

Chapter Two

1. Two unpublished versions of a short story, "Not You I Weep For," in the Berg Collection, New York Public Library. Although undated, the holograph note at the top of the first page of the second version reads, "Begun at age 18 (?)." Hereafter cited in the text as Berg 1 or Berg 2.
2. In notes to and telephone conversations with Abby Werlock during October and November 1990, Olsen recalled that she wrote these versions in Omaha. References to these conversations are hereafter cited in the text.
3. David Dillon, "Art and Daily Life in Conflict," *Southwest Review* (Winter 1979): 106; hereafter cited in the text.
4. Quoted in Abigail Martin, *Tillie Olsen* (Boise, Idaho: Boise State University Press, 1984), 6; hereafter cited in the text.
5. For examples of the confusion surrounding Olsen's origins, see such critics as Marilyn Yalom, "Tillie Olsen," in *Women Writers of the West Coast: Speaking of Their Lives and Careers,* ed. Marilyn Yalom (Santa Barbara: Capra, 1983), 57; hereafter cited in the text. Also Erika Duncan, *Unless Soul Clap Its Hands* (New York: Schocken Books, 1984), 36; hereafter cited in the text. See also Orr, 25; Rosenfelt 1981, 375; and Kamel 1985, 72, n. 13.
6. *Mother to Daughter, Daughter to Mother: A Daybook and Reader,* selected and edited by Tillie Olsen (Old Westbury, N.Y.: Feminist Press, 1984); hereafter cited in the text.

7. From an interview with Naomi Rubin, May 1983, quoted in Bonnie Lyons, "Tillie Olsen: The Writer as Jewish Woman," *Studies in American Jewish Literature* 5 (1986): 91; hereafter cited in the text.

8. Rosenfelt 1981, 376, and Erika Duncan, "Coming of Age in the Thirties: A Portrait of Tillie Olsen," *Book Forum* 4, no. 2 (1982): 212; hereafter cited in the text.

9. The notice is part of the Olsen material in the Berg Collection.

10. John L'Heureux, preface to *First Drafts, Last Drafts: Forty Years of the Creative Writing Program at Stanford,* prepared by William McPheron with the assistance of Amor Towles (Stanford: Stanford University Libraries, 1989), 63; hereafter cited in the text.

11. At least three critics say that she contracted the pleurisy after being imprisoned in Kansas City's Argentine Jail (Martin, 7; Yalom, 58). See also Kay Mills, "Surviving Is Not Enough: A Conversation with Tillie Olsen," *Los Angeles Times,* 26 April 1981, part 4:3; hereafter cited in the text.

12. Orr reiterates this information and asserts that Olsen was at home when she simultaneously became pregnant and began the novel (Orr, 31). Duncan says that she began writing *Yonnondio* in February 1932, but contradicts the others by saying the baby was born during the beginning writing (Duncan 1984, 39). Rosenfelt states that she moved to Faribault in late 1932 (Rosenfelt 1981, 380) and had the baby before she turned 20 in January 1933.

13. Robert Cantwell, review of "The Iron Throat," *New Republic,* 25 July 1934, and idem., "Literary Life in California," *New Republic,* 22 August 1934, both quoted in Burkom and Williams, 72.

14. Charlotte Nekola, "Worlds Moving: Women, Poetry and the Literary Politics of the 1930s," in *Writing Red: An Anthology of American Women Writers, 1930–1940,* ed. Charlotte Nekola and Paula Rabinowitz (New York: City University of New York/Feminist Press, 1987), 132; hereafter cited in the text.

15. From Joseph Kalar, "Worker Uprooted," reprinted in *Proletarian Literature in the United States,* ed. Granville Hicks et al. (New York: International Publishers, 1935), 170, quoted in Nekola and Rabinowitz, 132.

16. See also Orr's account of her interview with Olsen, 12 May 1984, described in Orr, 33.

17. Representative Martin Dies of Texas chaired the HUAC. For an account of the committee's research, see, for example, *Investigation of Un-American Propaganda Activities in the United States, Special Committee on Un-American Activities, House of Representatives, 76th Congress, 1st Session on House Resolution 282,* printed for the use of the HUAC (Washington: U.S. Government Printing Office, 1940), popularly known as the "Red Book."

18. "Investigation of Communist Activities in the San Francisco Area—Part I," *Hearing before the Committee on Un-American Activities, House of Representatives, 83d Congress, 1st Session, December 1, 1953* (Washington: U.S. Government Printing Office, 1954), 3080; hereafter cited in the text.

19. "Annual Report of the Committee on Un-American Activities for the Year 1953," 6 February 1954, prepared and released by the Special Committee on Un-American Activities, U.S. House of Representatives, Washington, D.C., Union Calendar #440, House Report #1192, 83d Congress, 2d Session, in *House Reports, 83d Congress, 2d Session, Jan. 6–Dec. 2, 1954, Vol. 1* (Washington: U.S. Government Printing Office, 1954), 1–195.

20. "Jack Olsen's Statement for the House Un-American Activities Committee," in Tillie Olsen's personal files; hereafter cited in the text.

21. Quoted from the announcement of Jack Olsen's death by the Board of Directors, St. Francis Square Apartments, Inc., 27 February 1989, in Tillie Olsen's personal files.

22. Proclamation recognizing 25 March 1989 as "Jack Olsen Remembrance Day in San Francisco," in Tillie Olsen's personal files.

23. *The Invisible Enemy: Alcohol and the Modern Short Story,* ed. Miriam Dow and Jennifer Regan (St. Paul, Minn.: Graywolf Short Fiction Series, 1989).

24. Ellen Cronan Rose, "Limning: or Why Tillie Writes," *Hollins Critic* 13, no. 2 (April 1976): 3; hereafter cited in the text.

25. From the preface to *Stanford Short Stories* (1960), quoted in Burkom and Williams, 75.

Chapter Three

1. "The Iron Throat," *Partisan Review* 1 (April–May 1934): 3–9.

2. Cantwell, "Literary Life in California," quoted in Martin, 7. Olsen described her encounter with the judge in "Thousand-Dollar Vagrant," *New Republic,* 29 August 1934, 67–69.

3. "The Strike," *Partisan Review* 1 (September–October 1934): 3–9; hereafter cited in the text.

4. These documents are now in the Berg Collection. Olsen has recently discovered still more notes and pages (Werlock interview, 1990).

5. Catharine Stimpson, "Three Women Work It Out," *Nation,* 30 November 1974, 565; hereafter cited in the text.

6. Afterword to *Life in the Iron Mills* by Rebecca Harding Davis (Old Westbury, N.Y.: Feminist Press, 1972).

7. Anne Hockmeyer, "Object Relations Theory and Feminism: Strange Bedfellows," *Frontiers* 10 (1988): 27.

8. Michael Staub, "The Struggle for 'Selfness' through Speech in Olsen's *Yonnondio: From the Thirties,*" *Studies in American Fiction* 16 (Autumn 1988): 131, 132.

9. See, for example, Annette Bennington McElhiney, "Alternative Responses to Life in Tillie Olsen's Work," *Frontiers* 2 (1977): 86.

10. Carolyn Rhodes, "'Beedo' in Olsen's *Yonnondio:* Charles E. Bedaux," *American Notes and Queries* 14 (October 1976): 24; hereafter cited in the text.

Chapter Four

1. From the interview with Mickey Pearlman at Olsen's home in San Francisco in 1987; hereafter cited in the text.

2. The possibility exists that the ironing mother (in "I Stand Here Ironing") is the daughter of Eva (in "Tell Me a Riddle"), sister of Lennie (in "Hey Sailor, What Ship?," "O Yes," and "Tell Me a Riddle").

3. Richard M. Elman, "The Many Forms Which Loss Can Take," *Commonweal* 75 (8 December 1961): 295; Yalom, 61.

4. The beauty of Olsen's most widely anthologized story stems in part from its nonspecific resonances. Although most critics assume that the phone call is from a counselor (e.g., Joanne S. Frye, "'I Stand Here Ironing': Motherhood as Experience and Metaphor," *Studies in Short Fiction* 18 [Summer 1981]: 287; hereafter cited in the text; and Vicki L. Sommer, "The Writings of Tillie Olsen: A Social Work Perspective," in "Tillie Olsen Week: The Writer and Society," 21–26 March 1983, 84; hereafter cited in the text), one critic insists that the story "depicts a nameless mother-narrator, who, having received a phone call from her daughter Emily's guidance counselor saying that Emily is an underachiever, pushes an iron across the board on which Emily's dress lies shapeless and wrinkled" (Kamel 1985, 59). Olsen's text contains no reference to a phone call (it could have been a note), or guidance counselor (it could have been a teacher), and we are not certain that the dress—described only as "helpless"—belongs to Emily. Lyons infers that a "heartless teacher who belittled Emily for her fear has 'curdled' in the mother's memory" (96). Neither the heartless teacher nor the word *curdled* appears in the text. And Rose Yalow Kamel, "Riddles and Silences: Tillie Olsen's Autobiographical Fiction," in *Aggravating the Conscience: Jewish-American Literary Mothers in the Promised Land,* ed. Rose Yalow Kamel (New York: Peter Lang, 1988), 92 (hereafter cited in the text), finds that Emily, "desperate for attention," "responds to the mother's suggestion that she try out for a high school play." Emily's desperation is questionable; the mother is uncertain as to who suggested that Emily audition; and we are told that she tries out not for a play but for an "amateur show" (92).

5. Sally H. Johnson, "Silence and Song: The Structure and Imagery of Tillie Olsen's 'Tell Me a Riddle,'" in "Tillie Olsen Week: The Writer and Society," 21–26 March 1983, 33; hereafter cited in the text.

6. Elizabeth Fisher, "The Passion of Tillie Olsen," *Nation,* 10 April 1972, 474; hereafter cited in the text.

7. Helen Pike Bauer, "'A child of anxious, not proud, love': Mother and Daughter in Tillie Olsen's 'I Stand Here Ironing,'" in *Mother Puzzles: Daughters and Mothers in Contemporary Literature,* ed. Mickey Pearlman (Westport, Conn.: Greenwood Publishing, 1989), 36; hereafter cited in the text.

8. According to Olsen, the source of the word "shoogily" originated with a toddler-friend of her daughter Laurie, who used the word as a synonym

for "comfort" (Werlock interview, 1990). See also Kamel (1985, 61), who suggests that "shoogily" is "rooted in Yiddish (shoogily—meshugah)."

9. Critics like Orr see the ending as an "opening" rather than a "closing" (77). Frye sees it as a paradoxical affirmation acknowledging the separateness of mother and daughter (291). Bauer sees it as a generous plea by the mother who, already a wife and mother at 19, includes no reference to relationships but simply asks that her daughter not be weak and dependent (37).

Chapter Five

1. Thomas Stearns Eliot, *The Waste Land,* in *T. S. Eliot: Collected Poems, 1909–1962* (New York: Harcourt, Brace & World, 1963), ll. 266–67; hereafter cited in the text.

2. Thomas Stearns Eliot, "The Love Song of J. Alfred Prufrock," in *Collected Poems, 1909–1962;* hereafter cited in the text.

3. I (A.W.) am indebted to Professor Madeleine Marshall, St. Olaf College, for suggesting this interpretation during several conversations in Northfield, Minnesota, during February and March, 1990.

4. Kathleen McCormack, "Song as Transcendence in the Works of Tillie Olsen," in "Tillie Olsen Week: The Writer and Society," 21–26 March 1983, 59–69, 63; hereafter cited in the text.

Chapter Six

1. Like the title "Hey Sailor, What Ship?," the title of "O Yes" derives from a refrain reverberating throughout the tale. Indeed, it may connect with Whitey's own use of the phrase in his conversations with Lennie: twice in the previous story Whitey sighs "Oh, yes" when he recalls that the friends of his youth have achieved success in the conventional sense of the word; his "Oh, yes" precedes his weary delving into the past.

2. Naomi N. Jacobs, "Olsen's 'O Yes': Alva's Vision as Childbirth Account," *Notes on Contemporary Literature* 16, no. 1 (January 1986): 7; hereafter cited in the text.

Chapter Seven

1. Mary K. DeShazer, "Tell Me a Riddle," in "Tillie Olsen Week: The Writer and Society," 21–26 March 1983, 21; hereafter cited in the text.

2. DeShazer (22) suggests that there are five linguistic features to Tillie Olsen's style: fragmentation and ellipses; parentheses and italics; pronouns, titles, and epithets; gerunds and participles; and repetition.

3. Sara McAlpin, "Mothers in Tillie Olsen's Stories," in "Tillie Olsen Week: The Writer and Society," 21–26 March 1983, 56; hereafter cited in the text.

4. Naomi Jacobs, "Earth, Air, Fire and Water in 'Tell Me a Riddle,'" *Studies in Short Fiction* 23 (Fall 1986): 404; hereafter cited in the text.

5. Jacqueline A. Mintz, "The Myth of the Jewish Mother in Three Jewish, American, Female Writers," *Centennial Review* 22 (1978): 346–55; quoted in Johnson, 35.

6. McCormack (60) notes numerous links between Mazie and Eva, both of whom see community in the metaphor of song, and both of whom then form kinship with others.

7. E. L. Niehus and T. Jackson, "Polar Stars, Pyramids, and 'Tell Me a Riddle,'" *American Notes and Queries* 24 (January–February 1986): 82.

8. McElhiney (83) sees the scene between Eva and Clara as reminiscent of the one between the ironing mother and Emily; Johnson (42) sees a similarity between Eva and Clara as mothers, as does McAlpin (67), who thinks Eva is more "isolated" and bitter than the ironing mother. Kamel (1988, 110) sees Clara as an "Emily hardened to bitter middle age"; McCormack (67) finds Clara and Eva more like Mazie and Anna.

9. These pages are part of the Olsen material in the Berg Collection.

Chapter Eight

1. Gelfant (quoted in Orr, 121) says that Stevie continues the quest of the Grandmother in "Tell Me a Riddle."

2. Gelfant says that "the resurrected boy and the dying woman [Eva in "Tell Me a Riddle"] are both searching for a transmittable human past that will give significance to their present struggle" (1984, 65).

3. Orr says that "Stevie and Wes, nephew and uncle, recall for us the shared mother-daughter perspective in *Yonnondio*" (123).

4. "Requa," *Iowa Review* 1 (Summer 1970): 56; hereafter cited in the text.

Chapter Nine

1. Annie Gottlieb, "Feminists Look at Motherhood," *Mother Jones* 1 (November 1976): 51.

2. Alix Kates Shulman, "Overcoming Silences: Teaching Writing for Women," *Harvard Educational Review* 49 (November 1979): 532; hereafter cited in the text.

3. Shelley Fisher Fishkin, cited above in Introduction, n. 2; and Sally Cuneen, "Tillie Olsen: Storyteller of Working America," *The Christian Century,* 21 May 1980, 573; hereafter cited in the text.

4. Joyce Carol Oates, review of *Silences, New Republic,* 29 July 1978, 33; hereafter cited in the text.

5. Phoebe-Lou Adams, review of *Silences, Atlantic Monthly,* September 1978, 96.

Selected Bibliography

PRIMARY WORKS

Novel

Yonnondio: From the Thirties. New York: Delacorte Press/Seymour Lawrence, 1974; Dell, 1975. Includes what can be considered an essay, "A Note about This Book."

Story Collection

Tell Me a Riddle. Philadelphia: Lippincott, 1961; reprinted, New York: Dell, 1961; Delta (paperback), 1989; Laurel, 1975; Delacorte (hardcover), 1979. Includes the stories "I Stand Here Ironing," "Hey Sailor, What Ship?," and "O Yes" and the novella "Tell Me a Riddle."

Novella

"Requa." *Iowa Review* 1 (Summer 1970): 54–74. Reprinted as "Requa I" in *The Best American Short Stories 1971,* edited by Martha Foley and David Burnett, 237–65. Boston: Houghton Mifflin, 1971. (This volume was dedicated to Tillie Olsen.) *Granta* featured "Requa" in the 1979 issue on American writers.

Poems

"I Want You Women up North to Know" (T. Lerner). *Partisan* 1 (March 1934): 4. Based on a letter by Felipe Ibarro published in the 9 January 1934 *New Leader.*
"There Is a Lesson" (T. Lerner). *Partisan* 1 (April 1934): 4.

Nonfiction

"A Biographical Interpretation." Afterword to *Life in the Iron Mills* by Rebecca Harding Davis, 69–174. Old Westbury, N.Y.: Feminist Press, 1972.
Mothers and Daughters: That Special Quality, an Exploration in Photography. Edited with Julie Olsen Edwards and Estelle Jussim. New York: Aperture Foundation, 1987.
Mother to Daughter, Daughter to Mother: A Daybook and Reader. Selected and shaped by Tillie Olsen. Old Westbury, N.Y.: Feminist Press, 1984.

Personal statement to accompany Manuscript Exhibit. *First Drafts, Last Drafts:* Forty Years of the Creative Writing Program at Stanford, 63–65. (see L'Heureux entry, below).

Preface. *Black Women Writers at Work.* Edited by Claudia Tate. New York: Continuum—, 1983.

Silences. New York: Delacorte Press, 1978; Delta, 1989. The first published version of parts of *Silences* appeared in *Harper's,* October 1965, 153–61; an excerpt appeared in *Ms.,* September 1978, 64–65; the title essay, "Silences: When Writers Don't Write," was adapted from the talk "Death of the Creative Process," presented at the Radcliffe Institute for Independent Study in 1962.

"The Strike" (T. Lerner). *Partisan Review* 1 (September–October 1934): 3–9. Reprinted in *Years of Protest: A Collection of American Writings of the 1930s,* edited by Jack Salzman, 138–44. New York: Pegasus, 1967. An essay.

"Thousand-Dollar Vagrant" (T. Lerner). *New Republic,* 29 August 1934, 67–69. Reprinted in *Years of Protest: A Collection of American Writings of the 1930s,* 67–69. An account of Olsen's sentencing by a vengeful judge after her involvement in a strike.

"Women Who Are Writers in Our Century: One Out of Twelve." *College English* 34 (October 1972): 6–17. Previously presented as a talk under the same title at the Modern Language Association forum "Women Writers in the Twentieth Century," 28 December 1971. Reprinted in *Woman as Writer,* edited by Jeanette L. Weber and Joan Grumman, 63–64, 66. Boston: Houghton Mifflin, 1978.

"The Word Made Flesh." Prefatory essay to *Critical Thinking, Critical Writing,* 1–8. Iowa: 1984.

Manuscript Collection

Portions of the manuscript version of *Yonnondio* are in the Berg Collection of English and American Literature in the New York Public Library.

SECONDARY WORKS

Articles and Parts of Books

Ackroyd, Peter. Review of *Yonnondio. Spectator,* 14 December 1974, 768.

Adams, Barbara. "Tillie Olsen: Wings of Life." *Ithaca Times,* 24–30 April 1980, 13.

Adams, Phoebe-Lou. Review of *Silences. Atlantic Monthly,* September 1978, 96.

Atwood, Margaret. "Obstacle Course" [review of *Silences*]. *New York Times Book Review,* 30 July 1978, 1, 27. Highly influential review that notes and perpetuates Olsen's saintlike status as a woman writer and "survivor." Repeats and endorses Olsen's view of Rebecca Harding Davis as a victim of motherhood.

Avant, John Alfred. Review of *Yonnondio. New Republic,* 30 March 1974, 28–29.

Banks, Joanne Troutman. "Death Labours." *Literature and Medicine: Fictive Ills: Literary Perspectives on Wounds and Diseases.* Edited by Peter W. Graham and Elizabeth Sewall. Vol. IX, 162–71. Comparing Olsen's "Tell Me a Riddle" and Tolstoy's *The Death of Ivan Ilych,* the article argues that the literary styles of the authors parallel the lifestyles of their characters, who in turn "partially revise the authors."

Baro, Gene. Review of *Tell Me a Riddle. New York Herald Tribune Books,* 17 December 1961, 8.

Barr, Marleen. "Tillie Olsen." In *Dictionary of Literary Biography,* vol. 28, 196–203. Detroit: Gale Research Co., 1984.

Bauer, Helen Pike. "'A child of anxious, not proud, love': Mother and Daughter in Tillie Olsen's 'I Stand Here Ironing.'" In *Mother Puzzles: Daughters and Mothers in Contemporary American Literature,* edited by Mickey Pearlman, 35–40. Westport, Conn.: Greenwood Publishing, 1989.

Bavilacqua, Winifred Farrant. "Women Writers and Society in 1930 America: Tillie Olsen, Meridel Lesueur, and Josephine Herbst." Paper given at the symposium "Tillie Olsen Week: The Writer and Society," 21–26 March 1983.

Bedway, Barbara. "Women Writers' Plight." *In These Times,* 6–2 September 1978, 21.

Bellows, S. B. Review of *Tell Me a Riddle. Christian Science Monitor,* 9 November 1961, 7.

Berger, Alan. "*Riddle* Will Tug at Heart" [review of the film *Riddle*]. *Boston Herald American,* 27 February 1981.

Bernikow, Louise. *Among Women,* 264–65. New York: Harmony Books, 1980.

Blustein, Bryna Lee. "Beyond the Stereotype: A Study of Representative Short Stories of Selected Contemporary Jewish American Female Writers (Yezierska, Olsen, Paley, Darwin, Ozick)." Ph.D. dissertation, St. Louis University, 1986.

Boucher, Sandy. "Tillie Olsen: The Weight of Things Unsaid." *Ms.,* September 1974, 26–30.

Buford, Bill. Reviews of *Yonnondio, Tell Me a Riddle,* and *Silences. New Statesman,* 31 October 1980, 23–25.

Burkom, Selma, and Margaret Williams. "De-Riddling Tillie Olsen's Writing." *San Jose Studies* 2 (February 1976): 64–83. Well-written and loving tribute to Tillie Olsen; the best discussion of her biography and early-1930s political poetry and essays. Short discussions of *Yonnondio,* the stories in *Tell Me a Riddle,* and "Requa."

Cantwell, Robert. "Literary Life in California." *New Republic,* 22 August 1934, 49.

Cassill, R. V. Instructor's handbook for *Norton Anthology of Short Fiction,* 166–68. New York: W. W. Norton, 1977.

Chevigny, Bell Gale. Review of *Yonnondio. Village Voice,* 23 May 1974, 38–39.

Clapp, Susanna. Review of *Yonnondio. Times Literary Supplement,* 10 January 1975, 29.

Clayton, John. "Grace Paley and Tillie Olsen: Radical Jewish Humanists." *Response: A Contemporary Jewish Review* 46 (1984): 37–52.

Coiner, Constance. *Pessimism of the Mind, Optimism of the Will: Literature of Resistance,* 48–57. Ann Arbor, Mich.: Dissertation Abstracts, 1988.

Coles, Robert. "Reconsideration: *Tell Me a Riddle"* [review of *Tell Me a Riddle*]. *New Republic,* 6 December 1975, 29–30.

————. "Tillie Olsen: The Iron and the Riddle." In *That Red Wheelbarrow: Selected Literary Essays,* edited by Robert Coles, 122–27. Iowa City: University of Iowa Press, 198?

Contemporary Literary Criticism 4 (1975): 385–87. On *Yonnondio.*

Crane, L. G. Review of *Yonnondio. Best Sellers,* 15 May 1974, 97.

Culver, Sara. "Extending the Boundaries of the Ego: Eva in 'Tell Me a Riddle.'" *Midwestern Miscellany* 10 (1982): 38–48.

Cuneen, Sally. "Tillie Olsen: Storyteller of Working America." *Christian Century,* 21 May 1980, 570–73.

DeShazer, Mary K. "Tell Me a Riddle." Paper given at the symposium "Tillie Olsen Week: The Writer and Society," 21–26 March 1983.

Dillon, David. "Art and Daily Life in Conflict." *Southwest Review* (Winter 1979): 105–7.

Doherty, Gail, and Paul Doherty. Review of *Yonnondio. America,* 18 October 1975, 236.

Duncan, Erika. "Coming of Age in the Thirties: A Portrait of Tillie Olsen." *Book Forum: An International Transdisciplinary Quarterly* 4 (1982): 207–22. Reprinted in *Unless Soul Clap Its Hands: Portraits and Passages.* New York: Schocken Books, 1984. This laudatory essay weaves selected passages from Olsen's published fiction with an examination of the author's early life, politics, and views of the family. Strong on biography; complete discussion of *Yonnondio.*

Edwards, Margaret, and John Gorman, transcribers. "A Visit with Tillie Olsen." Burlington: University of Vermont, October 1972.

Elman, Richard M. "The Many Forms Which Loss Can Take." *Commonweal,* 8 December 1961, 295–96.

Ferguson, Mary Anne. *Images of Women in Literature.* Boston: Houghton Mifflin, 1973.

Fisher, Elizabeth. "The Passion of Tillie Olsen." *Nation,* 10 April 1972, 472, 474.

Fishkin, Shelley Fisher. "The Borderlands of Culture: Writing by W. E. B.

Du Bois, James Agee, Tillie Olsen and Gloria Anzaldua," in *Literary Journalism in the Twentieth Century,* ed. Norman Sims. New York: Oxford University Press, 1990.

————. "Reading, Writing, and Arithmetic: The Lessons *Silences* Has Taught Us." Panel discussion entitled *"Silences: Ten Years Later"* at the Modern Language Association Convention, New Orleans, December 1988.

———— and Elaine Hedges, eds. *Listening to "Silences": New Essays in Feminist Criticism.* Forthcoming, New York: Oxford University Press, 1992. Includes essays by Mary Battenfeld, Robin Dizard, Shelley Fisher Fishkin, Diane Middlebrook, Lillian Robinson, and Deborah Rosenfelt.

Fowler, Lois J. Review of *Mother to Daughter. Women's Review of Books* 2 (June 1985): 12–13.

Frye, Joanne S. "'I Stand Here Ironing': Motherhood as Experience and Metaphor." *Studies In Short Fiction* 18 (Summer 1981): 287–92. Useful and powerful analysis of the limitations in understanding between mothers and daughters in fiction and in real life.

Gardiner, Judith Kegan. "A Wake for Mother: The Maternal Deathbed in Women's Fiction." *Feminist Studies* 4 (June 1978): 146–65.

Gelfant, Blanche H. "After Long Silence: Tillie Olsen's 'Requa.'" *Studies in American Fiction* 12 (Spring 1984): 61–69. Reprinted in Gelfant's *Women Writing in America,* 59–70. Hanover, N.H.: University Press of New England, 1984. Excellent, very useful analysis; the only available discussion of "Requa" as Olsen's "most innovative and complex work of fiction."

————. Review of *Yonnondio. Massachusetts Review* 16 (Winter 1975): 127–43.

Gitomer, Irene. Review of *Tell Me a Riddle. Library Journal,* 15 September 1961, 2963.

Glastonbury, Marion. "The Best Kept Secret—How Working-Class Women Live and What They Know." *Women's Studies International Quarterly* 2 (1979): 171–81.

Glendinning, Victoria. Review of *Yonnondio. New Statesman,* 29 December 1974, 907.

Godine, Amy. "Notes towards a Reappraisal of Depression Literature." In *Prospects: Volume Five,* edited by Jack Salzman, 217. New York: Burt Franklin & Co., 1980.

Gottlieb, Annie. "Feminists Look at Motherhood." *Mother Jones,* November 1976, 51–53.

————. "A Writer's Sounds and Silences: *Yonnondio.*" *New York Times Book Review,* 31 March 1974, 5.

Graulich, Melody. "Violence against Women: Power Dynamics in Literature of the Western Family." *Frontiers: A Journal of Women's Studies* 7 (1984): 14–20. Reprinted in *The Women's West,* edited by Susan H. Armitage and

Elizabeth Jameson, 111–25. Norman: University of Oklahoma Press, 1987. Although the passages on Olsen are the briefest of the four, she with the others is credited with having anticipated recent feminist scholarship equating violence against women with "patriarchal definitions of gender and marriage rather than of individual pathology."

———. "Somebody Must Say These Things: An Essay for My Mother." *Women's Studies Quarterly* 13 (Fall–Winter 1985): 2–8.

Grumbach, Doris. *"Silences." Washington Post,* 6 August 1978.

Hedges, Elaine. "Women Writing and Teaching." *College English* 34 (October 1972).

Holmquist, Kay. "Author Indignant at 'Waste of Human Beings.'" *Fort Worth Star-Telegram,* 20 April 1975.

Howard, Daniel F., and John Ribar. Instructor's manual for *The Modern Tradition: An Anthology of Stories,* 4th ed. Boston: Little, Brown, 1979.

Howe, Florence. "Literacy and Literature." *PMLA* 89 (May 1974): 433–41.

Howe, Irving. "Stories: New, Old, and Sometimes Good" [review of *Tell Me a Riddle*]. *New Republic,* 13 November 1961: 145–50.

Jacobs, Naomi M. "Earth, Air, Fire and Water in 'Tell Me a Riddle.'" *Studies in Short Fiction* 23 (Fall 1986): 401–6. A persuasive and tightly written analysis of "Tell Me a Riddle" as a "profound spiritual rebirth" showing Olsen's belief that humans need "not only bread but roses."

———. "Olsen's 'O Yes': Alva's Vision as Childbirth Account." *Notes on Contemporary Literature* 16 (January 1986): 7–8. A brief but helpful reading of "O Yes" in terms of Olsen's skillful use of a birthing metaphor.

Johnson, Sally H. "Silence and Song: The Structure and Imagery of Tillie Olsen's 'Tell Me a Riddle.'" Paper given at the symposium "Tillie Olsen Week: The Writer and Society," 21–26 March 1983.

Jones, Beverly. "The Dynamics of Marriage and Motherhood." In *Sisterhood Is Powerful,* edited by Robin Morgan, 49–67. New York: Vintage Books, 1970.

Kamel, Rose Yalow. "Riddles and Silences: Tillie Olsen's Autobiographical Fiction." In *Aggravating the Conscience: Jewish-American Literary Mothers in the Promised Land,* 81–114. New York: Peter Lang Publishing, 1988. A revised version of the article "Literary Foremothers and Writers' Silences," the Olsen chapter discusses the influence of two forces on Olsen's work: Rebecca Harding Davis and Judaism. Contains extended discussions of *Yonnondio, Silences,* and the *Tell Me a Riddle* stories with, despite some factual errors, fine insights into "Tell Me a Riddle."

———. "Literary Foremothers and Writers' Silences: Tillie Olsen's Autobiographical Fiction." *Melus* 12, no. 3 (Fall 1985): 55–72.

Kaplan, Cora. Introduction to *Tell Me a Riddle.* London: Virago, 1980.

———. Introduction to *Yonnondio.* London: Virago, 1980.

Kapp, Isa. Review of *Silences. New Leader,* 22 May 1978, 5–6.

Kelley, Anne. Review of *Tell Me a Riddle. Chicago Sunday Tribune,* 29 October 1961, 6.

Kirschner, Linda Heinlein. "I Stand Here Ironing." *English Journal* 65 (January 1976): 56–59.

Koppelman, Susan, ed. *The Other Woman.* New York: Feminist Press, 1984.

Leonard, Vickie. Review of *Mothers to Daughters. Off Our Backs* 16 (October 1986): 21.

Lester, Elenore. "The Riddle of Tillie Olsen." *Midstream,* January 1975, 75–79.

Levy, Laurie. Review of *Silences. Chicago* 27 (October 1978): 210–12.

Lhamon, W. T. Review of *Yonnondio. Library Journal,* 15 April 1974, 1150.

L'Heureux, John. Preface to *First Drafts, Last Drafts: Forty Years of the Creative Writing Program at Stanford University,* prepared by William McPheron with the assistance of Amor Towles. Stanford: Stanford University Libraries, 1989.

Loercher, D. Review of *Silences. Christian Science Monitor,* 18 September 1978, B9.

Lyons, Bonnie. "Tillie Olsen: The Writer as Jewish Woman." *Studies in American Jewish Literature* 5 (1986): 89–102. Analysis of Jewish references and allusions in *Silences, Yonnondio,* and the *Tell Me a Riddle* stories, with emphasis on "Tell Me a Riddle," arguing that Olsen's combined experience as Jew and woman is essential to her fiction.

McAlpin, Sara. "Mothers in Tillie Olsen's Stories." Paper given at the symposium "Tillie Olsen Week: The Writer and Society," 21–26 March 1983.

McCormack, Kathleen. "Song as Transcendence in the Works of Tillie Olsen." Paper given at the symposium "Tillie Olsen Week: The Writer and Society," 21–26 March 1983.

McElhiney, Annette Bennington. "Alternative Responses to Life in Tillie Olsen's Work." *Frontiers* 2 (Spring 1977): 76–91. Very unsophisticated but elegaic discussion mainly of the *Tell Me a Riddle* stories and of *Yonnondio.* Relatively error free.

McNeil, Helen. "Speaking for the Speechless" [review of *Silences*]. *Times Literary Supplement,* 4 November 1980, 1294.

Malpezzi, Frances M. "Sisters in Protest: Rebecca Harding Davis and Tillie Olsen." *Artes Liberales* 12 (Spring 1986): 1–9.

Manning, Gerald F. "Fiction and Aging: 'Ripeness is All.'" *Canadian Journal on Aging/La Revue Canadienne de Vieillissement* 8, no. 2 (Summer 1989): 157–63.

Marcus, Jane. "Still Practice, A/Wrested Alphabet: Toward a Feminist Aesthetic." In *Feminist Issues in Literary Scholarship,* edited by Shari Benstock, 79–97. Bloomington: Indiana University Press, 1987.

Martin, Abigail. *Tillie Olsen.* Series 65 in Western Writers Series. Boise, Idaho: Boise State University Press, 1984. A short, concise introduction to Olsen's biography and publication history, this useful and articulate pamphlet contains plot synopses, excerpts from reviews, and brief comparisons to Virginia Woolf, as well as to "western" writers John Steinbeck and Willa Cather.

Meese, Elizabeth A. "Deconstructing the Sexual Politic: Virginia Woolf and Tillie Olsen." In *Crossing the Double-Cross,* edited by Elizabeth Meese, 89–113. Chapel Hill: University of North Carolina Press, 1986. A "formalist-feminist" discussion of "women's (the 'outsiders') relationship to culture" and to the literary text, using extended examples from Virginia Woolf's *Three Guineas* and *A Room of One's Own* and Olsen's *Silences.*

Miller, Lynn Christine. "The Subjective Camera and Staging Psychological Fiction." *Literature in Performance* 2 (April 1982): 35–42.

Miller, Nolan. Review of *Silences. Antioch Review* 36 (Fall 1978): 513.

Mills, Kay. "Surviving Is Not Enough: A Conversation with Tillie Olsen." *Los Angeles Times,* 26 April 1981, pt. 4, p. 3.

Mintz, Jacqueline A. "The Myth of the Jewish Mother in Three Jewish, American, Female Writers." *Centennial Review* 22 (1978): 346–55.

Mitchell, Sally. Review of *Silences. Library Journal* 103 (August 1978): 1512.

Moers, Ellen. *Literary Women,* 28–29. New York: Doubleday, 1976.

Moran, B. K. "Women Writers of the West Coast: Speaking of Their Lives and Careers." *California Magazine* 9 (January 1984): 86.

Moss, R. J. Review of *Mothers and Daughters. Psychology Today* 21 (November 1987): 80.

Nekola, Charlotte, and Paula Rabinowitz. *Writing Red: An Anthology of American Women Writers, 1930–1940,* 179–81 and 245–51. New York: Feminist Press, 1987. Contains brief introductions to sections on women writers (poetry, fiction, nonfiction) in the 1930s; includes Olsen's "I Want You Women up North to Know" and "The Strike."

Newman, Mordecai. Review of the film *Tell Me a Riddle. Present Tense* 9 (Winter 1982): 20.

Niehus, Edward L., and Teresa Jackson. "Polar Stars, Pyramids, and 'Tell Me a Riddle.'" *American Notes and Queries* 24 (January–February 1986): 77–83.

Nilsen, Helge Normann. "Tillie Olsen's 'Tell Me a Riddle': The Political Theme." *Etudes Anglaises: Grande-Bretagne, Etats-Unis* 37 (April–June 1984): 163–69.

Oates, Joyce Carol. Review of *Silences. New Republic,* 29 July 1978, 32–34. Excellent review of *Silences,* one of the few to look dispassionately at both the strengths and weaknesses of Olsen's art. Admires the generous impulse behind the writing of *Silences* but finds the numerous shortcomings in a work hailed as a "literary manifesto of the women's movement" both "saddening and inexplicable."

O'Connor, William Van. "The Short Stories of Tillie Olsen." *Studies in Short Fiction* 1 (Fall 1963): 21–25.

Olsen, Violet. "The Writer and Society." Paper given at the symposium "Tillie Olsen Week: The Writer and Society," 21–26 March 1983.

Orr, Miriam Elaine Neil. *Tillie Olsen and a Feminist Spiritual Vision.* Jackson: University Press of Mississippi, 1987. Based on *Tillie Olsen's Vision: A Different Way of Keeping Faith,* 46–52. Ann Arbor, Mich.: Dissertation Abstracts, 1985. The first book-length study of Olsen's work, it interprets her fiction in terms of a religious or visionary quest and an "opening" of women's possibilities; it also argues that the reader can supply what is missing in the text and "transcend" to Olsen's "prophetic vision." Contains some useful biographical details.

Pace, Stephanie. "Lungfish; or, Acts of Survival in Contemporary Female Writing." *Frontiers* 10 (1988): 29–33.

Parker, Dorothy. Review of *Tell Me a Riddle. Esquire,* June 1962, 64.

Park-Fuller, Linda, and Tillie Olsen. "Understanding What We Know: *Yonnondio: From the Thirties.*" *Literature in Performance* 4 (November 1983): 65–74. A "production record" of the 1982 film version of *Yonnondio* made at Southwest Missouri State University. Concentrates on discovering a "phenomenological method of literary analysis" to determine "experiential patterns" in the novel that were appropriate for the film.

Park-Fuller, Linda. "Voices: Bakhtin's Heteroglossia and Polyphony, and the Performance of Narrative Literature." *Literature in Performance* 12 (November 1986): 1–12.

———. "An Interview with Tillie Olsen." *Literature in Performance* 4 (November 1983): 75–77.

"The Passion of Tillie Olsen" [review of *Tell Me a Riddle*]. *Nation,* 10 April 1972, 472–74.

Pearlman, Mickey. Introduction to *American Women Writing Fiction: Memory, Identity, Family, Space,* edited by Mickey Pearlman. Lexington: University Press of Kentucky, 1989.

———. Introduction to *Mother Puzzles: Daughters and Mothers in Contemporary American Literature,* edited by Mickey Pearlman. Westport, Conn.: Greenwood Publishing, 1989: 1–10.

Pearson, Carol, and Katherine Pope. *The Female Hero in American and British Literature,* 44–45. New York: Bowker, 1981.

Peden, William H. Review of "Tell Me a Riddle." *New York Times Book Review,* 12 November 1961, 54.

———. "Tell Me a Riddle." In *The American Short Story: Continuity and Change, 1940–1975,* 2d ed., 64–65. Boston: Houghton Mifflin, 1975.

Peters, Joan. "The Lament for Lost Art" [review of *Silences*]. *Nation,* 23 September 1978, 281–83.

Register, Cheri. "American Feminist Literary Criticism: A Bibliographical Introduction." *Signs* 6 (Winter 1980): 277.

Rhodes, Carolyn. "'Beedo' in Olsen's *Yonnondio:* Charles E. Bedaux." *American Notes and Queries* 14 (October 1976): 23–25.

Rhodes, Carolyn, and Ernest Rhodes. "Tillie Olsen." In *Dictionary of Literary Biography Yearbook, 1980,* edited by Karen L. Rood, Jean W. Ross, and Richard Ziegfield, 290–97. Detroit: Gale Research, 1981.

Rich, Adrienne. *Of Woman Born: Motherhood as Experience and Institution,* xx, 284. New York: W. W. Norton, 1976.

Robinson, Lillian. *Sex, Class, and Culture.* New York: Methuen, 1987.

Rohrberger, Mary. "Tillie Olsen." In *Critical Survey of Short Fiction,* edited by Frank N. Magill. Englewood Cliffs, N.J.: Salem Press, 1981.

Rose, Ellen Cronan. "Limning; or, Why Tillie Writes." *Hollins Critic* 13 (April 1976): 1–13. Discussion of the issues in *Silences,* particularly of sight/insight and of the *Tell Me a Riddle* stories, *Yonnondio,* and Olsen's involvement with Rebecca Harding Davis's *Life in the Iron Mills.* Discusses Olsen's "current feminist articulation" of her "real aesthetic."

Rosenfelt, Deborah. "From the Thirties: Tillie Olsen and the Radical Tradition." *Feminist Studies* 7 (Fall 1981): 371–406. Reprinted in *Feminist Criticism and Social Change.*

———. "Divided against Herself: The Life Lived and the Life Suppressed." *Moving On,* April–May 1980, 15–20, 23. Examines the contributions of Agnes Smedley and Tillie Olsen to a "socialist feminist tradition" extending from Charlotte Perkins Gilman to Marge Piercy and Alice Walker. Contains very useful discussions of Olsen's life and work, particularly *Yonnondio* and "Tell Me a Riddle."

Rubin, Naomi. "A Riddle of History for the Future." *Sojourner,* July 1983, 1, 4, 18.

Ruddick, Sara, and Pamela Daniels, eds. *Working It Out.* New York: Pantheon, 1977. Contains Olsen's "One Out of Twelve: Women Who Are Writers in Our Century."

Russell, P. A. "Millennialism, Utopia, and Progress." *Canadian Journal of History* 20 (April 1985): 116–17.

Salzman, Jack. "Fragments of Time Lost." *Washington Post Book World,* 7 April 1974, 1; *New York Post Book World,* 19 April 1974. Discussion of *Yonnondio,* which Salzman calls "the best novel to come out of the so-called proletarian movement" of the 1930s.

Schaumburger, Nancy Engbretsen. "An Australian Tillie Olsen?" [review of *The Home Girls, Loving Daughters* and *A Long Time Dying* by Olga Masters]. *Belles Lettres,* July–August, 1988, 2.

Schwartz, Helen J. "Tillie Olsen." In *American Women Writers,* vol. 3, edited by Lina Mainiero and Langdon Lynne Faust. New York: Ungar, 1981.

See, L. "Publishers Weekly Interviews." *Publishers Weekly,* 23 November 1984, 76.

Shanahan, Thomazina. "Tillie Olsen: In Mutuality." *Heliotrope,* May–June 1977, 1–5.

———. Review of *Mother to Daughter. Belles Lettres,* January–February 1986, 7.

Shulman, Alix Kates. "Overcoming Silences: Teaching Writing for Women." *Harvard Educational Review* 49 (November 1979): 527–33.

Sommer, Vicki L. "The Writings of Tillie Olsen: A Social Work Perspective." Paper given at the symposium "Tillie Olsen Week: The Writer and Society," 21–26 March 1983.

Staub, Michael. "The Struggle for 'Selfness' through Speech in Olsen's *Yonnondio: From the Thirties*." *Studies in American Fiction* 16 (Autumn 1988): 131–39. A classic misreading of *Yonnondio* as a "presentation of a working-class feminism" and a story about "women and girls of the working class [who] will never identify their own concerns at home or in the society at large . . . until they can create forums where their individual stories are heard, shared and debated." Also has Mazie descending "into trancelike madness over the course of *Yonnondio*."

Stimpson, Catharine R. "Three Women Work It Out." *Nation,* 30 November 1974, 565–68. Overview of *Yonnondio* as a "recovered" text and fine analysis of the political angle of Olsen's vision.

———. "Tillie Olsen: Witness as Servant." *Polit: A Journal for Literature and Politics* 1 (Fall 1977): 1–12. Reprinted in *Where the Meanings Are: Feminism and Cultural Spaces*. New York: Methuen, 1988.

———. Review of *Yonnondio*. *Nation,* 3 November 1974, 565.

Stone, Elizabeth. "Olsen on the Depression, Roth on the Couch" [review of *Yonnondio*]. *Crawdaddy,* September 1974, 88–89.

———. Review of the film *Tell Me a Riddle*. *Ms.,* March 1981, 22–24.

Stone, Judy. "End of a Riddle and the Beginning of a New Career." *San Francisco Examiner and Chronicle Datebook,* 13 January 1980, 20–21.

"Tillie Olsen on the Privilege to Create." *Radcliffe Centennial News,* July 1979, 9.

Trueblood, Valerie. "Silences." *American Poetry Review,* May–June 1979, 18.

Turan, Kenneth. "Breaking Silence" [interview with Tillie Olsen]. *New West,* 28 August 1978, 56–59.

———. "A Riddle Wrapped in Mystery." *New West,* 14 July 1980, 17–19.

Van Buren, Jane Silverman. *The Modernist Madonna: Semiotics of the Maternal Metaphor*. Bloomington and Indianapolis: Indiana University Press, 1989. Using feminist psychoanalysis and semiotics to examine the maternal metaphor in the texts of Harriet Beecher Stowe, Louisa May Alcott, and Mary Cassatt, the book contains a section comparing Alice Walker and Tillie Olsen. It examines Eva of "Tell Me a Riddle" as Olsen's "alter ego" to demonstrate the conflict between "mother self" and "woman self" that frequently impedes artistic impulse. Contains some serious factual errors, however.

Van Horn, Christina. "Writer Tillie Olsen: Upbeat on Woman's Future." *Boston Globe,* 31 May 1981, 6A.

Vincent, Sally. "Tillie Not So Unsung." [London] *Observer,* 5 October 1980, 34.

Walker, Nancy. "Language, Irony, and Fantasy in the Contemporary Novel by Women." *Lit* 1 (Spring 1990): 33–57.

Wood, Ann Douglas. "The Literature of Impoverishment: The Women Local Colorists in America, 1865–1914." *Women's Studies* 1 (1972): 21–22.

Yalom, Marilyn. "Tillie Olsen." In *Women Writers of the West Coast: Speaking of Their Lives and Careers,* edited by M. Yalom. Santa Barbara, Calif.: Capra, 1983. Contains essays on 10 West Coast writers from Jessamyn West and Kay Boyle to Maxine Hong Kingston and Joyce Carol Thomas. A fine overview of Olsen and a tribute to her life and work, focusing on her style and "tremendous" impact on audiences wherever she speaks.

Yeager, Patricia. "Writing as Action: A Vindication of the Rights of Women." In *Honey-Mad Women: Emancipatory Strategies in Women's Writing,* 149–76. New York: Columbia University Press, 1988.

Zeidenstein, Sondra. *A Wider Giving: Women Writing after a Long Silence,* xiii–xiv. Goshen, Conn.: Chicory Blue Press, 1988.

Reviews

Mother to Daughter, Daughter to Mother: A Daybook and Reader

Journal of Education, Fall 1985, 112.

[London] *Observer,* 10 November 1985, 25.

Publishers Weekly, 12 October 1984, 48–50.

New Directions for Women 13 (November 1984): 20.

Women's Review of Books 2 (June 1985): 12.

Silences

American Book Review 1 (March 1979): 7.

American Poetry Review, May 1979, 18.

Choice 15 (December 1978): 1372.

Christian Science Monitor, 14 May 1979, B5.

Georgia Review 33 (Winter 1979): 958.

Harvard Educational Review 49 (November 1979): 527.

Kliatt 14 (Winter 1980): 25.

Library Journal 103 (August 1978): 1512–13.

New Statesman, 31 October 1980, 23.

[London] *Observer,* 1 March 1981, 32.

Publishers Weekly, 1 May 1978, 80.

New York Times Book Review, 17 June 1979, 35.

Southwest Review 64 (Winter 1979): 105.

Times Literary Supplement, 14 November 1980, 1294.

Yale Review 68 (Winter 1979): vi–iv.

Tell Me a Riddle

Christian Science Monitor, 9 November 1961, 7.
Critic 38 (August 1979): 6.
Guardian Weekly, 21 December 1980, 22.
Kirkus Reviews, 15 August 1961, 745.
Kliatt 23 (April 1989): 33.
Ms., September 1974, 26.
Nation, 10 April 1972, 474.
New Listener, 14 August 1964.
Observer, 1 March 1981, 32.
Studies in Short Fiction, Fall 1986, 401.
Time, 27 October 1961, 101.
Times Literary Supplement, 14 November 1980, 1294.

Yonnondio: From the Thirties

Best Sellers, 15 May 1974, 97–98.
Black Studies, 15 May 1974, 97.
Washington Post Book World, 7 April 1974, 1.
Library Journal, 15 April 1974, 1150.
Ms., September 1974, 26.
New Republic, 30 March 1974, 28.
New Statesman, 31 October 1980, 23.
New York Times Book Review, 31 March 1974, 5.
New Yorker, 25 March 1974, 140.
Village Voice, 23 May 1974, 38.
Virginia Quarterly Review 50 (Autumn 1974): 120.
Wilson Library Bulletin 48 (June 1974): 803.

Index

Critics in text are indexed last name, first name. Characters are indexed first name, last name.

The Authors

Mickey Pearlman received her Ph.D. from the City University of New York. She is the editor of *American Women Writing Fiction: Memory, Identity, Family, Space* (1989) and *Mother Puzzles: Daughters and Mothers in Contemporary American Literature* (1989), the author of *Reinventing Reality: Patterns and Characters in the Novels of Muriel Spark* (forthcoming), and the coauthor of *Inter/View: Talks with America's Writing Women* (1990). She is also editing three forthcoming volumes: *The Anna Book: Searching for Anna in Literary History, Canadian Women Writing Fiction,* and *British Women Writing Fiction.* She publishes regularly in literary and regional magazines. She is now working on a book of interviews with American, British, and Canadian writing women for W. W. Norton.

Abby H. P. Werlock received her D.Phil. from the University of Sussex, England, and is a member of the English Department at St. Olaf College, where she teaches writing and American literature courses. The recipient of a National Endowment for the Humanities fellowship (1984) and a Joyce Scholar award (1990), she has been a James Fenimore Cooper Fellow (1986) and an NEH Visiting Scholar (1987). She is currently writing a book on mixed marriages in American fiction.

The Editor

Warren French (Ph.D., University of Texas, Austin) retired from Indiana University in 1986 and is now an honorary professor associated with the Board of American Studies at the University College of Swansea, Wales. In 1985 Ohio University awarded him a doctor of humane letters. He has contributed volumes to Twayne's United States Authors Series on Jack Kerouac, Frank Norris, John Steinbeck, and J. D. Salinger. His most recent publication for Twayne is *The San Francisco Poetry Renaissance, 1955–1960.*